A ROSIE LIFE IN ITALY 3

SHOULD I STAY OR SHOULD I GO?

ROSIE MELEADY

ENVY PUBLISHING

For Dad

CONTENTS

BEFORE YOU START...

See more from Rosie and join her newsletter on: www.rosiemeleady.com

Social Media: @ARosieLifeInItaly

On Rosie's website and newsletter you'll find she likes to talk about buying a house in Italy, renovating, travel in Italy, restoring furniture, life and pets in Italy.

While this book is based on fact, the author has used poetic licence, has exaggerated and created some fictional scenes and people. Some names of real characters and places have also been changed for protection... of the author.

TO STAY: STARE

"**B**loody hell, you are huge! And, my Lord, your legs are very hairy," I can't help but react aloud to the sight in front of me when I open, for the first time, the cobweb-strewn letterbox that has hung outside the impressive wrought-iron gates for close to a century.

The scorpions don't bother me, nor the fuzzy-wuzzies with thousands of legs – chunkier and fluffier versions of their tamer looking centipede cousins back home in Ireland. But the giant black spiders with visibly hairy legs, like this one, still make me wince. Not run a mile, just wince. Although I'm not scared of them, they are fast, which freaks me out. I've dealt with her type a lot in the past six months of renovating the Sighing House.

I reach inside the letterbox and attempt to use a leaf to brush her off a festively red envelope. But she stands firm. She must really like that envelope. I try again with a bit more force. She pounces on my hand and makes a run for my face. Not a move I was expecting.

Of course, the neighbour with the golden retriever passes at this very moment. He's trying not to look at the mad, mysterious Irish woman, who bought the stone mansion that has stood derelict on his road for over ten years, dancing some crazy ritual with no music, wiggling like something has electrocuted her whilst yelping "GET OFF GET OFF..." which, to be fair, is stupid on my part – as it's an Italian spider so she obviously can't understand my request. And bugger me if I could say it in Italian. After four years of living here, I still can't string a sentence together.

She thuds to the ground. Yes, she was big enough to thud. She dashes towards the loose end of my pyjamas. I need to move fast. If she makes it to my leg, I will have no choice but to pull off my bottoms here on the street, golden retriever or no golden retriever. I grab what's in the letterbox, leap over the eight-legged Jurassic beast and shudder my way into the house with "OUUU OOOUUU OUUU" getting louder with each quick step. The golden retriever man catches my eye and averts his look, probably afraid I'll hex him, which isn't a gift he wanted this Christmas Eve.

I open the red envelope and momentarily savour the card from my childhood friend Denise, before placing it beside the two other precious Christmas cards that had arrived from my mam and dad and from my brother Jim and his wife Ingrid.

I am about to dump the bundle of promotional material I also collected during my grab-and-run, but decide to sift through and see if there are new words that will help expand my limited Italian vocabulary.

Amongst the flyers, there are two other long envelopes with my name handwritten on them. They are not the right shape for greeting cards.

In the only warm room of the house–the pellet-heated sitting room–I open the first envelope. It's from our builder Antonio. It looks like an invoice for €15k... but it must be a receipt as he is paid up to date. I open the second one. It's from Danny Boy's plumbing and electric company. Again, it looks like an invoice but must be a receipt for €11k. Both finished four months of renovation work a few days ago, just in time for us to move in to the 22-roomed villa for Christmas. There's still a lot to be done, but at least we now have a solid roof, updated electrics and plumbing on two of the three floors.

I am already an old hand at the ridiculous amount of paper-work dealing with an Italian company creates. I decide that is what this is, fold them up, and put them in the drawer.

Of course, I wake at 3am on our mattress on the floor. The mystery documents are playing on my mind. They are receipts, right?

I can't stop mulling it over in my head...

The two bills come to the exact amount we are due to be refunded on the 50/50 government reimbursement scheme. If they are new bills for extra work, none of that work was autho-rised or discussed.

Over my first cup of morning tea, I take the letters out and look at them again. There are a few lines of detail. With my Google translate app, I read Antonio's; €9k is for filling in holes and repairing the walls after the plumber's and electri-cian's work.

3

Well that's definitely a mistake. Returning the walls to their original state was part of Danny Boy's quote. And there is something about drainage and piping. Again, Danny Boy's responsibility I am sure.

They should sort these cross-overs out between themselves. Antonio must be required to bill it through me to fulfil the never-ending requests of Italian bureaucracy, just as I thought. I stick the folded papers into the drawer.

After Christmas, I will look at it and sort it out. I won't tell Ronan about it. There's no point in worrying him too, as it's already sitting in the back of my mind, casting a little grey cloud over an already cloudy Christmas morning. We had spent the last month trying desperately to get our daughter Izzy home to us from London but failed miserably thanks to missing passports and borders being closed because of a new Covid variant, and we were now to spend Christmas missing a piece of the family puzzle.

A text comes in from Antonio crazy early. He must be just going to bed after Christmas Eve celebrations with his family, including his father Giovanni, who was our landlord until a few days ago. "I went past your house yesterday evening and saw the Christmas lights on the balcony, and it made me very happy. Merry Christmas."

I feel like replying to him; "I went past the letterbox this morning and your confusing surprise bill/receipt made me very anxious. Merry Bloody Christmas to you too."

I know he is proud of the roof he made, and the fact they got offsite so that we could move in for Christmas Eve. It was a push. They all thought we were mad, but we made it, even with the floods of rain and our project manager, Tomaso, going AWOL.

It doesn't feel like Christmas. After watching the sunrise over the lake behind the house, I open the drawer to get a spoon to squeeze the tea bag of my usual second cup of the morning and Antonio's bill semi-unfolds in front of me. I can't help but look at it again.

What if it is true? What if we do owe them this for work that is done? We'd be f**ked. We don't have €26k hiding in a mattress or a secret offshore account, and the bonus refund we are due is to cover the tonne of additional work that's required to make the house habitable. At the moment, we can survive knowing this will end when we can continue the work in the spring and get rid of the mould, get functioning windows and doors, and the million other things that need to be done.

With that, my phone buzzes. It's a text from my cousin Dawn, the daughter of my mother's only sister. Our mothers were born nine months apart, making them Irish twins - a term given to two siblings born within the same year. They were always close like twins, bickered like sisters and were each other's best friends.

My eyes sting with dollops of salty tears as I read; "Mam passed away this morning. Typical of her to hold out to Christmas day to enjoy the drama of it." Gorgeous Aunty Rita, my mam's sister and best friend, had left us. My thoughts rocket to my mother. She must be devastated. I can't call her number quick enough.

"Merry Christmas," she and my dad echo down the phone. I say the same, and they continue on a jolly note. In the background I text my cousin, "Have you told my mam yet?"

"Yes, I was on to her first thing this morning."

"Mam, I know about Aunty Rita," I say as soon as there is a pause in my mam and dad's jolliness.

They become more sombre. "Who told you? We didn't want anyone told until tomorrow. We wanted yous to enjoy Christmas."

This is typical of my parents, especially my dad. If we ignore the fact someone has died, then we can pretend they are still alive.

Bad news and kissing were immediately switched off the TV when we were growing up. Not that they were anti-sex... obviously not, as they had five of us. And they were still one of the most romantic couples I knew, even after 66 years together. They had stayed in Covid lockdown isolation for the last nine months without letting anyone else pass through their door. They spent their days pottering in the garden, Mam cooking, Dad trying to improve the operations of Netflix with his TV repair man background, and both playing Scrabble every evening.

In the late afternoon, if it was at all sunny, Dad called Mam out to the sunroom to watch the birds feed from the new feeder he had designed and to pretend they were on a cruise. This involved them leaning back in their armchairs, closing their eyes and, with the sun on their faces, falling asleep. They'd sprinkle their day with video calls to us, their adult children dotted around different parts of the world. "Well, if we were on a cruise, that's what we would be doing, wouldn't it? Not that we ever wanted to go on a cruise, did we, Mar? Stupid ol' things."

"The nearest we got on a cruise was the night of our wedding," Mam often recounted to anyone listening. "After the church, it was a good Mass, we had tea and sandwiches back in the house and then our only friend with a car, Jean, dropped us into town for a knickerbocker glory and then we got the bus to the boat for Blackpool. I was expecting a cabin to be something like the luxury suites I'd seen pictures of on the Titanic, but instead, the ferry over had a tiny cabin with bunk beds. Bunk beds for our first night together... but we managed." She laughed hysterically every time she recounted it.

Considering a knickerbocker glory and a good Mass were my parents' idea of foreplay for their first night of passion together, I wasn't surprised that my dad did not approve of acts of passion on the telly. But he also wanted to protect us from bad news.

"Mam, Christmas is pretty miserable already this year. It's not spoiling anything, and I'd be pretty annoyed if I wasn't told so that I could ring and comfort the cousins. Especially as I won't be able to get to Ireland for the funeral because of bloody Covid."

"Well, don't tell the boys. Leave them with their families to enjoy the day."

"That's ridiculous... but okay... but how are you? Are you okay?"

"Let's get through the day and talk about it tomorrow."

"Will you change your mind about spending Christmas by yourselves? I am sure Jim could still fit you in for Christmas dinner."

"No, no, it's too risky with all this Covid mess. We got this far without catching it and being on our own. Christmas family get-togethers is what they are warning everyone about. Jim and them are all out working during the week. They could be carriers without knowing. No, we are fine on our own. We'll eat a bit of turkey and ham, have a few drinks for my sister and I'll win your dad at a game of Scrabble... But not a word to anyone, do you hear?"

Christmas day was like every other except dipped in grief for my lovely aunt. Later, we did a live call with Izzy, where I unwrapped her presents that I had carefully wrapped for her, and she unwrapped the ones that she had equally carefully wrapped for us. Via video link, we showed the gifts we got one another that never made it to under the tree. The sadness of my aunt and not having Izzy with us made me forget about the possible looming bills folded in the drawer.

The day after Christmas without Izzy, after receiving astronomical unexpected bills, and after hearing my gorgeous closest aunt died, I feel claustrophobic and on the verge of a meltdown. I had to get out of the house and go for a walk alone in the fresh air.

However, there were so many Covid rule updates in Italy about what we can and can't do over Christmas, that I am not sure what is permitted.

Trying to figure it out when you can't read the language is an extra challenge. I spend an hour searching, but I still can't find clarity on whether 'not permitted out' means staying inside your house or not going on a road trip. As shops are closed and we have no family or friends to visit anyway, I had no intentions of going outside the house, so I wasn't paying too much attention to the updates of what we can do the day after Christmas. But now I needed out.

So I post on an 'Expats in Italy' Social Media group. "Can someone tell me if we can take a walk outside our homes today?"

"Oh my God, why don't you read the news? Why don't you just Google it?" some grumpy old witch responds. Her profile picture is deceivingly pleasant.

Someone else chimes in on this comment, "I know, right? It is unbelievable how someone can research what they are going to watch on Netflix but can't look up basics." Their jibes between each other about how ignorant, stupid and lazy people (i.e. me) can be continue back and forth until one of them has to go cook Boxing Day lunch for their family who got over from the UK before the closure of borders the previous week. She goes off topic to tell the other witch she is so relieved they got here before flights stopped, she would be out of her mind otherwise.

I keep telling myself they are expats, not Italians. This is not a reason to develop a dislike for our new home country. But, I'm wondering if I will ever make any friends here in Italy. Covid lockdowns were lonely. They kept us away from people, away from socialising, joining groups or classes, away from work stuff, away from experiencing the culture and history of this country we want to call home.

I knew making a new circle of friends as an adult was going to be difficult. I didn't expect to make floods of Italian friends, especially as we couldn't speak the language, but I thought perhaps a few expats—immigrants in the same boat as us. But if these Facebook witches were anything to go by, I was now less keen.

We've been in Italy three years but I feel we haven't lived in Italy. We moved here three weeks after making the decision and we basically continued our Irish life from Italy, stuck behind our computers in our home offices, communicating with friends and family in Ireland online. It's not that we are unsociable, we just had no opportunity to break in through the shell. It has probably taken us the entire three years to simply get over the shock of moving here in such a hurry. We haven't integrated; we are bobbing in our inflatables around the perimeter.

I had dipped in and out of an ex-pat yoga group and met a few friendly faces. Most were retired and at least ten years older than me, but far more supple.

It is understandable why people have to wait until retirement to move to the sun. We were lucky to be self-employed with an online based business, and few people my age would have an agreeable teenager, willing to uproot from their home and move to a different country. We were fortunate with our son Luca.

The cruelty of these two social media witches made me lose faith in even making friends with ex-pats. If this was the typical expat who did not take into consideration that it's Christmas, people are separated from family, that the person they are responding to might be struggling with the language and dealing with debt, doubt and death, then making friends with even expats was not for me. Their cutting words were enough to smash the thin surface glass that was holding me together.

It punches so hard in my already over-sensitive stomach I crumble into bed. This wasn't how our Italy adventure was supposed to be.

2

TO BUY: COMPRARE

"It is from my mother's house. I live in Spain. It is better for me there than here in this shit-hole of Italy, but I have had to return to sort out my mother's estate. They are all fighting over it."

The well-groomed man in his fifties is untying a gold monstrosity from his roof rack, whilst his partner, a thinner, silver-haired chap, starts merrily pulling long parts of the heavy antique brass bed from the car boot. "In Spain, we live a nice life. I cannot wait to go back and not be here listening to my family fight. Italian families always fight. My siblings do nothing, so I had to come back and clear the house so we can sell it."

It's late, but I'm glad it has arrived. Sleeping on our mattress on the floor is doing nothing for Ronan's back, and the waft of damp old plaster mixed with stuffy dust makes it difficult to sleep.

As we brought only what we could fit in the camper van from Ireland and then lived in a furnished house for the first few years here in Italy, we have to start from scratch with furnishing the Sighing House.

With so many rooms to furnish, I have kept everything that was left in the abandoned house, no matter how cobwebbed or wood-wormed, hoping divine inspiration will strike and I will have the time to turn it into a show-stopping piece. This has led to at least two rooms on each floor being stuffed to capacity with these 'treasures' which most sane people would have cleared to the dump before starting to renovate. The rooms look like badly planned, overcrowded flea markets.

But now that push has finally come to shove, the dark wooden beds left behind look like they could be haunted. Not something I want to put my mattress on in case I woke up dead. They will be dumped.

Joseph, one of the Moroccan guys that worked on the roof, was horrified that Ronan was going to let his wife move into a house in such disarray and with such old furniture.

Antonio, the builder boss, regularly had his eye on things, asking if I would like him to throw it out. Conveniently, he only seemed to ask this of the things that might hold value, like the gramophone and antique washstand. Not of the things that genuinely should be dumped, like the coffin-like sideboard-thing that stretched the entire length of a wall in the big downstairs room. Its dark, shiny veneer wasn't even veneer but imitation veneer wrap, and it had a display cabinet on each end, lined with plush red imitation polyester velvet used by the same companies that make cheap roulette tables.

Underneath each display cabinet was a fold-down door, which I'm guessing could be a drinks cabinet, and three inoperable drawers under each. Between the two cabinets, joining both into one piece of furniture, was the long sideboard, with two large glass door cabinets above and three long drawers underneath. All held up on spindly legs and adorned with fake brass press-on flowers in each corner and fake-wood beading.

I didn't know how fake it all was until we eventually decided there was absolutely nothing we could do with it, as it was too big and hideous for any of the rooms in the house. We decided to be brave and to smash it up, only to discover the fake veneer was over a thin layer of plywood with corrugated cardboard in-between to make it appear as a thick piece of wood.

I kept the two end cabinets though, to recycle as mini writing bureaux with bookshelves above. I'll probably spend the same amount on materials that a new writing bureau would cost, before deciding to dump them.

There were things we needed to get quickly, such as a bed. Not only because of the health hazards floor-sleeping was causing, but our floor-mattress had quickly become, not just a bed for us, but also for our two dogs and two cats.

The week after Christmas, Ronan surprised me with this brass bed he'd bought secondhand from Marketplace.

"It was only €100, and they were so keen to get rid of it they said they would deliver it."

I've seen brass beds, but nothing like this. It looks like something from Aladdin. It's big, shiny and knobbly. King-size and heavy.

"It is good quality," says the taller guy with grey hair.

"And he should know," chimes in the cheery, shorter guy. "You know his face?"

"No," I say hesitantly.

"Ah, if you were Italian, you probably would recognise him. He is on a TV program about antiques. He knows everything about antiques and architectural history."

"Ha, you might find looking around this place interesting then," says Ronan as the three of them lift the heavy headboard section into the kitchen.

"May I? I would love to." The grey-haired guy needs no more encouragement. He's immediately stroking the shabby looking wooden interior doors.

"These are very ancient. Madonna doors."

"Yes, I've heard," I growl. These doors, the ones that went missing during the sale of the house, nearly made us walk away from the deal. I was now secretly planning to replace them with well-fitting doors that could be cleaned and, when closed, stayed closed.

I had spent half a day with every cleaning product known to man scrubbing and polishing a few of the doors, but years of dust and grime had embedded in the grain so much that nothing will lift their spirits. They still look dusty and grimy with their greened brass handles that no longer latch. The recent additions of cement and mud splatters add to the eyesore of these rare doors that I should appreciate, but instead, really want to get rid of.

"I think they are the originals from when the house was built in 1923," I say, trying to sound enthusiastic about them.

"No, they are older than that. They were antique doors when the house was built. You cannot get doors like this anymore."

"Oh, really?" Ronan is suddenly interested. "So the thieves knew what they were doing when they tried to take the doors."

I held back on saying, "who would want to have doors like that?"

I hadn't yet told Ronan my plan to replace them all, but I was guessing he would in time get sick of them too and think the same, longing for doors that closed snugly, swung the correct way, could be wiped clean and had locks that worked.

"Thieves?" Antique Guy looked up, surprised.

"Well, the previous owners... It's a long story."

Antique Guy's attention was already lost.

"Oh mio Dio... your staircase..." He is nearly swooning, standing on the first landing. "It is hand-cut local stone."

I'm surprised he can distinguish it under all the building dust. Maybe he's also an archaeologist and can recognise shapes under layers of silt.

"No one can get this stone anymore. Your staircase is very... important. You don't see these staircases very often."

"But this..." his hand wiggles the banister. "This is shit."

He continues to walk up our rare staircase, the one Ronan had been Googling ways to cover because, like me with the doors, the worn steps were an eyesore to him, whereas the doors didn't bother him... yet.

I follow the guy as he peers into each of the bedrooms. "These floor tiles, they are fantastic, they were only put in the houses of rich people. The terracotta tiles were for the common people."

I'm not that fond of the tile patterns for rich people in the bedrooms. I would prefer if the tiles for the common people were throughout. Again, I don't voice this.

"Four siblings lived here. The rooms across the hallway have the common terracotta ones in. Perhaps the brother who lived in this apartment was richer than the brother who lived across the hallway." I say in half-jest but thinking maybe that was actually the case.

"But look...look what they did here," I say, leading Antique Guy into one of the tiled rooms of commoners across the hallway. "They painted the terracotta tiles." I point to where the tiles from the doorway switch from the sweet, nearly ripe clementine tone to a deep ruby red.

"Ah no, it is not paint, it is Amaro. The drink. They used it in the old days to stain their tiles."

"Why?"

"To make them red," he says, as if I am stupid. "To make it look less like the tiles of the common people."

"Can it be removed?"

"Maybe by sanding off the top layer... You have many pleasant features in this house, it will be beautiful when finished." He starts down the stairs, but I want to make the most of him and his English-speaking explanations.

"Can you tell me what this is?" I say, grabbing one of the many mystery objects we have discovered in the house: a weird shaped wooden, light thing. It is about two feet long with four flat wooden laths, creating a 3D shape of a squashed oval with pointy ends. In the centre, there is a flat, square piece of wood. It looks like a half-made rocking toy for a child or some sort of weird shelf.

"Ah, it is a Suora e Prete— a Priest and Nun," he smiles. "You are missing the nun. It was for warming the bed or getting the dampness from the sheets in the old times when everything got damp from humidity. You just have the priest, which is this wooden structure. The nun was a metal container in which you would put hot coals and ashes from the fire. The 'nun' would then be placed here, under the priest." He points to the square wooden shelf inside it. "The structure kept the blankets away from the hot coal container and allowed the heat to move to more areas of the bed without the bed going on fire."

"Why is it called the priest and nun?"

"You are asking me why the priest goes under the blankets on top of the warm nun?" He laughs. "We Italians can be very irreverent, even in the early 1900s when these were named!"

The two guys bid us fond nights in the Aladdin bed and take their leave. The shorter guy says how much they can't wait for this pandemic to be over so they can get back to Spain, where the weather is better than this. He waves to the clear star-studded sky that is cool but is better than many Irish summer nights we have experienced. It is chilly and getting colder now the sun has gone down.

The pellet stove is welcoming, we are exhausted from sorting stuff and trying to make the house somewhat more habitable. The construction of the brass bed will wait until the following day.

Asha, our large black long-haired German Shepherd, plops down in front of the pellet stove. She has spent the day wandering around like a bit of a lost soul looking for my desk. It's normally where she parks herself during the day, acting as a foot warmer while I work.

With no designated office space amongst the rooms that are all too cold and damp and full of... stuff, my desk has not been put back together yet.

After the Aladdin bed delivery and watching telly for a while on the diarrhoea sofa, we reluctantly open the wobbly door held closed with string, step into the refrigerated hallway and run up the important, rare, freezing cold stone stairway and try to remember which room we last moved our mattress into, in order to escape the damp. Ronan already had already turned on one of the Dalek gas fire heaters, which, even though is lit correctly, still leaves a stench of gas in the air.

As I plonk down on our mattress on the floor and wriggle between sheets dampened from humidity, I find myself wishing for something I never thought I would want. A priest and nun to warm my bed.

3

TO SNOW: NEVICARE

"They must be receipts. There's no way we could owe them that much. I mean, that would bring Danny's bills to-date up to the original quote he gave us for the entire project. And the top floor and solar panels still have to be done and bits finished. No, his bill is a definite mistake."

I had at last mustered the courage to show Ronan the invoices that had been bugging me since Christmas Eve.

"Phew, I'm glad you agree. I have been searching for the original quote, but I can't find all the pages of it. I am finding parts of first versions and parts of second versions and nothing is matching up."

I am usually careful about these things, but moving everything around and not having a desk or shelf that remains in one place and cement free for more than two days has caused things to be spread out.

"And as for Antonio's bill, €9k for repairing the walls after the electrics and plumbing gouging? When we didn't want them so gouged in the first place? Putting the walls back to their original state was definitely something Danny said he'd do. If I knew he was going to charge that much, I would have done it myself."

I can't find it mentioned on the pages that I have found of his quote. I search through them again, looking closely at my detailed handwritten translations above the words, trying to find the words for stone and brick. But there are pages missing.

"Perhaps it wasn't written in the quote but I remember him saying it when we were walking around with Tomo," says Ronan, also shuffling through pages but he's looking at the ones without translation so I'm not sure what he is looking for as he can't understand a word.

"It was the time the two lads were here, the ones that caught Covid... So Danny has to pay Antonio that amount, if he subcontracted the work to Anto's guys."

I'm glad I have not gone mad. "We'll have to wait until after the 6th January to discuss this with them as they are still off for the Christmas break."

The week between Christmas and New Year is the time I love most. It's like a series of Sunday mornings. It completely confuses Asha, who, since she was little and through all our moves, knows exactly when Sunday is. During the week she'd lie under my desk keeping me company and keeping the loneliness away that working for yourself from home can often bring.

But Sunday was different. It has always been the day I stay in bed with my laptop writing for enjoyment rather than work stuff until after noon. Emails would not be opened and Ronan brought me breakfast in bed. Asha would lie beside me, for girlie time, and to protect my precious me-time from any disturbance.

It will be a long time before we have those routines again in this house. The bedroom is purely for sleeping in, too damp, ugly and cold to have a leisurely lie-in.

And as for a desk and an office space, who knows when I will have that again.

When the long Italian Christmas break is over, I ask Danny to get his office to send me through the original quote, explaining I feel there is some duplication in the bills that he and Antonio have sent. Sure enough, there's my signature on two pages. In the preceding pages I can't find mention of repairing the walls. It's a long process going through the 20+ pages of detailed building terms and translating them.

The electric works and the plumbing are quoted separately, and they add up to €33k not the €24k. How did I miss this? How did I get it so wrong?

I take a chance and call Tomo. He's as cheerful as ever and delighted to hear from me. He is somehow ignoring the pandemic and is planning a trip to Thailand. "Yes, I remember we both agreed €24k was a very good price for all the electric and plumbing work. But looking at the PDF Danny has sent through, I can see how we messed up. We thought the central pages were a subtotal as it is in smaller writing. But it is at the end of the quote for the electrics. And the plumbing total at the back is €24k. That is bigger writing, which made us think it was the totally total. It was a stupid mistake by us. Anyway, how was your wonderful Christmas?"

I wish I had his attitude. If I did a job and missed something that was going to cost my client €13k I would be mortified, not skipping over to a friendly chat. But for some reason I really like Tomo, he gives me a sense of optimism.

Eventually, we accept we owe Danny the €11k, with a further €5k's worth of work still to be done to finish the top floor and install the solar panel.

But Antonio's bill is definitely a mistake. He is charging us €9k for the plasterwork repair and €6k for a new drain system running around the house to collect the rainwater. Surely this was also included in Danny Boy's original quote and plans?

We search Danny Boy's quote again, but cannot find any mention of a drain system for the gutters.

It's something we will deal with in a few weeks, when Antonio gets back from extending his ski trip onto the already extended Christmas holidays. I am sure there is a logical explanation. We are thinking it might be something formal that he has to issue for his accounting system. All I know is that I must get back to work and earn some money to pay even the basic bills when they start to arrive.

I sit, wrapped in a blanket with a fan heater on, at the end of the diarrhoea sofa with my laptop and I answer any emails that need to be done to rearrange booked weddings a second time. I reward myself with a couple of hours to write my blog each morning with Asha by my feet, Looney, our bichon frise, by my side and the cats doing their best to sit on my keyboard, open notebook or lie on any paper I am looking at.

January is usually the busiest time for me after Christmas engagements but this year people are sitting on the fence, unsure of what Covid will do to their destination wedding plans. Instead of taking calls and handling emails about new bookings I have assumed the role of counsellor to couples concerned about what Covid will do next. I don't know why they think I know more than anyone else, but talking about it seems to help them.

That is, all except one couple. It's the bride more than the groom. She is determined their wedding will go ahead. Covid or no Covid they will be dragging their guests kicking and screaming halfway across the world to witness them getting married.

As I don't have an office, the kitchen is the only place I can take a video call away from the dust and Victorian asylum-style backdrops of mould and cobwebs.

While I am on the call with the determined couple, I see two men in high-viz jackets over red boiler suits standing in our garden.

"It must be the gas men," Ronan says in an excited whisper, as he puts on a mask and goes out to greet them. Out of the corner of my eye I can see him talk to the first ever visitors to our house, hand gestures all over the place. I go back to focusing on my bride and groom call who want to know what flavours of gelato they have to choose from for the welcome night of their guests' arrival.

"Is it true that there's Tiramisu-flavoured ice cream?"

"Yes, there's also English trifle."

"I think we'll go with something everyone will enjoy Darling... how about strawberry and chocolate?"

"But Freddy, I want Tiramisu."

I'm sure I heard her stamp her foot. She pouts and I can see his eyes glaze like a puppy dog who wants to be adopted.

I hear Italian voices in the hallway, they are talking loudly at Ronan. There's commotion and then I notice the vehicle they have arrived in.

"I'm sorry, I am going to have to call you back in a moment." I slam my laptop shut just as Ronan opens the door and ushers the men into the kitchen, pointing them to the gas stove.

I stand up to a hysterical chorus of "Mascherina, mascherina," being shouted at me by the two men. I grab a mask from the counter and put it on at breakneck speed.

"Che c'è? Cos'è?" I ask, already knowing I will not understand their response.

I guess correctly. They are both saying things. They show me their clip board.

"Not here," I say in Italian and I tell them our address. They attempt to leave through the front door but, having pulled back the draft blocking curtain and saying "Mamma Mia" in unison at our Star Trek efforts of keeping the north winter wind out with duct tape, bubble wrap and Styrofoam, they leave through the back door in a hurry.

"Are they not the gas guys?" Ronan is miffed.

"Ronan, what the hell? Did you not notice what they arrived in? The big yellow thing with blue lights on the top? An ambulance?"

He looks out the window and sees them take off at high speed, the siren now going.

"Oh yeah, I thought it was one of those emergency gas vans."

Seeing ambulances speeding along on otherwise empty roads is becoming less frequent. The news is promising. The first batch of vaccines have started to be administered to health workers and the over 90s in Italy. I'm getting hopeful that we will soon be able to travel freely again.

The following day it's snowing–not something that happens around here too often. The clothes on the washing line are frozen into monstrous shapes overnight and Spooky is fascinated by the white stuff falling from the sky. It was supposed to be a sunny winter day for our last push to get our house move finished, as we realise we have left some things in Giovanni's attic, but it's too cold to budge away from the warm stove.

I don't feel the house is our 'home'. As long as we are still moving stuff from the other house, we are still connected there.

"I've created a small pile of things we brought by mistake from Giovanni's that are Giovanni's and not ours," I say to Ronan, trying to achieve something that will count as progress towards the massive task that is making this ruin feel like a home. Ronan looks over, "What? My favourite plant? It will die out there, and I thought that was ours."

"No, it's Giovanni's... and it's plastic."

"Plastic? I've been watering it for the last three years. I was very happy with myself that it stayed alive."

Before getting distracted by trying to declutter, I had again tried painting an undercoat of white paint on the entrance hallway walls. I was sick to the back teeth of the crack-den-style look created by the graffitied instructions spray-painted on the walls by the electrician and plumber. But I abandon my efforts when the cold in the hallway makes being there unbearable and the paint which should dry in a couple of hours stays wet for days. Asha and the cats all have white streaks on their black coats from exploring the craved smell of freshness the paint promises.

Other than a quick visit, but long enough to get covered in paint, the pets avoid the hallway and the rest of the cold house. Moonface has taken to walking across the mantle, sleeping beside the bronze Buddha head and jumping on Ronan's shoulders whenever he bends to fill the pellet stove. She droops sets of legs on either side of his neck and wraps her tail across his face, just under his nose like a big moustache for extra balance. She stays there for hours, sleeping while he's on the computer or watching the TV. Ronan doesn't complain, it keeps his neck warm.

Opening the front door that the ambulance men experienced won't happen again until the spring, so the redecoration will wait for now, we'll stay in hibernation until this cold spell is over.

We'll keep the cats in for a few weeks. They have come from being surrounded by fields to living close to a busy road and a railway track out the back. I'm nervous, but hope they are intelligent enough to eventually be left out by themselves without venturing outside our fenced garden.

Looney still comes up to sleep on our bed. Asha came upstairs on the first day, but she has been limping and when we go to bed, she is reluctant to attempt the stairs. So we make a bed for her in front of the stove. "We better take her back to the vet. The anti-inflammatory medicine seems to have stopped working on her leg, she's limping a lot again."

"I'll call Moira and make an appointment once the holidays are over."

Luca has been busy going up and down the stairs with boxes of stuff. I have no idea which room he sleeps in each night. Like us he drifts from room to room carrying his mattress with him like a turtle, finding the least offensive smelling room of the day. "Have you finally decided which room you want as your own?"

"Yeah", he says satisfied. "The big one on the second floor."

"NO, you can't have one on the second floor," I say, startled.

"Why not?" asks Ronan, lugging the plant back outside which he wanted to double check was actually false by burning one of the leaves which promptly melted.

"Because his name is Luca... My name is Luca I live on the second floor?" I sing the last line as badly as I ever sing.

They both look blankly.

"The Tracy Chapman song? About the kid being beaten up by his parents? Great song but very depressing."

"Soooo... if I move onto the second floor, you are going to beat me up? Is that what you are saying?" Luca has destroyed my illogical argument so I try something more practical.

"But there's no electricity up there."

"It's okay I have the left-over Christmas candles." He continues up the flights of stairs.

"He's going to become even more of a recluse up there by himself. He needs to get out, we all need to get out." This was my real fear showing itself. With a full floor to himself, we'd see him less. He would become independent of us.

"Tell that to the pandemic," sighs Ronan.

The evening train passes. I can see it from the sitting room window. It slides by with its illuminated windows looking like an old-fashioned film strip, each frame holding an element of someone's story. The train station is within walking distance – five minutes – so the train entering and leaving the station is always slow and quiet.

I like it – the train is life during a time when the world is staying quiet, holding its breath waiting for this thing to pass. But when I look closely at the slow passing train, and the next and the next, I notice there is no life on them, no one is allowed to travel except for essential service workers. The trains that would normally be bustling with people going to Florence are just golden-lit empty carriages, empty of adventures.

4

TO MEET: INCONTRARE

This is the third house move our trusty 21-year-old Hi-Ace campervan has helped us with, and she ran up and down the road full to the brim each time. She now needs a bit of encouragement to wake up in the mornings with a tap of a hammer on the starting motor. We do our last run from Giovanni's, bringing back his now slightly melted plant and other odd bits before retrieving the boxes of memories forgotten in his attic. I had brought them from Ireland as essential items and hadn't opened them since.

"During the summer I am going to redo the inside of the camper," says Ronan, trying to untangle a rusting chainsaw blade from around the once pretty camper's sofa-bed leg that I had carefully painted duck-egg blue many years previously.

We have used the van as a tool shed since we arrived in Italy three years ago. Sweeping her floor was like a therapy session for me, having finished removing the last of our stuff so that she can soon go back to being a campervan. She had got us to our forever home and now she could rest. We could rest.

"It's looking shabby and grotty and I have an idea for a new layout."

"Do you not think we are going to be little busy this summer with a slightly bigger project?" I nod towards the house.

"We'll be finished that by summer."

"You think??"

"Sure. Once we have the heating on and the walls dry out, we can start painting one room a day. Twenty-two rooms is twenty-two days. Finished within a month. Well, the bathrooms will take longer and we are bound to come across a hiccup or two, so maybe two months...three at max."

I am usually the optimistic one in our relationship, but I am thinking Ronan has forgotten a major hornet sized fly in the tiny jar of ointment.

"And where is the money coming from to do this lightning-fast decoration schedule?"

"The 50/50 restoration refund."

The 50/50 restoration refund is a somewhat elusive payment scheme the government set up to bring houses in Italy up to the seismic and energy efficiency standards. You get fifty percent back in tax reductions over ten years, which is pretty useless unless you are paying a lot of tax. However, there is also the option of a bank buying the tax credit from you for ten percent.

"Ronan, if those bills in the drawer are correct and they have to be paid, then that uses up all the 50/50 payback we were relying on to finish the house."

The house is still in bits. Nothing is finished, or close to being finished other than the very expensive roof we cannot see, the bathroom I have tiled and the kitchen which is beautiful. The sitting room is done to a standard we can sit in, but it will eventually need work. Even if we had the money, it would take more than a month or two to finish. I think a year or two would be more realistic. And that doesn't include replacing the smaller roof over the spooky attic, which we put on hold to save us €24k.

Ronan's face has lost its spark. "Well then, I should definitely do up the campervan, as we might end up living in it. On a positive note, it would be easier to heat. "

As his arm strains to slam the reluctant back door of the van, my phone buzzes with a text from Antonio. "Speak of the devil," I say to Ronan before reading his text aloud.

"Happy new year Rosie. When will you pay the invoice?"

It's time to face the elephant with tusks in the room.

I type back. "I hope you had a nice Christmas. I just want to be clear this financial statement you left on Christmas Eve is for work done to date and paid for by the two recent instalments we made?"

"Nooooo. It still needs to be paid."

The creeping fear of the horrible shadow just proved itself to be an actual monster. But I was not going to go down without a fight.

"We need to meet with Mick Kelly at the house and talk about this. We feel there is a crossover of work with Danny Boy's invoice."

Nothing gets a builder out to your house quicker than suggesting you might not pay his bill.

The meeting starts with Mick Kelly translating that Anto has done a lot of work he has not charged us for.

Antonio seems to have a tendency to do work he feels should be done without discussing it with us first. It is good to hear he was not charging us for it.

"É Bella si?" Anto says, as he points to the open ceiling hole entrance to a small attic above the stairwell, where the mandatory skylight window is to give access to the mandatory roof lifeline pole, that cost four thousand euro. He has lined the attic space with pine wood and beams.

Anto is enthusing in the background with lots of hand gestures about how he is going to build very steep stairs to the hole, there on the landing for us. Mick Kelly is disagreeing with him about it and insisting he should put in a spiral staircase and then they are both opting to knock down a wall to make room for the staircase to this well-lined hole.

I am trying to find a break in their conversation to interrupt, but as with all Italian conversations, they somehow keep the conversation going even though they're both talking simultaneously and neither is taking a break for a breath.

With ten minutes wasted on a thing they have not discussed with us yet again, I use the only solution I have found works, which is to raise my voice above theirs making me sound irate.

"It's nice yes, but what's the point?" I shout. They both look at me, shocked at my voice raising. "What is the point of it?" I gesture towards the pine-lined, most finished spot of the house. "No one is going to see it, it's going to be covered with a ceiling hatch."

"You do not want a stairs up there?" Mick Kelly says puzzled with amazement.

"Why would I want stairs up there? It's small, high, dangerously close to the three-storey stairwell and I have 22 rooms to go into. Why would I want stairs to an attic space that is even too small for me to stand up in or to swing a cat in?"

"You want a swing for your cat in it?"

"No! Never mind. Look, I appreciate he hasn't charged us for it, but I feel it was a waste of their time. Can we go downstairs and discuss the things he has given us the surprise bill for?"

Back outside, Anto points out the trench of new cement along the side and back of the house and up to the front door where they have put the new drainage system for the roof drainpipes to enter around the house.

"So, you guys did this, not Danny's crew?"

"Sì sì, we did it, it had to be done, the one that was there was old and did not match up with Danny's work."

"Then if you were in charge of this and also in charge of the gutters and drainpipes coming from the roof, why the hell didn't you match them up?"

I'm pointing to the long copper drainpipe from the roof that stops five feet short of the ground level. The drain system that he has put in doesn't go as far as the down pipe. There is no hole in the ground for the short down pipe to meet up with the ground drain. We point this out.

"Yes, he will fix this," says Mick Kelly. The length of copper pipe which was obviously for this section had been whisked away from our garden with every other left-over tile and length of pipe. They all now lay perfectly stacked at the end of Giovanni's field behind the house that we used to rent, along with twenty years of other left-over building supplies from their family building company projects.

There is also a drainpipe from the back roof going nowhere, except onto our flat roof causing rain to flow down from that onto the French doors and into our sitting room.

"This will connect to the drain when the other roof is done," explains Mick Kelly, who I think is starting to feel guilty about recommending Antonio to us.

"Yes, but we need something temporary to stop the waterfall outside our back door every time it rains. We also want the level of the concrete raised outside the front gate to stop the water from the whole street forming rapids into our garden every time it rains. This was something he was going to do."

"Okay, we understand the work on the drainage system was necessary, but the work and price were never discussed. We were of the belief it was part of the plumbing works that Danny Boy would do, that it was part of his job agreement," explains Ronan, with a few 'o's' sprinkled onto the end of the words to make it sound Italian.

"Also, the €9k you are charging for doing the wall filler work, this is something you should discuss with him as he subcontracted your company to do it, I presume?" My face is rigid. I'm not backing down on this.

Mick Kelly is translating what I have said to Anto whose shoulders are past his ears as he is talking a mile per minute, protesting with his hands out.

"I think perhaps we have a meeting with Dan and Antonio together at my office to work this out," says Mick Kelly while Antonio launches into another lengthy spiel and shoulder shrugging session.

"We also need to get started on applying for the fifty percent restoration bonus refund."

Mick Kelly nods, "Yes, that would pay for the bills."

"No," I say adamantly. "The bonus is to pay for future work in the house. This bill is still questionable." My voice is raised again. It's becoming obvious that Italians bring out an angry side of me.

Mick Kelly introduced us to a bank that participates in the 50/50 bonus scheme in our town. I went through the two-hour process of opening an Italian bank account, and with the help of the lovely, patient cash desk assistant, Roberta, I had made all the payments for the work done, using the special complicated forms that the cashier completes for each invoice instalment.

During my last visit in November, after spending €70k, I used Google translate to ask the bank manager –leering Marco– when the refund will come through. Marco likes the fact that all his good-looking female assistants giggle at his every word, except for Roberta, she's older and wiser. I didn't need Google translate to understand his response of 'ten years' in Italian.

I think he knew by my face that I was not expecting this. Roberta looked awkward.

I rushed back across the square to Mick Kelly's office.

"He said it would take ten years for the refund to come through!"

Mick Kelly laughed. "I hope not, as I am also relying on this for my house too later this year."

"So what do we need to do?"

"I will talk with him."

"What is the usual length of time for the money to come through?"

"I don't know, I have never claimed it before."

"But you are claiming for your house too?"

"Yes, but after I see how it's done for your house."

"Well, what about the bank? What did he say was the usual time-scale when we first met him?"

"He doesn't know as they've never done it either. I will talk to him."

I left Mick Kelly's office feeling like a guinea pig in a science lab.

Anto tells me there is a meeting scheduled next week to discuss the surprise invoices. I'll wait until the meeting to discuss the paperwork needed for the bank as we are going to bring Lucia to ensure there is nothing lost in translation. This is going to be a battle.

TO ARGUE: LITIGARE

I 'm all on edge. When I am on edge, I am ready for things too early and today is no different. I have arrived for our meeting at Mick Kelly's office a half an hour too early. Even before Ronan, as I decided to walk to the office to burn off some energy in case I explode at them.

Now that we are living in the house, I need to get garbage bins and as the town hall is just across the square from Mick Kelly's office and I have my battle head on, I feel ready to be brave and try to figure out how to request bins for the house. There are a group of four people chatting behind their masks and standing apart in the entranceway. Other than that, the lights are off in most of the offices.

One of them asks in Italian, "Can I help you?" while I am looking along the names of departments, guessing which one I need to go to. "I have just moved into the town and I want to get garbage collection," I say, using my pre-prepared Google translate line.

Instead of answering me, he jests with the group about who should deal with me, "That is TARI. They are on the second floor. You are resident now?"

"No, I am not a resident, but I have bought a house."

The group looks puzzled at each other and has what seems like a heated discussion about my need of bins as a non-resident. Only residents create rubbish apparently.

"You need to be resident to get bins, but this is the office that deals with it. You need to call them and make an appointment because now it is closed." He says all this in Italian with some English sprinkled in between, which allows me to semi-comprehend what he is trying to tell me.

I write down the number with no intention of calling them. They won't speak English and my lack of Italian has muted me.

My determination is still high when I get to Mick Kelly's office. Antonio is late, so I sit pensively as Ronan fraternises with the enemy, talking about football with Danny Boy and Mick Kelly.

By the time Antonio arrives, I am ready to take someone's head off. I launch straight into the issue. I have no time for small talk.

As soon as I say that Danny Boy was to do the filling in and so it is his responsibility to pay Anto, they both go into a chorus of 'no no no's' with an undertone of laughing.

My eyes shoot from one to the other. That was too much of a well-rehearsed response. They've discussed this. These two are two peas in a pod. There are photos of them fishing and drinking together on Facebook. They have this well tied up; they have planned answers, rehearsed and performed so badly that both should never consider a career in acting.

I realise we will not win this one. There is no way around it, our only option is to negotiate the bills down as much as possible, get them to agree a timescale to finish the house and get the payment time put off for as long as possible.

Danny Boy's bill is fixed. There is no negotiating it down.

With Anto, I argue that this work was never agreed.

"But it needed to be done."

"But it still would have needed to be quoted and agreed. Do you think I have a spare €20k sitting in a drawer?"

"But the project manager, Tomo, was gone, and I thought we had a good relationship for us to do what is necessary."

While I am fuming and going for throats like a trapped mink, Ronan is having a laugh with Danny Boy.

Mick Kelly does a great job arguing some points with Anto and gets €5k knocked off the bill, all the time Anto doing his neck jutting movement. Numbers are being jotted down on the A4 negotiating page.

Anto acts like he is doing a massive favour with this discount, especially as he has done extras he has not charged us for, like the pine-clad attic space no one will ever see and where I want to install a swing for my cat, apparently.

We agree with a final number. I tell him I can't pay it until June. He says April, but I insist on June. By then we will have some weddings completed and our bank account's 'payments in' column will be out of its stagnant state.

"Stop being negative and oversensitive, they are not trying to rip us off," says Ronan in a loud whisper, while the four Italians in the room are having a full conversation about something which I can't make out as they are all talking at once, not leaving a pause for each other to make their point and not listening to the responses.

"It was work done, and it needs to be paid for. The 50/50 will cover it and then our income will cover the next stage of works."

I resign myself to the fact that our restoration grant will be gobbled up by work already done. I console myself with the thought that we can claim fifty percent back on these invoices also, so we only really will pay €12k for the surprise work. This will leave us with some money to use for the next stage. With that thought I feel better, less hard done by.

Time is ticking on and we've been here long enough for me to have a splitting headache from trying to follow negotiations in a different language.

"Mick Kelly," I shout above the Italian banter. Of course, it comes out just as there is the only pause in the entire meeting. So I am the irate Irish woman again, but I don't care. "For us to make the payment of these invoices, we need to get the 50/50 refund. I have tried to message you about this, but you never respond."

"Yesaa... to get the refund, the bank needs the paperwork from the authority that looks after planning permission etc. to say the project is finished."

"Okay, so give it to them."

"But the project is not finished."

"The house will never be finished," I say, knowing from past renovation experiences. "But the roof, windows, plumbing and electrics are finished enough for you to sign it off as done."

He thinks about this for a moment. "Okay, so we need a meeting to close the project."

"We are in a meeting now. What do we need another meeting for?"

"We need a meeting to discuss because you need to have all the invoices for the work done."

"Yes, I have them."

"But you need to have paid them all."

"Yes, I have paid them all."

"But you need to have all the receipts from the bank to say you have paid them with the particular forms."

"They are all in there." I shove a well organised red folder across the table to him.

The others are both laughing. They understand what is going on and I understand their jeers, "Ah Mick Kelly, you have to work now. There is no way out."

Perhaps the Italians are not used to someone being so organised. I know for sure they are not used to people paying invoices as promptly as we have all the way through the project.

That night I dream that the fine cement that hangs in the house's air, coating my long hair and keeps it in whatever position I put it in, combined with the humidity, makes my hair solid, standing upright in a cone shape. No washing will help it. It's a solid cement obelisk on top of my head. I wake from the dream coughing from inhaled dust and mould, trying to think of how to say to an Italian hairdresser, "Not so tall and perhaps paint it a colour."

6

TO PRUNE: POTARE

The first thing we bought new for the house were the electric white goods. The fridge, the dishwasher and the washing machine.

After a month of being in our 'new' horror movie style house, the novelty of having a dishwasher hasn't worn off. We spent the previous three years in a rental with a tiny kitchen last updated in the sixties with no surface space and just a sink and an old range cooker.

We all love filling the dishwasher, pressing a button and having clean stuff to put back in the cupboards an hour later. The new kitchen, the only finished room in the three-storey house, remains surprisingly clean.

The washing machine took a few more weeks to become a joy. For the first few uses, it bounced around the dungeon hole we named the utility room, banging off walls and making the noise of a drummer falling down five flights of stairs.

My dad is on a video call with me, watching it bounce off the wall before it hops back across the room and bounces off the other side with the noisy drummer boy still stuck inside. "Have you removed the screws from the back?"

"What screws? There're no screws mentioned in the instructions?"

"They stabilise the drum during transport. They need to be removed before you use it."

"Why wasn't it mentioned in the instructions? Ronan even read them to try to figure out why it was bouncing around."

"Ronan read instructions? Is he well? If only I could be over there with you, I would have that fixed for you in a jiffy." My nearly 87-year-old dad sighs. Their plans to come to live with me are still scuppered because of Covid lurking outside their doors, ready to pounce on them if they attempt to travel until vaccines are developed enough.

The February weather is temperamental. It teases us into spring with some days reaching the high teens and then the following week it is snowing. On the first day of warmth, a balmy 18 degrees, we are immediately outside planning how to turn our football-pitch-sized space into a fabulous garden. The Italian passers-by still wrapped in their winter coats and scarf look at us in bewilderment. I think I even see fear or concern in some of their faces, wanting to warn us of the colpo d'aria – the Italian draught that will cause cold, fever, stomach ache, a limb falling off or possible death.

. . .

At the moment, the garden resembles a neglected wasteland that unscrupulous people used as a dumping ground for years. This hasn't been the case. The rubbish in the garden is only from the house, but there is a lot of it. Ivy has taken over outbuildings, low walls and a large part of the area we want to turn into a courtyard. Shrubs and pampas grass have grown into giants, roses left unpruned. Once carefully planted spring bulbs are buried under piles of fallen leaves and branches. The lawn has turned to long scutch grass and the ground beneath is bumpy from snake and rodent holes.

The only part outsiders have contributed to are where dog owners have carefully picked up their dog's business, neatly tied the top of the bag and thrown it into the overgrown front garden of the derelict house, rather than carry it home or to a bin. These get stuck in my rake as I pull the years of magnolia leaves and seed pods into piles to be composted.

There's also a lot of windswept rubbish blown in from the road, aged plastic packaging, a McDonald's cup from God knows where, considering there isn't one for about fifty miles.

I used to think Italians were careless with the environment and thought they just threw their rubbish out their car windows or dumped the odd bag of garbage on the roadside judging from the amount of litter I would see stuck in weeds of the roadside ditches. But having experienced the strong wind gusts when living at Giovanni's that knocked over our heavy garbage bins and sent litter soaring, and having seen carefully left out plastic bags ready for collection rolling down the street faster than a Ferrari, I realise it's the freak Italian gusts that are the biggest littering culprits.

There are already some features in the garden that just need fixing, tidying and amending to become part of the vision which I can't yet visualise. We want a courtyard outside the backdoor where we can eat alfresco under the shade of the persimmon tree. The area is already nearly enclosed by sheds on either end, the house on one side and overgrown hazelnut and bay trees on the other. There is a sizeable gap between the house and one of the sheds, which you can see the road and driveway through, so the first thing it needs is for the back garden to be sectioned off with a short wall to form a courtyard.

We were going to build it ourselves, but Ronan's back is still a bit dodgy and it would have taken us about three weeks of arguments to get it finished.

The building trade is booming now that Covid restrictions have been lifted and I can't ask Anto for help, so I hedge my bets and call Tomo to see if he knows someone who will do it as a nixer. "I'm in Bangkok. A guy will be at your house tomorrow." Tomo is magically travelling the world when the rest of the world find it impossible.

How happy was I to see Omaroberto turn up at eight the next morning. Omaroberto is the brilliant Moroccan stone mason who worked on our roof. We'd saved the stones that had to be removed from the eaves of the house for the new roof to be fitted and it is these he works with all day to build a perfect corner for our courtyard. It looks like it has been there forever.

The following day he returns to plaster the courtyard side of the wall with cement, which we'll paint white and grow bougainvillea against. We're very happy with the result. But being the people we are, we are both thinking the same thing, looking at the wet cement on the wall. Ronan voices what I am thinking, "We should write something in it."

I'm immediately over at it and I write our initials: RM 'heart' RS. It's cute and will be there for generations to smile at when they're eating alfresco in the garden with their friends.

Later that evening, after a couple of glasses of wine, I'm outside again walking the dogs and looking at the stars. I spot the wall and I'm thinking I should put the initials of our kids in the cement too before it dries. So underneath my earlier masterpiece, I scroll RM + RS 'heart' and I put the initials of both our kids. I get carried away and do one for the pets.

The following day Ronan walks outside to have his morning coffee. I follow with my tea.

"Rosie, why on earth did you write that one?" He is staring at what I scrolled in the now dry cement wall. He gets the kids initials and the Looney and Moonface one once explained, but he's pointing at the one I had done for Asha and Spooky and the last name of our family initial, 'S'. Now generations to come, when they're eating alfresco in the garden with their friends, will look at it puzzled and discuss why great-great granny and grandad felt the need to declare in concrete, for all to read, that RM and RS loved ASS.

Asha approves of the wall. It is the perfect suntrap and she immediately finds a spot where she slowly lowers herself to the ground, groaning at her leg and sleeps. It's taking her longer and longer to find a comfortable spot to sleep and her dark eyes have become bluer and her jowls peppered with white. Our beautiful girl is ageing fast.

She now prefers to stay there rather than follow me down the garden when Shelly from my yoga class arrives with her husband Sherwin, to show me how to get my unruly vines in order.

Shelly is the closest in the group to my age and still works full-time in editing for a TV company in Rome. Having planted a small vineyard on their own land, Shelly has done a vineyard course and knows the basics of pruning.

Our five vines are heavy and the builders have clipped the thick rusted cordon wire holding the vines up to bring their digger through to the other side of the garden. This sent the wire spiralling back like a trapped snake. Now the wires just hang, stick out and hide, ready to pounce and take your eye out in one step or movement. Sherwin is taller than Ronan, so the two men are the perfect height to reach, bend and wind the threatening rusty wires holding up the vines.

In the crisp warmth of spring sunshine, we enjoy a glass of wine together while the lads tame the wires and I get a crash course in vine pruning. Four canes to each branch and prune back to the sixth leaf notch of each twig.

Sherwin and Shelly have had a holiday house up the hill for ten years and moved there full time three years ago when Shelly got her new job in Italy. As she works in TV, she has an insight into the backstories of what is happening in Italy.

Of course, we talk about the vaccine and the possible end to the bloody pandemic. There is a delay in the vaccine roll out as there is now a political row about 300,000 supplies not arriving and they are still vaccinating people over 80 years old.

"It's true what they say about Italians having one of the longest life spans in the world. The supply of over 80-year-olds for the vaccine just seems never ending," exclaims Sherwin in his thick London accent. "We went back to the UK for our vaccines. Shelly gets a diplomatic pass because of the news projects she works on, so we've been able to go back and forth. We have some spare Yorkshire teabags and Bisto if you need any?"

He didn't need to ask twice. The last of our rationed Bisto gravy granules were used on Christmas Day and my teabag supply was running dangerously low. "We're having a BBQ this weekend with some of the others from yoga. Come along and we'll load you up with rations then?"

With the common need of decent tea and gravy I can see this couple understand us... We may have just made our first friends in Italy.

7

TO UNDERSTAND: CAPIRE

W e haven't socialised in so long, I'm wondering if we will still remember how to speak with strangers at a BBQ. Ronan has dressed for the occasion wearing a vest top he bought in the Chinese shop and the shorts he was wearing two days previous while plastering the shed. He has washed them – it's a special occasion, after all.

They are an eclectic bunch of Welsh, English, and Scottish. We, as the Irish contingent, complete the four nations and a zillion jokes.

The strange thing about living abroad is that you end up hanging out with people who you'd never encounter in your normal life at home.

"I used to work for MI5," announces Sherwin. "I was the full-time chef for the building." Shelly worked on all the TV programs I used to watch as a child and knew all the presenters on a first name basis.

"I know all about you," chips in Daisy coyly, giving Ronan a fist bump greeting. We both remember her from her stint as a soap opera TV actress before they killed her off. She then went on to be a singer working on the cruise ships.

"I've read Rosie's book."

"Me too, I know all about you too," laughs Ruth, the yoga teacher, handing Ronan a glass of fizzy water. Ronan does a weird nervous smile I have never seen him pull before. He hasn't read my book, so he has no idea what people know about him.

"He's brave. It's a bit early in the year for bare legs," I say, nodding towards the kilt-wearing chap on the other side of the garden.

"Oh, that's Ivor, Blodwin's husband," explains Ruth. "They were sheep farmers back home in Wales, but retired here to become olive farmers instead."

"Ivor wears kilts all the time. It's an interesting mix when we are helping them prune their olive trees and he's up a ladder," smirks Daisy.

"He is right, men need to air their balls," states Helga the German, the only non-native English speaker amongst the group, but who is probably more fluent than any of us at English, never mind her perfect Italian. She is the one that gets her legs behind her head in yoga and makes all the advanced moves look easy.

She fits into the stereotype perfectly by milling her own flour to bake bread and wears kaftans. I don't have a clue how she understands her husband, Calum, who has the thickest Scottish accent I have ever heard. I have an easier time understanding Italian than deciphering what he is saying.

Like us, they have been stuck here in Italy since Covid kicked off and haven't got back to Scotland to see their clatter of grandchildren, much to Calum's dismay, but not to Helga's. "The world is overpopulated enough. I do not understand why my two children have had to add ten more to the problem."

We all bond over renovation and Italian bureaucracy stories. Our nine missing doors story goes down a treat, with Daisy and Ruth both chipping in parts I have forgotten, but they remember as they read about it in my book. The group is a collective encyclopaedia of knowledge and a packed Rolodex of contacts for anything we might face in Italy.

"Just avoid the idea of ever suing anyone," says Daisy.

"My ex, the arrogant sod," she says, referring to her fourth husband who lives somewhere near Rome, "sued his builder as some building work wasn't done correctly on his house. The court went in favour of the Italian builder and F**k Face was slapped with a €30k solicitor's bill. He then sued the solicitor as he did absolutely nothing except file the paper-work as far as my husband could see, and that case is still going on two years later with his solicitor bills mounting... serves the bastard right but still a worthy lesson to learn from."

"Court cases and trials of any type in Italy should be avoided," nods Ruth, passing the carbon neutral avocado chocolate mousse Helga had brought along to the feast. "One Italian family I know has been in lawsuits with each other for twenty-six years. It started about a section of a house and continued with counter lawsuits about treatment of their cats and a horse."

The BBQ was a weird experience, not because of the people, they were all lovely, but because we hadn't been around other people socialising for a year. We both felt exhausted by the time we got home.

Looney runs to greet us and Asha whacks her wagging tail up and down off the ground. She attempts to get up, but I can see it is causing her pain, so I pet her on her bed instead. "Don't worry girl, we have an appointment tomorrow for a check-up on your leg. Moira, the lovely vet, will make it all better for you." She recognises Moira's name and her tail thumps harder.

Asha knows the vet's surgery so well by now that she automatically goes and stands on the scales. Moira rubs her fondly behind the ears.

"You have lost weight. That is good." She's referring to the dog, not me unfortunately. "I don't know Moira, it's not because of more exercise. If anything, she is walking a lot less, sleeping a lot and her eyes have become bluer in the centre."

"The medicine for the ligaments is not working?"

"No, not anymore. Can you give her something stronger?"

Moira looks concerned. "They are strong. I think an x-ray would be a good idea. It could be something we can't see. I do not have a big enough x-ray machine, but there is a vet's clinic in the next town that has one. They are very good orthopaedic surgeons for animals."

Within days, we have an appointment at the mega vets. It seems better kitted out than a lot of hospitals for humans in

Ireland. It's a husband-and-wife team clinic where both greet us like old friends. They are younger than me and have an obvious passion for what they do and ambitions to become the best clinic in Umbria.

First, they x-ray Asha and take bloods. The x-ray results are not good. The bone in her back leg has become very thin and could snap at any time. It's a strong sign of cancer, but we won't know until we get the blood results back.

However, the vet is upbeat. The leg can be amputated. Dogs can manage very well with three legs. I look at my old girl. She has visibly aged so much in the last year. Her whiskers have greyed and white hairs have dispersed through her sleek blue-black shiny long-haired coat. Her once strong wide back, which we used to joke about getting a saddle for, now has a ridge of bone showing in places. She's still a heavy dog. "I don't think she would be able for three legs, and it's major surgery. I don't want her to suffer."

"We have done it many times. Recovery is quick. But first I think we need to do a CAT scan... it is expensive. I am sorry. But it will show if there is cancer and if it has got into her spine. If it is not in her spine, then I think you should consider amputating the leg. Talk to Moira about it."

While they prepare to sedate Asha for the CAT scan, we call Moira and tell her the result.

"I think she could manage with three legs. It could prolong her life for another one or two years."

"Only one or two?"

"She is already nine, Rosie. A German Shepherd's life expectancy is usually nine to thirteen years."

We know this. We had a German Shepherd before, Chaska, who reached thirteen and that was old. Like Asha, Chaska had gone downhill rapidly. Kidney failure had got her, and she died in Ronan's arms at the vets twelve years ago. We said never again, but here we are... possibly again.

Asha is sedated for the scan and Ronan drives me home as one of us needs to be there for a delivery. He returns to the vets.

I wait for his call, but it doesn't arrive. Two hours go by. I'm pacing the floor like a guy in a fifties movie outside a maternity ward. And then I hear the car pull up, Asha sitting up straight in the passenger seat, one ear up and one ear down, tongue hanging out, smiling, stoned out of her head. And then I see Ronan's face. I have never seen such sadness in his eyes.

"Oh, no... it's cancer?"

"It's in her spine. They can't do anymore for her." He manages to get the words out before leaning into my waiting arms and sobs like a baby.

"But they said she's in good form, so we still have some time with her. Weeks, perhaps a month or two."

"Is that all? She must be in a lot of pain, the poor thing."

I think back on the mornings where Asha has woken me frantically pawing at my arm, her eyes pleading with me. And me thinking she wanted to go out to pee and not understanding she was telling me that something is terribly wrong.

I open the door and Asha steps out of the car with wobbly ease. She leans against me and I pet her floppy ear. She's smiling, still drugged.

"Let's make her comfortable and give her lots of time and love, and when she gets to the stage of being in pain we will ask Moira to come out to the house."

I'm trying to be brave, but it's no use. My arms are around her neck and I'm blubbering into her shoulder so much that her hair is sticking to my eyes, cheeks, and nose.

But we don't have as long as we think. They needed to manipulate her leg for the scan and X-rays and it has inflamed her leg and joints. The following days we give her painkillers and she lies at my feet crying while I try to work on my laptop. She stands in front of me and looks into my soul, her eyes pleading with me. I can't do this anymore. I text Moira. "It's time. She's in too much pain."

"I understand. Come on Wednesday. I can do it at 4pm."

Wednesday. Ash Wednesday.

8

TO BURY: SEPPELLIRE

"I want to bury her in the garden." I am telling Lucia about our sad news. She loves our dogs as much as we do and has been our doggy sitter many times over the years.

"You cannot bury animals in your garden. It is not permitted," Lucia informs.

"Then what do you do with them?"

"The vet looks after getting them cremated. You can get the ashes if you want."

I am really uneasy about just leaving her body to others to dispose of. All my life we've buried our much-loved pets, hamsters and goldfish to cats and dogs, in our garden.

We fed her steak for dinner the night before and a full roast chicken in the morning.

"Does she not need to be fasting?" I ask off hand as she starts gnawing as best she can on a huge ham bone Ronan just gave her. She was already in heaven.

"In case she dies during the procedure of euthanasia?" he responds, his eyebrows undulating at my stupid question. But that is where my head is at.

The high level of pain killers we are giving her are wearing off and she's lying at my feet whining again. The clock ticks by slowly. By three I'm breathing like I just jumped into ice cold water.

It's time to say goodbye. Luca loses the fight against his tears. She has been with him since he was three. He can't remember his life without Asha in it. She is still a pup at heart. Her bark makes her seem like a great protectress, although she wouldn't hurt a fly. A creaking door or someone sneezing would have all 50kg of her on my lap within seconds. She is a big baby and a huge part of our lives, including four house moves in two countries.

As we walk into the garden, the cats circle and weave through her legs, rubbing their ears against her. And then Looney jumps at her, puts her front two paws on her shoulder and licks her face. The pets have never behaved like this before. We are all a blubbering mess.

Ronan helps Asha into the back of the car. She sits with her tongue flapping in the wind, smelling the air as we pass our first home in Italy; Giovanni's house. And Dogana, where we had walked the olive groves many times. The lake where she swam. And down the winding road we drove that night nearly four years ago to arrive in our new home after a three-day journey across Europe.

For the moment, she has forgotten her pain and is lapping up the scents. She had got us here, the kids she had protected and been a forever friend to, were now grown. Her job on this earth was done.

We take her into Moira's surgery. Because of Covid it is by appointment only, so we are the only ones here, thankfully.

Asha goes and stands on the scales and Moira is cuddling her head at the cuteness. We are both blubbering messes again.

"Maybe it is best she stays in the car. It would be better to do it there?" Moira says.

"But then we would have to lift her out and she is heavy."

"Oh, you want me to look after the em..." Moira is trying to find the right word in English. "The funeral? If so, I have not planned it. I need to book the service to come to take her. I could ask them to come on Friday, but you would need to bring her back then."

"I don't understand. I thought it was something you would arrange automatically. What are we supposed to do with her body?"

"You have a garden, no?"

"Yes, but we were told it is not permitted to bury pets in the garden."

"No, it is allowed, of course. Horses and farm animals no, but pets, yes."

"Oh, so we can take her home to her garden?" To me, it is a relief, but not to Ronan.

"Rosie, I can't. I can't dig her grave." He is sitting on the floor, hugging and petting Asha. His heart is already breaking and I understand by his drawn face that he might as well dig a hole big enough for them both to fit in if he had to do this task.

"Give me a moment." I walk outside and do a message recording.

"Lucia, we are at the vets. She said we need to take Asha home and bury her in the garden. Ronan can't dig the grave by himself. Could you ask Alessandro to come to help us?"

Immediately, I get a response. "Of course, leave it with me. Do you have shovels at the house?"

"Yes, Luca will show you where they are."

It was peaceful.

Lying in the back of the car ready for her next adventure, we sit on either side, loving her as she closes her eyes and her breaths become slower. Two of Moira's next customers arrived with their lively pets ready to be seen, but when they realised what is happening by our swollen wet eyes, they step back and bow their heads in sympathy and respect.

We drive back from the vets. Her body is still warm and supple and pain free. "She had a good life, and she really enjoyed being here in Italy. She made peace with cats, had big fields to run in and then got us to the new house," I say, trying to keep both our hearts from sinking.

"I'm glad she'll be in the garden. It's where she belongs and, as I always say, a house is not a home until it has a pet buried in the back garden."

Actually, that is the first time I have ever said it. Why would I have ever said it before? It is like that annoying habit I have of saying "It will all be fine, everything will be okay" when clearly it won't be. Such as the time my sister Eileen was found dead, and I had to tell my parents. Worst day of my life, but as they sobbed, I found myself saying "It will all be okay" when clearly it wasn't going to be. I tend to say it out of habit at the most obscure moments.

We pull in through the gate. There is a mist in from the lake hovering in the garden. Down at the end, we could see a light. It is Lucia and her boyfriend Alessandro with their phone's torch propped behind a bottle of water to magnify the low beam. We angle the car, so the headlights shine down the garden, giving them more light. There they are, spades in hand, standing with Luca. "I need my coat."

By the time I've returned with my coat, Ronan has returned from the end of the garden with the wheelbarrow – Asha's last chariot. "They have it already dug."

"Here, let's put this in first. It will make it easier for us to lift her out." I lay Asha's favourite blanket in the wheelbarrow and let it fall amply over the sides.

'She's still warm," I say, petting her forehead. "I don't want to bury her while she's still warm."

"Okay, but let's move her into the wheelbarrow. Moving her 50kg deadweight body isn't easy. "I don't want to pull her legs... in case I hurt her," I climb into the car and push while Ronan wraps his arms around her chest and lugs her out into the wheelbarrow.

I move her head so that it looks more comfortable. "Poor girl," I whisper and kneel down, kissing her head. "You were the best, we'll miss you, baby."

I gently remove her collar. "Come on Rosie, they're waiting on us."

We wheel her down the garden in her chariot to where the grave diggers wait. I put my hand on her chest. It is completely still. The three boys lift the corners of the blanket and with a bit of a topple, she lands in her final resting place. This time Lucia adjusts her head, so she looks comfortable. She takes the blanket from me and tucks her in, bends down and kisses her head. "Arrivederci, Amore."

As they drop the clay on top of her body, I sing a croaky version of the 'Our Father'.

A train passes slowly and I wonder if any passengers or neighbours are watching and what they are thinking... Four people with shovels at the end of the garden digging a grave with the fog hanging around us exaggerated by the headlights of the car... "We're probably going to be reported for burying a body. Is it possible to twitch shutters the same way neighbours would twitch curtains?"

Mam and Dad call later. They know how difficult it is as they had to make the decision for their 16-year-old mutt Topsy only weeks ago and they were both also very attached to Asha. I try to focus on the positives.

"The vet was wonderful, and we buried her in the garden this evening."

"The vet?" asks Dad.

"No Asha. We buried Asha in the garden, not the vet." I'm not sure if he was serious about the question, as he seems to think

Ronan joining the mafia is part of the package of moving to Italy.

We had all lost one of our best friends, a much-loved family member. We will miss her loving eyes and one ear up and one ear down. She brought so much love and happiness to our lives. Ash Wednesday will be Asha Wednesday to us forevermore.

9

TO CREATE: CREARE

The only time I get an urge to clean is when a chapter ends in my life. It's weird and doesn't happen very often, but the following day the sitting room and kitchen get the full brunt of it. I empty the vacuum twice of Asha's drifts of long black hair before I sit down to do emails on my laptop.

"We've decided to postpone." Reading the same words for the fifth time this week makes me close my laptop and take a deep breath. Normally at this time of year, I would be busy completing wedding plans for the summer, doing venue visits with excited couples and taking bookings for the following year.

The Irish and English governments had made some off-the-cuff remarks during the week about the possibility of people not being permitted to travel until 2023, and are advising people not make any travel plans for this summer, sending my business into free-fall again.

With the fear of travel restrictions, quarantine on return and the slow rollout of vaccines, couples are making the hard decision to postpone their weddings for the second time, now to 2022, some to 2023. Two of my couples have kept at least one of their life plans on schedule and have got pregnant. They'll have ready-made ring bearers before their new wedding dates.

This also presents a major dilemma. The original long-term plan was to wind up my Irish business before applying for residency in Italy and start something new, possibly not wedding-related at all. As Ronan is due his pension the following year it was going to be the perfect time for a new start.

The reason for not wanting to run my wedding business in Italy is because, as a sole trader they would tax me on everything that goes through my business account. They don't allow for expenses. In Ireland I am taxed after all expenses are deducted.

This is especially important for a business like mine where my clients pay for their catering, hotel, transport, etc., through me. So, for each client I could have €30k going through my account with €28k of this being paid directly out to other providers.

In Ireland I'm taxed on the €2k remaining - my profit. In Italy I would be taxed on the full €30k. Multiply that by 20 clients and I am paying tax on €600k rather than €40k. This would mean not only is my profit gone but also I would need to find additional money elsewhere to pay the tax man. I am no accountant but this is my understanding of the situation.

So running my wedding planning business the way I had it currently structured would not work. I would need to change it so that clients paid for services directly. At the moment, I couldn't do this. Thanks to Covid, all my weddings for the year I was due to wind up had been pushed to the following two years and I was contracted to all postponed clients to provide the easy peasy package service that I was known for.

By the time some of the weddings happen, I will have been dealing with them for five years when usually my longest commitment is eighteen months. However, some clients have decided it's all too unstable and to just get married at home.

The result is we will be without clients for the second year in a row and I have a business I can't close. I still have work to do, re-planning their weddings for a second and for some a third time; contacting venues, bands, photographers and at least ten other services to check availability for new dates, renegotiate contracts, working out new prices, creating booking forms. This is what I usually earn my fee doing. Never in my business planning did I ever have to re-plan twenty weddings, which is as much work as planning them the first time. I am doing all the re-planning at no charge, so basically the first planning fee is paying for two or three wedding plans for the same couple. With so many postponements, it doesn't leave any room for new clients and fresh income.

Once the re-planning is done, I will be unwillingly 'free' for the summer, free to work on the house, which we will need to be creative with. Without income, our renovation budget has shrunk drastically. I also need to put my thinking hat on and find a new income stream. Savings will only stretch so far.

The house could be the solution. Running a B&B is the obvious choice but can't happen with Covid. I do like the idea of groups coming to stay for a week... 'Life is Short Retreats' in

Italy for women in their wiser years and workshops for writers.

Within a few hours I have an idea sketched out... A few times a year I will send the lads off on a holiday and the house will become a hogan where women or writers can meet like-minded souls; do activities, relax, chat, make new friends, share their stories.

But none of these ideas solve my immediate income problem as it involves people travelling, strangers gathering and becoming friends – things forbidden because of Covid which we can't see an end of. Also, the house will need major work before it becomes a welcoming space.

I take refuge in writing. It comforts me. I write my blog regularly which I started on the day of the first lockdown in Italy, nearly twelve months ago.

I hadn't written creatively in years because I never had the time. I can get lost in writing all day and it was my 'some day when I have time' thing to look forward to, the thing I hungered to do most. Covid Lockdowns cancelling my wedding bookings and keeping me indoors gave me all the undistracted time in the world. I had no excuse not to write. The blog got the words flowing daily and by June I had turned my blogs into a story which developed into a book. I found an editor and a cover artist and on the third anniversary of us arriving in Italy full time, I self-published my first novel: A Rosie Life In Italy.

It was to be a one-off book; my 'write a novel' item on my bucket list ticked off. Sales have been consistent. And now, in its fourth month, it has covered its costs and any sales after this will be passive income.

I like to nurture and, in my mind, non-fiction books are the only ones that Indie authors can really sell effectively. So I decide to try to make some money focusing on creating self-help books.

I start writing 'How to Have a Fabulous Midlife Crisis'; I'm writing chapters on how to live your best life after your kids are grown, dust off your old ambitions and give them new life. I also create a 'Post Pandemic Planner' to help people through the gloomy days they may have during Lockdowns.

As the weeks go on and wedding enquiries cease completely, I decide I am having one of those days where I need some of my own medicine and open the 'Post Pandemic Planner'. I start to fill in the section: 'List a hundred things you have always wanted to do'... At first I can think of two things: sail around the Greek Islands and spend time exploring Costa Rica... but then the list starts to expand: Have a beautiful courtyard as an outdoor living space, become semi self-sufficient, make gorgeous meals everyday ...

Costa Rica and the Greek Islands will have to wait a while, but building a courtyard and a veggie patch is something I can work on now.

The weather has been perfect all week, so after the last cancellation call, I take a deep breath, go out to the garden and whack ivy for the morning, releasing frustration. Ronan focuses on gathering the remaining meters of thick rusty wire hanging from the metal poles that held up the vines many years ago and now has repurposed itself into a supporter of the eye patch industry by potentially taking out an unsuspecting eye or two.

By trying to avoid being one such client, I step on the rake and live out the classic cartoon scene of being bonked hard in the middle of the forehead by the handle. Ronan walks away trying not to laugh with the excuse of having something important to do in the winter sunroom... well, it is currently a shed, but I have a good imagination, so I call areas by the name they will eventually be.

I sit in our cement-splashed sun chair and imagine how to turn the current mud and scrap heap around me into a courtyard.

I'm not very good at sitting doing nothing and neither is Ronan. Within a half hour we are having arguments about whose giant step is closer to a meter as we pace out our courtyard to be. Eventually we resort to a measuring tape, watch a YouTube video on how to lay a patio and Google flagstones and pebble prices to get an idea of what we need to budget. We realise we will need 140 flagstones and a few tonnes of sand and pebbles to get it in shape, costing us over €1,000, so we keep remeasuring and redesigning until we are considering putting just twelve stones around the persimmon tree which will take centre place in the courtyard.

I work out I will need to sell 137 more copies of 'My Post Pandemic Planner' and memoir to pay for the courtyard flagstones. So it will have to wait, hopefully not as long as Costa Rica and the Greek Islands.

I move my focus onto something that won't cost much – the veggie patch (known as an 'Orto' in Italy). There is fantastic soil where I've hacked the ivy away so I dig it up and barrow it down the garden while Ronan constructs a makeshift raised bed out of old wooden fence poles piled in the garden.

Tomatoes, lettuce, green beans and courgettes will be planted in it, with a herb garden developed closer to the mud-heap-soon-to-be-courtyard.

I search news announcements daily, waiting to hear when Italy will allow tourists from the UK to arrive and for the UK to allow people to go on holiday. At the moment, there is a risk of being fined up to £5k if they even found you in a UK airport without a valid reason: health or work. And with Covid out of control in the UK, Italy is not allowing casual visits.

There's talk to indicate a green passport within the EU from July. The UK says there may be a possibility of travelling to some countries at the end of June. They release their list of permitted counties people are currently allowed to travel to without being fined. They are obscure places like the South Sandwich Islands.

"This list is not compiled so that people can go off to lie on a beach," says a UK government person. Families being kept apart for a year or not being able to get back to elderly parents seems to be considered as the same frivolity as lying on a beach. Although I think many people could do with lying on a beach right now, including me. I look up South Sandwich Islands, maybe it has nice beaches, but then realise they are down near Antarctica... I'll stick to my muck heap garden.

10

TO RECOVER: RECUPERARE

I zzy has got her work schedule. She starts mid-June and will work full time until Christmas. It is in perfect unison with the date the UK and Italy say they will permit travel. This means we won't get to see her until her contract ends next Christmas.

I am not a person who has ever suffered from depression, but I can feel myself spiralling down.

"What if there's another variant by the winter? What if she can't travel then either?" I voice my fears to Ronan, who is looking equally glum.

It's already been nearly a year since we've seen her. If it was planned, I could cope, but the not knowing is killing me.

I try to throw myself into developing the new business retreats idea and I do an online business refresher course, but no matter how hard I try and how much time I spend on developing it, it feels like holding a floppy fish. I just can't get enthused about it no matter how hard I try.

"What's the point?" I find myself saying every time I go to do something in the house. "Nobody is coming to visit until Christmas and by then the whole world will probably be in lockdown again."

Responding to emails from wedding clients is like dragging my feet through sludge. I can't feel enthusiastic for them like I usually am, as they are not enthusiastic either. They are worried and down and I absorb their feelings and add them to my own. I am a fixer by nature and I can't fix this.

 Reading a nice review about my book or reading a complimentary comment about it on social media keeps my head bobbing above the black sea of lonely despair. I am doggy paddling in our freezing cold house with its mouldy walls and lots of potential. That and being able to video chat with my parents and Izzy every day has been my saving grace. But I no longer want to just chat to them, I want to hug them; I want to scratch the smiling surface we painted every day for each other and touch them, sit with them and know that they are all really okay.

I was beginning to feel the need to avoid the daily call; the surface was cracking and I could not keep up this pretence any longer that everything was alright. It wasn't.

I abandon 'My How to Have a Fabulous Midlife Crisis' book project. How can I write about something that is no longer real for me? I am in the depths of misery and there's nothing fabulous about it.

I hear about a new 'social media' app called Clubhouse. My initial thought is 'not another one', but then I discover it's as if a radio station and a podcast had a baby. No faces, just live voices in topic rooms you can participate in.

I join Clubhouse and immediately I'm addicted. I join 'rooms' discussing business, entrepreneurship, motivation, midlife. Networking with people again, laughing with strangers and sharing stories raises my spirits and satisfies my craving for some sort of social interaction. But while the rooms are interesting and the chats encouraging, nothing raises my enthusiasm for business. I am burnt out.

I continue to write my blog and interact with readers of my book. They catch me every time my head goes under a giant wave. It's not ego, it's just a feeling that I exist and my words are keeping the readers' heads above water too. They tell me how much I have helped keep them afloat, but they don't realise how that comment keeps me from going under too. A circle of support.

It's the 10th March. My maternal grandmother's birthday, the first anniversary of the day we were supposed to sign for the house but Covid happened and it has now turned into the first anniversary of the day the world saw Italy, the first western country, go into Covid lockdown. And we were in the middle of it.

I had returned from Ireland only days before, as the pandemic was taking hold in Italy. My parents had had the news on all day every day and the only thing on every Irish radio and TV show were talking about 24/7 was the crisis in Italy. By the time I was leaving Ireland, I was exhausted by the bombardment of news. I couldn't wait to get back to Italy with its then 1,600 cases. The news had freaked me out so much I patted my parents on the head to say goodbye rather than hug them because I was afraid I would give them the virus.

Also, I knew by the sounds of how things were progressing I would not get back to them before the summer; it was going to be quite a while before I saw them again, and a hug would have broken me and turn me into a snivelling wreck. I never imagined I would sit here a year later, still not knowing when I will return to hug them.

Chatting to people again and networking lifts my feeling of complete isolation after a few days. Not only my head, but my shoulders too, bob above the wave of positivity coming from people reading my book. It's ranking number one in categories to do with Italy. I haven't lost my writing mojo after all.

I decide to throw myself into the house and prepare for when people will come. On Saint Patrick's Day I hang my Irish Tri-Colour from the front balcony.

I buy green paint and begin preparing a bedroom for when Izzy will come. I don't know when it will happen, but she will return at some point and we need to get things ready. I call it the jungle room.

There's an Irish Clubhouse room playing Irish music and chatting with people. I join in the chat. It's been a long time since I've had a laugh with strangers. It's a huge part I miss about my Irish self.

I blast Irish music and feel a rise in my heart for being Irish again. For the first time in Italy, I miss Ireland.

I sing out loud and cry out loud as songs bring back memories while green paint splashes on my clothes and drips on my face.

The window is open and I don't care what passers-by think about the wailing green woman they spotted in the derelict house; it includes a glance from the neighbour with the golden retriever. I have just added to his weird collection of memories of me.

With March in full swing, spring blossoms are dotting the landscape and our garden.

It's time to get back outside and clean up the yard and start making it into an outdoor space we can enjoy.

I find Asha's hair under the tree from the last time I groomed her. The rain had flattened it, but when I rake the large clump, it springs up and reveals its soft dry inner. I reach down and pet the soft hair warmed by the sun. Hot chubby tears burst through and roll down my face. For a moment she is with me again, lying under the tree in the sun beside my chair, my hand automatically petting her.

I pull up the decent sized rug of matted hair, roll it and carry it down the garden to the compost heap. If it is too much for me to handle emotionally, I know it would knock Ronan for six.

By the time I am back up the garden to the house, the boys have come outside with a cup of tea for me. Perhaps one of them saw me cry and called the forces to raise my spirits. Tea is always a good start.

"God, it's a gorgeous day. Will I put up the hammock?" says Ronan enthusiastically.

"It's a bit too soon for the hammock, I think?" I sit on the Formica kitchen chair they have brought out.

But Ronan is not listening. He tempts fate and hangs my Fatboy hammock on its free-standing poles plonked under the persimmon tree.

I throw myself onto it and loudly exhale with the words "this isn't too bad," which sends an automatic cue for the poles, that have not connected properly, to collapse, folding me neatly in the hammock like a burrito and bonking me on the back of the head with the metal pole. Second bonk in a week.

It's a laugh or cry moment for me, but for Ronan there's just one option as he's bursting his sides laughing. I'm still not quite at the laughing stage as we reconstruct the hammock, and I lower myself more gingerly onto it.

Luca hands me my tea and we all sit in silence for a few moments, each of us with our faces to the sun, eyes closed, soaking up one of the main joys of living in Italy; sunshine.

I hear a sound I have never heard before, but know what it is. "Listen guys, do you hear that?"

They fall silent and, as if on cue, there's a distinct "cooo kooo...coo koo."

"It's a cuckoo! That's a sign spring has arrived."

"Are cuckoos actual birds?" Ronan asks in all seriousness, squinting towards me.

"What? Yes, of course... what do you mean?"

"I thought they were only in clocks."

Gulps of tea reverse simultaneously from mine and Luca's mouths and up our nostrils, both of us choking while laughing. When we recover, I lie back in the hammock again, still tittering. I quietly notice my mouth is smiling. I was afraid these muscles would never work again. The laughter, with the help of the sun, has cleared a blockage. The last wave of the sea of gloom that had been soaking my body for months evaporates into a puff cloud, blows away and disperses into the blue.

11

TO MEASURE: MISURARE

I 'm completely Covid confused at this point. Umbria was in red for weeks after Christmas while the rest of the country enjoyed lighter tones of orange and yellow. Then a new colour was created for Umbria, 'Dark Orange', which no one really understood. Those who bathed in lighter shades have plunged into hot red again, while Umbria pales from dark orange to orange.

All I know is I haven't been able to enjoy the luxury of eating in a restaurant or having a drink at a bar since last September. I haven't travelled outside thirty miles of where we live in over a year and even those brief encounters were just to go to a DIY shop or Lidl.

Trying to renovate during this time of ochre-shaded rainbows is quite a challenge. We grab lulls between colours to rush to OBI, the bigger DIY store twenty-five miles away, and while we go with a list, our shopping there always becomes random. Anything major like tiles have to be ordered as their stock seems slow to be replenished.

So, a month ago, we ordered tiles for the second bathroom. They were a random choice and I've already questioned it one hundred times. We got notification they had arrived while I was painting the Jungle Room. I've heard rumours of Umbria going red again, so we grab the opportunity and go to OBI. I have a list. On the way into the shop, masked and trollied, Ronan spots garden flagstones, "Oh they do paving here."

Paving was not on our list, but we immediately go right towards the garden centre section rather than left towards the tiles.

I go to the outdoor section and Ronan searches the indoor section, which I follow him into as it's bloody cold outside.

"I found some," calls out Ronan, standing in front of shelves with display blocks and slabs. We amazingly both agree on the same one – the colour is right for us and if you bought more than ninety pieces; they were €3.50 each rather than €6.50. Or €22 per square meter.

"Okay, so how many do we need?" Ronan asks.

"Oh Jezuz, not this again."

We have measured and calculated the area five times with four different scenarios over the last month and, as we hadn't intended patio shopping today, neither of us had the piece of paper with the measurements.

While Ronan was schooled in feet and inches, I was in school on the cusp between Ireland changing from imperial to metric measuring, so I flip between feet and meters, centimeters and inches.

"The middle bit is 13 by 13," I recall.

Ronan is on his calculator 13 x 13. "That's 169 square meters."

"Okay..."

"At €22 per square... that is €3,718."

"What?"

"That can't be right. We're just doing the back garden, not the whole town. 13 feet by 13 feet?"

"Oh, I thought you were in meters."

"Okay, so what is that in meters?"

Ronan is calculating again out loud..."13x 13 divided by 3. Or should we divide 13 by 3 first?"

"I don't know, I'm confused now... Let's start again... so let's say 4 by 4, or 5 by 5 to be on the safe side."

"Five whats?"

"Five meters."

"Ok, so that is 25 square meters, which at €22 per square meter would be €550."

"Well, that sounds about right, and we set our budget at about €500 for the courtyard. So that's good!"

"But that's only the centre bit, not the stone around. The bags of 20kg stone are €5.50 per bag. How much would a bag do?"

"I have no idea... maybe two square feet?"

"We're back to feet again?"

"Yeah, so six square meters, no feck. I've got to divide by three rather than multiply... Let's just buy forty bags."

Ronan knows there is no logic behind the quantity but agrees. It sounds like a doable number.

The shop is practically empty and seems to have double the amount of staff than customers at the moment, but none of them are looking our way. I eventually catch someone's eye in the distance and wave at them. She shouts that her colleague will be with us.

A few minutes later, a blocky assistant arrives. I immediately apologise for my bad Italian. "Mio Italiano é brutto." I'm still unsure if sometimes I am saying 'Italians are ugly' rather than 'my Italian is brutal'. I've stopped using the word cattivo as Luca told me it means evil, although I am not sure if it is better to say to an Italian's face that I think their entire nation is ugly or evil.

He nods. I say in my awful Italian, "We want these. Twenty-five..." I don't know how to say square meters in Italian, so I say it in English.

He looks like I just called him ugly. He then babbles quietly in Italian. It is hard enough trying to learn a language, but with mask-covered mouths it makes it more difficult and if somebody speaks fast or quietly, it is near impossible to understand.

"Piano," I say, asking him to speak slower, but instead he just talks more quietly and quicker. And then louder and longer. I eventually figure out what he is asking.

"He wants to know how many slabs we want."

He is standing staring at us as our heads are completely jumbled with feet and meters, and now he wants to know how many pieces.

Ronan repeats the square meterage of 25, and I am saying loudly no,no,no, as the man now inputting '25 slabs' into the computer.

I guess 160. We multiply 160 by €3.50 and get €560, so it's about right. We agree on 160.

I ask if he delivers. What I have said in Italian doesn't make any sense, it doesn't even sound Italian. I mimic a steering wheel and make van noises. He's still standing, looking at me.

Ronan says it in broken English and suddenly, he understands and opens a ledger, while saying they are heavy, it will be expensive.

We know they are heavy, that is why we need them delivered. To our town it is €120.

I say we also want 'sacchi piatri' again. I do not know if this makes sense, so I lead him to the stone samples and point to the one we want.

He goes to the computer and calls it up and babbles away behind his mask. I have no idea what he is asking, so I walk around to his side of the computer and there, written in red Italian, it states discontinued.

He ushers us outside.

"It's funny how we both pretend we can understand what people are saying when we really don't know what the hell is going on," says Ronan as we follow him, not sure where we are going or why.

"I know. It is because we desperately want to understand and speak Italian, so I think our brains have decided to fake it until we make it."

We walk through a large outdoor courtyard to the area where there are sacks of stone. I point to the one that I was looking at inside and say we want forty bags. He counts the ten bags that are there, he's throwing his hands up in the air.

"Can we order them?"

I seemed to have offered a genius solution.

"Sì!"

He really is not getting that we don't have a lorry outside waiting to take away twenty tonnes of stone and slabs. We go back inside to the computer. I notice the stone we have ordered is the same one on display inside beside the one we originally wanted. I am not sure why we had to go outside for our hike across the yard. The one we wanted was yellow, this one is more pink. I am so confused by feet, meters and kgs that I feel I haven't thought this colour scheme through enough and the design I had in mind has gone out the window, I've decided to just go with the flow and hope for the best.

The guy gives me the order printout from the computer. I sort of figure out what he is telling me. I've to go pay €370 now and then the rest when the order arrives. Hopefully around the first week of April, but who knows with Covid?

It was the same story with the bathroom tiles, normally twenty days, but who knows with Covid? They arrived around day twenty so all was well and here we are to collect the tiles, but we've got distracted by garden slabs.

We head toward the tiles, which are at the other end of the warehouse-size store. On the way, something catches my eye and triggers me to say, "You know the floor tiles in the Jungle Room we are doing up? I hate them."

"So do I! Why don't we cover them with this?" says Ronan happily as we pass the aisle of floating laminate flooring.

"We've put it down in previous houses. It's quick, easy, effective and doesn't require any gluing or nails so we would not have the guilty conscience of ruining the old tiled floor." He sounds like an advert, but may be on to something.

I drift down the aisle. This had not been in the game plan, so I have had no time to think of how it will look or what shade of wood would go with the room. Ronan is going for grey tones, I'm going for warmer browns, so we go with neither and settle on a dark oak.

We're doing the feet into meters again. This one is easier as the room is just 10 x 11 feet. We work out we need five boxes. At €22 a box, we will have a new floor for just over €100. My head is hurting. I look at my list, and do a quick dash around the store getting the bits and pieces we came for, including a hot glue gun and staple gun I had promised to buy myself as a birthday present.

I have to pay for the paving separately to everything else as it is an order. So I pay at the cash desk and then go over to the other desk that prints off the invoice, with the receipt of the payment I just made stapled to it.

I'm wondering how I pay the balance.

"When they arrive, we will call you and then you come and pay."

"But I want them to be delivered?"

"Yes, so you come and pay and then we arrange delivery."

So another day will be wasted to come and pay the balance and confirm we still don't have an articulated truck to collect the tonnes of paving.

We're in the car on the way home with the back filled with wooden flooring that we didn't know we needed and two receipts in my hand, one for the paving and stones we hadn't come for and one for the tiles... which we had come for but have now forgotten to collect.

I feel drained talking about meters and feet, trying to understand Italian and deciding about things we didn't come to buy. I'm not turning back. We'll return tomorrow to collect the tiles.

12

TO TILE: PIASTRELLARE

W e return the following day. Of course, we are halfway there when I can't find the order invoice. I was sure I had left in the car, but I have an email from the shop reminding me to collect my order. So we again take a trip around the shop, buying things not on our list before reaching the tile counter. Thankfully, the girl speaks very good English. I show her my order and she says, 'ah yes, you placed your order with Marco'.

Marco had been very patient and helped us work out the exact amount we would need to tile the shower and walls and how many boxes of mosaic trim tiles we would need. We ordered three boxes of the mosaic trim tiles instead of two just in case we felt creative and wanted to tile around a mirror or some-thing later on. I already secretly know this will never happen and the extra box of mosaic tiles will be left in the corner of the shed for generations to come.

"If you go out and around the side of the building, my colleague will bring them out to you." We do as she says and clear space in the back of our car for the order we had been waiting twenty days for.

The guy comes out with four packs of tiles, three of the mosaic and one ordinary that would just about do the size of the back-splash. "Where are the rest?"

"You want to rest? I can lift them for you?" he offers, taking the light boxes off the forklift.

"No, we ordered much more. Where are they?"

He points to the order.

"This is it," he says in Italian. The girl who speaks better English comes out and we tell her we ordered enough to tile a complete bathroom. She is very apologetic, there must have been some mistake and tells us to come back inside.

This involves re-parking the car and walking back through the maze of the warehouse-style store to her desk where she checks her computer and we go through the measurements. Marco hadn't changed the quantity in the designated area on the screen, which was at default at one. Silly helpful Marco.

"So, when will we have our tiles?"

"It will take twenty days."

"Again? Is there no way of rushing them considering the mistake?"

"No."

"Can we get free delivery considering it was the shop's mess up?"

"I am afraid not."

"But we have guests coming. I need tiles. What do you have in stock?"

"None."

"None?"

"Well, none of that quantity."

"But you have a bloody big warehouse out there. What do you keep in it?"

"Where we have coffee? Lots of things, but not tiles."

I resign myself to the Italian way and ask the next steps.

As this is now classed as a new order, we will need to go over to the order desk, cancel this one, get a credit note for the amount – which is like a physical gift card – and then use that gift card to pay for the lot when they arrive in twenty days.

"Can this amount just be paid off the new order?"

"No, that would mess up the system. It is better this way."

There is confusion at the desk as the cash till girl is messing up and giving us a gift card for the new higher amount and getting frustrated with me as I try to explain her mistake in Italian. We call the English-speaking girl and I explain she is crediting us for much more.

"Ahhh," she is now very grateful to me for saving her skin.

Having a flimsy gift card with several hundred euros in my possession is treacherous, considering I mislaid the large order form between the house and car earlier.

Back in the car, I'm trying to remain calm and patient.

"We need a second bathroom, especially if we have Izzy or anyone else coming to visit. I don't want to leave everything to the last minute. We can't wait another twenty days for the tiles. We can use them for the third bathroom when they arrive, but let's go to the other DIY superstore and see what we can find off the shelf."

We are in Italy and when in Rome we need to do as the Romans do and put up with the twenty day lulls and the over-complicated systems for the simplest of things. Whereas, in Ireland, we were used to walking into DIY shops and coming out with everything we needed to get the job started and finished the same day.

"Why do you think they will have anything in stock?"

"They are a French company, so maybe they will have a different structure. And thankfully they don't close for a three-hour lunch so we can go there now on the way home."

At the second store, I find a packet of mosaic tiles, with what looks like Irish green marble set amongst beige pieces. Close by, there are boxes of tiles that look like an old brick wall.

"These remind me of the dry-stone walls in Connemara, together with the green marble mosaic tiles. We can do an Irish themed bathroom."

"They don't look anything like a dry-stone wall in Connemara."

"I know, but they've triggered the idea of making a bathroom look like you are outside in the Irish countryside."

"Outside showering in Ireland? You'd be bloody freezing. We can save money by not putting a radiator in there to give it the same effect and we could just install a hole in the ground for the loo like they used to have in the country outhouses. How about that?"

"Honestly, it will look good... I think... look, I am trying to make the most of my imagination with these tiles, as they are the only ones that are readily available in the shop."

Ronan is happy to go along with my bossy decisions, as usual. "How many boxes will we need?"

I'm doing the calculation on my phone. "I think about evelen boxes of them."

"Okay," says Ronan as he loads the boxes onto our trolley from under the display tiles.

"Should we not get an assistant? They probably need to approve us taking these and give us twenty dockets."

"Let's say nothing and just go to the cash desk with them and see what happens."

Sure enough, us arriving at the cash desk with eleven boxes of tiles throws things into chaos.

"Where did you get them? Did you go into the warehouse?"

There are a string of phone calls and someone from the tile department is summoned to the cash desk urgently. It might be a French company but when in Italy they are doing things the Italian way.

The guy arrives and I think he says that the new guy put the pallet of tiles out on the shop floor by accident rather than in the warehouse and they had decided to just use them as a display island rather than move them all again.

We act dumb to the Italian way of needing a million dockets and twenty days to reconsider what we have done. Ronan just keeps pushing the tiles forward on the conveyor belt, then a handbasin, followed by the vats of paint and rollers we are buying to cover the mould. None of these things were on a list.

She's in a fluster until the guy comes back with an emergency docket, releasing the eleven boxes of tiles into our care.

We feel very accomplished having gone tile shopping and returning home with actual tiles, even though it took about four hours. I've also got myself a top of the range staple gun, something I have long wanted in anticipation of doing all the upholstery projects I have lined up, even though I have never upholstered. But it's time to start, or throw the threadbare, cobwebbed sofas taking up space in the rooms onto the dump heap.

13

TO COLLECT: RACCOGLIERE

E ach week there are more minutes of light before sunset. Clocks have gone forward and with every additional minute of light in the morning and in the evening, life feels a little easier.

The new vaccines which are now being rolled out are giving the most hope. Italy seems to be flying along giving over eighties the vaccine.

 I read an article where it says they will start vaccinating over sixties by the end of this month, and everyone over forty in Italy will be vaccinated by the summer, which means I will be able to travel back to Ireland. I'm ecstatic until I see on social media chat rooms that non-residents in Italy can't get the vaccine. It seems ridiculous. It's not like we can't catch it or spread it and we are EU citizens, so I'm sure it is within our right to get it.

I spend hours trawling through articles, trying to find correct information. I'm on the website where people register for the vaccine. But trying to translate it into something understandable is difficult. It says the website has an English and German option but there is nowhere to click for these options. To register for the vaccine for when your age group's turn comes, you need to enter your name and your Codice Fiscale and then, on the next page, they require your Tessera Sanitaria number.

The Tessera Sanitaria is the Italian health card which allows you to access a doctor, amongst other things like getting a bin collection service for your house apparently. When you become a resident, you automatically become entitled to one in most regions, but not in Umbria.

I am still not clear on the acrobatic moves I will need to perform to get a Tessera Sanitaria. I think I need to be paying tax for five years in Italy as a self-employed person before I can get it. But there is a loophole. I have been told as soon as Ronan gets his pension, and then applies for residency, he will get a Tessera Sanitaria automatically and I will also get one as his spouse. If we can hang on for another year when Ronan gets his clock, then we will be all set and get our golden ticket. Then we can get bins and get a GP.

Getting our Codice Fiscales was a lot easier. This is another number you need in Italy to do anything. When we signed up to rent a house, the estate agent got our Codice Fiscales for us.

The Codice Fiscale is the first thing people need to get when they move to Italy, as you need it for a lot of general stuff. For instance, if you want to buy electrical goods, even a phone, you need your Codice Fiscale. If you want to buy a mattress or a piece of furniture, it is not as easy as just walking in to a shop and saying, "okay we'll have that one," and walk out with it. Oh nooo, this is Italy.

Like the tiles, buying a mattress or piece of furniture was quite a new experience too. We soon learned the steps: You go to the furniture store, pick the thing you want, write down the code, then find one of the store workers wandering around, tell them you want this, they'll then lead you to a computer on a table and spend at least twenty minutes taking all your details. If you want delivery, add another fifteen minutes. Details they will want are your name, address, your Codice Fiscale, sometimes your date of birth, where you were born and sometimes ID.

They will then print out the page with your order on it. Just hope their printer doesn't jam, as this could add another thirty minutes to your purchasing experience, like it did us.

You take the paper they give you, which has a carbon copy attached, to the cash desk. Here they will give an option to pay the full price or, if it is not in store, you can pay a deposit and then come back when it is ready for collection and pay the rest. If it is in store and you want to take it then, they will give you the receipt and one page which they will have used one of their many stamps on. This all takes about ten minutes while they find the right stamp and stapler to stick the receipt and page together along with the printed directions to their warehouse five kilometres away.

When you arrive at the warehouse, you give the man your page with stapled receipt. He has no computer, so he does not know that you are arriving or have what you want lined up. Which, to me, would be an obvious thing to help workflow, but, hey. You then wait another ten minutes before he finds what you have bought.

The second time we bought a mattress we didn't want to go through this whole rigmarole, so we tried another shop. We showed the store woman what we wanted; she checked on the computer ... it will be here in twenty days. Again, we can pay a deposit and the rest when it arrives. You want delivery? Delivery for stores seems to be outsourced, it never seems to be included. From the store to our house fifteen minutes' drive away, it will be €40.

"No, we will pick it up."

"Okay, you need to call in the afternoon on the day to see if it has arrived and then you can come to pick it up."

She takes lots of details, including our address, even though we are not getting a delivery.

Applying for a Codice Fiscale just requires an ID. They give you an A4 certificate with your name and your Codice Fiscale number on it decorated with several colourful stamps. It costs nothing. They take your address to send you the Codice Fiscale card. It's a plastic card the same size as a bank card, I believe. I don't know, because we never received ours. We requested it to be sent a few times but they never arrived, so Ronan cut a piece of card out of a cornflake box and wrote my Codice Fiscale on it for me.

When anyone requests my Codice Fiscale card, I hand them the Blue Peter cornflake box one. I get looks, but I explain I have never received the official card. They nod knowingly, as if it is a common occurrence. Some apologise to me for all of Italy.

For Luca's Codice Fiscale, we trekked to the Agenzia delle Entrate in Cortona at 4pm, after lunch on a Friday, only to read on the door sign that it is only open in the mornings. So we trekked there again on Monday. There was no one in reception except for a man who sensed our cluelessness and informed us that the Agenzia delle Entrate was across the road, but because of Covid it is only open on Friday mornings, and we need an appointment. Two women greeted 'Rob', the guy helping us, who had followed us out to the street to give us the opening times of a similar office in Arezzo, and its phone number and where to go in the building. All in English and all from memory, as Rob was completely blind.

Everyone in the town greeted Rob as they passed him by, and he greeted them back by name.

Luca needed the Codice Fiscale that week. We couldn't wait or he'd lose his college place.

I'd heard it was possible to get one of these essential numbers online so we went home and Googled Codice Fiscale. After inputting some details, a number generated immediately. I felt it was too easy, so I went onto the government site to verify it. It was unable to verify it, so I think we will still need to get an appointment at the office. But we've never got around to it. Luca's computer-generated Codice Fiscale worked for getting him into college and that's all he needs it for, for now.

14

TO PLAN: PIANIFICARE

"We couldn't get anything done last year, so we're going to get the flat roof replaced on the extension and I want a new kitchen and we're going to get a new car." My mam is telling me their plans for the summer.

"But why are you doing all that when you are coming over here?" I'm confused. We were doing up the bathroom as a wet room, a small kitchen, bedroom and sitting room on the ground floor in the house for my parents to move into as soon as Covid allowed them to travel safely again. Now Mam was planning major renovations to their house in Ireland.

"Well, I won't be coming over in the summer. It would be far too hot for me. It will be September before we go over."

"But if you are coming here, why are you buying a car?"

"Well, we're not coming to live."

"This is news to me. I thought that was the plan we discussed."

"Nooooo! Look, we are not getting any younger, Rosie. We'll stay put in our familiar surroundings."

"But you'll come for winter?"

"Everything is up in the air at the moment with this Covid thing. Let's wait and see what happens."

My heart sinks a little. Indeed, they were not getting any younger. Dad was approaching 87 and Mam was going to be 85 next birthday. Having not seen them for a full year and with Covid ebbing and flowing, I wanted to get them over to us as soon as possible to wrap them in a bubble of virtual cotton wool and look after them.

I also couldn't wait to hear Dad's view on everything, even the plane ride. I'd never been on a plane with him, even that would be fun. He and my brother Jim both viewed the world through eyes like a child, fascinated by everything new, ready for new experiences and exploration. I was similar, I suppose, so I get a buzz for life when around these two.

The only thing Dad didn't want new experiences of was food. He never wanted a dinner that did not include ample potatoes, meat and a vegetable all plainly cooked. No fancy sauces or flavourings, just cooked the way Mam could do it for him.

I resigned myself to the fact that perhaps they would never move over. Immigrating in your late eighties was a big ask.

I needed to remodel the vision of having Mam and Dad at our long Italian dinner table with family visiting regularly for big, leisurely Italian meals in the courtyard under the persimmon tree.

It was one of the many things that drew me to Italy, the love of family. The commonality of three generations living under the same roof, growing together, supporting each other like a tribe. It was how I grew up in Ireland and it is how I longed to be again, together with my extended family. But now I'm thinking, what was the point of having a big house if Mam and Dad were not going to share it, and Jim and Ingrid and their kids were not forced to visit often as a result and enjoy the house with us.

Of course, they would probably visit anyway, but not as regularly as Ingrid hates flying. Jim would come at the drop of a hat. We were the same in that sense, wave a plane ticket in front of either of us and we get as excited as a dog over a meaty bone.

I'm feeling low and even lower when I read on the same day that the notice I had seen about anyone in their forties being vaccinated by the summer was a hoax or very wishful thinking. That age group probably won't get vaccinated until the end of the summer and again I am reading about non-residents finding it impossible to get vaccinated without a Tessera Sanitaria card.

Work wise, I am fully booked for the next two years but without income, as they are all postponements. And I can't start working on the Summer Club for Women idea nor the writers' retreats, as we need to wait until the house is finished which, looking at the derelict state it is in, God only knows when that will be.

My mood is at an all-time low. I desperately want to get home to see my parents. I want Izzy to get over to us.

Shelly has heard rumours that travel from the UK may be possible from May if Izzy can get the vaccine.

The UK has done a massive rollout of first dose vaccines and now there is a dispute between them and the EU about exporting vaccines. So nobody is winning this battle so far, except America, Israel and the UAE which are all flying along with vaccinations. I hear from a friend that, in Kentucky, they have opened the vaccine centres to anyone over sixteen who wants it and you can choose between three different brands, while we sit in Italy where it is still limited to over 80-year-olds. There just seems to be a lot of eighty pluses in Italy to get through. It's taking forever to get to the next age group as we anxiously wait for Ronan's opportunity to come up and find a way for him to get vaxed. With him being diabetic, we are staying to ourselves as much as possible and not taking any chances.

Izzy has grown up before my eyes via video chat. I was missing out on her life, but more so, I was missing precious time with my parents. It was never the plan to be away from them for any length of time. That was the beauty of moving to the sun within Europe; I could get home, back to them regularly. I could get back within twenty-four hours if they needed me. This pandemic had made that concept alien.

There was nothing for it. For me to get home, I needed to apply for residency in Italy and then at least I could get into Ireland as a citizen and back to Italy as a resident. I'll deal with the consequences of the tax implications afterwards.

With new determination and enthusiasm, I walk to the office in the Comune to apply for residency on Monday morning. It is shut because of Covid with no opening date shown.

My mood plummets. No residency means no vaccine, and no vaccine means no travel.

My love for Italy is morphing into frustration. I am stuck here, and it is beginning to lose its sheen.

15

TO SEARCH: CERCARE

The house renovation has come to a standstill since Christmas. We had given all the paperwork to Mick Kelly, who did whatever he had to do to upload the information for the 50/50 renovation scheme.

Two months have passed and most of my constantly harassing emails to check that everything has been approved have been ignored. Then, at last, Mick Kelly sends me a letter about the bonus with no explanation.

There is a lot of small print. I do not know what it is saying and after an hour of translating with Lucia's help, we figure out it is notification that all the documents have been approved.

I message Mick Kelly excitedly.

"Great, so when can we get the money back from the bank?"

"The documents have been approved by the outsourced company, but the bank still needs to approve it."

"Right, so I'll go to the bank tomorrow and see what they need."

I arrive at the bank armed with Lucia as an interpreter. But the door to the bank is closed, and it is pitch black inside. "That's strange. I always come to the bank at this time... where has the notice gone with their weird opening times?"

"We'll come back on Monday, I suppose," says Lucia.

I go to take money out of the bank's ATM, so I can at least buy Lucia a coffee for coming in, and I haven't had a cappuccino since last August.

But the ATM is... gone.

"Where's the bank machine?"

I step back to see if they possibly moved it around the corner or further along the street. It's then I notice the signage with the name of the bank that ran across the width of the facade above the door and window is also gone.

"What the hell? They've gone. The bank is gone. Where have they gone?"

We are nothing short of looking under the shrubs running along the lake front trying to find where the bank has lost itself to.

We call Mick Kelly, whose office is just across the square. But, of course, he doesn't work on a Friday.

We ask an old lady, who has stood behind us thinking we were queuing for the ATM, if she knows where the bank has gone, but she doesn't know either.

"It was here last week," she says, as puzzled as us.

So we go to the pizzeria next door, which can't currently sell pizza because of restrictions, only coffee and croissants to take away. We ask the guy if he knows where the bank has gone. "Yes, it has moved over there." He points to a pink building on the street corner past the town hall.

"You'd think they'd put a 'we have moved' sign up in the window."

"This is Italy," is the only explanation Lucia can give.

We go to the building the guy pointed at, but there is no signage to say it's the bank. There was another bank there previously, but it seems my bank has now gobbled it up in a merger and removed any evidence that a bank is still operating there.

It's a slightly bigger building. Marco, the bank manager, is there, but there is no Roberta. The lovely friendly cashier who is patient with my Italian efforts and has helped me navigate the minefield of forms during the last six months, is gone.

But it is not Roberta I need to talk to today, it is Veronica. She was the one with the office beside the director in the other building. She's young, false eyelashes, heavily made up. She taps away at her computer with her badly chipped gel nails. "Yes all the documents have been approved," she smiles.

"Okay great, so when will the money be in?"

She clicks her Hello Kitty pen incessantly staring at the screen, I think she is waiting for divine inspiration. After what seems like an eternity she says in Italian, "I just need signatures. Come back next week."

Lucia can't make it the following week, so her father Emanuele who is a professional translator, comes along.

At that meeting Veronica gives me several documents to sign. "So how long will it take for the money to arrive in the account?"

"Perhaps about eight weeks."

"Eight weeks?"

That's a long time, and it brings me right up to the deadline of paying for the work done up to Christmas.

"Can I get a bridge loan from the bank?"

"You want a mortgage?"

"I think I need to be a resident to get a mortgage?"

"Yes."

"I am not a resident. Can I just get a small loan?"

"Most people have a mortgage who gets this bonus," she says, stabbing her matching Hello Kitty mouse mat with a paperclip.

"I don't want a mortgage, just a bridge loan for the amount."

"It would take the same amount of time to get the loan as it will be waiting for the reimbursement," she explains through Emanuele.

"Would I need to be a resident to get the loan?"

"Yes."

"Well, that rules that out too then."

Veronica shrugs an I-can't-do-anything-to-help look.

"So we will just have to wait until the reimbursement comes through."

I thought this was going to be easy. With a sigh, I leave the office. I have it marked on the calendar to contact Veronica at the bank in eight weeks' time - the first week of June.

Emanuele needs to leave, so I'm left with Veronica to sign the necessary forms. She moves me into the director Marco's office next door to hers. As I am signing the multiple forms, a call is put through to her in the office. She is swivelling on the chair back and forth listening to the customer and answering her back before the customer has finished any sentence. Her chair doesn't swivel in her own office. She's swivelling more rapidly and her voice is rising.

Through Veronica's responses, I can make out that the woman calling is complaining that money has been taken out of her account as a direct debit and she wants it back. Veronica explains for a second time that the bank cannot reimburse a direct debit and the woman needs to cancel it directly with the company. Veronica is now having an extended shouting match with the customer and then slams down the phone. She must have missed the class about the customer always being right.

There's a message from Lucia waiting for me on my phone when I leave the bank. "Antonio has called me asking to tell you that the gas company comes in two weeks in the morning to put the gas on and he said that next week you need to pay his bill."

"I cannot pay his bill! We agreed at the meeting to pay it in June. I know it was June because we thought we would have money coming in from wedding work in June, if the bonus had not come through."

"Anyway, he said he texted you to tell you and asked me to remind you."

"Why the hell is he contacting you about my bills with him, anyway?"

I text Antonio. "Antonio, please do not contact Lucia about our business together. She is not my secretary, she is a friend who helped me and I don't want that to be abused. You have my number and we have always communicated perfectly well by text using Google translate."

"Okay, but when are you paying my bill?"

"We agreed in writing the 13th June. Why are you asking for it in April?"

"I thought you could pay it in April when you get the reimbursement."

"The reimbursement has not come through yet, and even if it had, we had agreed June."

Back home, I search through my papers on the shelf I have designated for building paperwork and find the agreed date and reduced amount noted on the page in his handwriting. I send him a photo of it.

"Okay. I will not contact Lucia again."

If I let my mind wander to the dark side, I might think he was trying to shame me into paying it earlier by telling my friend I had not settled his bill. But I won't let myself go there... yet.

16

TO CONNECT: COLLEGARE

"**Y**ou need to send me a photo of your box." I am about to delete and block the sender until I realise it is from Antonio. "What box?"

"The box outside for the gas. The silver one."

So I go outside and take photos of the metal box in the front corner of the garden from all its best angles and send it on. Fair play to Antonio for still helping with trying to get our gas installed for us. It's one of those extras he has done for no charge.

The box must not have met the approval of the higher powers, as a day later I spot Omaroberto in our front garden, slicing neat lumps out of our front fence with a grinder and fixing the box into the perfect-sized hole he's made. The result is that the two-way box can now be opened from the road with no one entering our garden. However, all an inspector has to view at the moment inside are a few spiders and emptiness.

Two weeks later, there is a mystery man standing at my gate in a boiler suit. He is stocky with tight black wiry hair and stubble, with a bulbous nose, or what Italians call a potato nose, big lips and bulging eyes enveloped in lids that seem to only open halfway.

His van is parked on the road and he's trying to look over our gate rather than through it, which would be logical for someone our height as the bars are slim and spaced out and stop above his head. I run out excited at the idea that this could be the one, this is the man who is going to bring warmth to my life and allow me to walk around in my underwear, have showers with reckless abandon without overthinking the coldness I am going to feel when I step out.

I will no longer need to race from the sitting room through the arctic hall up the stone steps and dive under the duvet once I remember which mouldy room we are sleeping in that night.

He says something gruffly. I can't understand him but see the word 'gas' on his boiler suit. It is him, my hero. He says it again and I recognise 'tubi' as the word for pipes. I am ecstatic the gas man is here even though he has his mask pulled below his big nostrils, freeing possible Covid into my breathing space if I get close enough to understand him fully.

"Sì sì, I am very happy to show you my pipes," I say in my best Italian. I usher him in through the gate and lead him to the corner of the front garden, to where the plumbers have installed the pipes, the builder has installed the box, the plumbers again did something else, some mystery guy came and took a photo of it and the builder came back out and sliced up my fence.

"Here it is," I say with a Taa-Daa ring to my words.

He's talking gruffly again and seems angry and is waving his hands around at my box. I am sweating and frustrated that my Italian is still so bad that I can't understand a word he is saying.

He looks like he is about to leave, so I jump in front of him, blocking his path and use the word for WAIT with a hand upright nearly against his half-masked face as I desperately call Lucia in a panic with the other hand. "I am sorry I have tried to do it without calling you, but the gas guy is here and I can't understand a word he is saying. But he seems like he's about to leave without connecting the gas, please can you talk to him?"

"Okay, but I am in the middle of buying chickens."

I hand him the phone and there seems to be a heated discussion, his hands flailing. He nearly throws my phone towards the fence to show Lucia how inept and lacking my box is.

Eventually, he hands my phone back to me and nods. Lucia is still on the line. I put her on speaker as there is no way I am putting my spit coated phone near my face. He is still grunting as he makes his way closer to the box with his tool kit.

"I could not understand him either. He is from Sicily and talking mostly in dialect. And when not in dialect, his accent is very thick," Lucia says, slightly out of breath from talking so rapidly to him.

"He said it is not his job to make the connection to the meter. The pipes are not ready and he should not install the meter until they are in the correct place. But he reluctantly agreed he will do it this time... As if there is going to be another time! He said this was an exception. I used my sweetest begging voice to get him to do it, 'Oh thank you thank you'," she says sweetly, imitating her worst self.

"I wanted to tell him to f**k off." There's the Lucia I know back. "But why do I have to do this? Why does the asshole not make the connection when he is there and can do it?"

I smile and nod at the reluctant Sicilian, as Lucia spits these words out like venom across the speaker and I just hope he really can't speak any English.

"Bloody Italians... but he is from Sicily, so he will not count himself as Italian. Bloody Sicilians." She's now out of breath from anger, frustrated at having to use womanly charm to get someone to do their job while she's busy buying fowl.

I retreat to the house, and within five minutes, the guy is gone. I go out and check the box. It has a meter in it, but the pipes are not connected to it. I text both Danny Boy and Antonio. "We have gas. Well, I think we have gas, but the pipes are not connected. The guy said they were not in the right place."

Danny Boy texts back, "I could not put the pipes into the box because then you cannot use the bombola gas. I will come next week to do it."

I go into the kitchen, resigning myself to not have piped gas for another week, but when I try to turn on the stove, there is no gas. I text Danny Boy again, who explains back, "Now it is closed so you can't use the bombola."

"So we can't cook or shower for another week?"

I can nearly hear Danny sigh heavily through his text. "Mario will come this afternoon to make the connection."

So just to recap how to get gas connected to your house in Italy: The builder attaches the box, the plumber runs the pipes, the gas company fits the meter, a mysterious guy takes a photo for his wall or the Comune or something, you sign up with a gas utility supplier to get the gas and then the plumber needs to come back and do something else and then you should have gas.

Sure enough, Mario in his fog of chain smoke and chesty cough arrives and squeezes his large body into our Star Trek control-centre room a few times. He waddles back and forth to the gas meter box and bombola connecting and disconnecting gas pipes with a constant lit cigarette hanging out of his mouth and smoke squinting his eyes. Within an hour, our radiators were clicking to the sound of hot water and air bubbles for the first time.

I ring my mother, as it has been an ongoing concern for her. We were all freezing for the last few months. "But at least you were freezing in Italy," she has said consoling herself on more than one occasion... as if freezing is at a higher temperature in Italy.

"Mam I have gas!"

"Gaviscon is good for that or if you stand on your head, you can..."

"No, I don't mean farty gas. I mean heating gas! I had a feeling it would happen just as the weather is starting to warm up."

"Oh, that's great news. You'll be warm for the summer then!"

I never thought I would be so happy to get gas. The first thing I do besides putting the heat on full blast is to strip the front door of all its duct taped insulation and let the daylight shine through its many gaps and cracks.

The promise of not being cold again has given me new energy. Even though it is warm out, we put on all the radiators and sweat as we jog from room to room, draining the trapped air out of them.

Over the next few days, the house becomes a sauna as we need to leave the heat on to finally dry out the walls. Having the walls dried out means the builders can come back and start finishing rooms, we can start decorating, we can start making the house less like a tenement slum house from the early 1900s. We will soon be mould free!

17

TO DOUBT: DUBITARE

My phone is ringing and I'm surprised to see my dad on the screen rather than my mam who is the usual face who calls. "Is everything okay?"

"Yes", he says with a grin, "We'll be over on Sunday." I knew he was joking, but the penny dropped as to what he meant by his words. They were getting their long-awaited vaccine.

"Ahhh, when are you getting it?"

"Friday."

For the last year, my dad would not speak of coming to Italy. We were all in a 'place' of thinking that with Covid, it may never be possible, but now I can hear hope in his voice. "So put the kettle on and that heating you have now."

Even though I am missing his birthday for the second time due to Covid, just the news of them getting their vaccine makes me happy as it has made such a difference to their mood already.

My mam is excited to go grocery shopping again as the shop keeps on delivering the wrong brands and she enjoys a browse.

She's also looking forward to letting Ingrid in to wash her floors for her as neither she nor my dad have the strength to do it anymore.

The number of Covid cases is dropping and they are talking optimistically again about coming over to Italy, perhaps in September and perhaps they'll stay.

"Now tell me Rosie, I know you said there are no pubs over there, but in the bars along the lake is there a bit of craic? Like a bit of an ol' sing song?"

"Dad I've told you before, sing songs in bars are not a 'thing' in Italy, but I am sure they wouldn't object to you starting one..."

He decides to take that as a "yes the Italians are known to break into song together at every opportunity." He's watched too many Mario Lanza movies.

"But would I know the words that they'd be singing? Would they know 'Daisy, Daisy' or would they be singing all Italian songs?"

"Dad, it's different here... you know, it won't be the same as Ireland?"

He's not listening. "And tell me again, what do you eat? I don't want any of the pasta and pizza crap. I'd need me spuds every day, made by your mother. I wouldn't trust you cooking them, you'd burn them."

It's our family's humour to be as insulting as possible, all said in jest but with an undercurrent of truth running through it. My brothers and parents regularly jeer at my lack of cooking skills except when they come to eat it. Fifteen of us would gather for Christmas dinner at my house for the years I lived in Ireland and everyone would go away satisfied and asking for recipes. But because I have worked for myself full time all my adult life and Ronan was the house parent and did most of the cooking, they have it in their heads that I can't cook. Now and then I'll take over the kitchen and follow a recipe and if it is good, I make it so much that everyone gets sick of it.

I decide to tackle the idea of Dad wanting a replica Ireland in Italy at a later date, when they are actually here. "We'll figure it out. Don't worry."

"And what about books?" He asks, ignoring me again. Could I get good books in English over there, something with a bit of a story to it like 'The Great Escape' or a mystery, nothing too heavy? They are all crap over here. I like to read before I sleep, but with book shops closed and what have you, all I can find is crap." Why he thinks he is going to find a large selection of fantastic escape novels and mysteries that he can't find in book shops near him, written in English in Italy, mystifies me.

The vaccine continues to roll out in Italy, and even though there is no sign of us being able to get it soon, I live in hope and plan to go back to Ireland in August. I'll granny-nap my parents back to Italy, where I can wrap them in cotton wool and spoil them rotten. There is the niggling fear that Dad may find the food difficult, so I take no chances.

I go out to the garden and plant two ridges of potatoes in preparation for my parents' arrival in the early autumn. While I am digging, I listen to a new Clubhouse room I discovered for indie authors. There are established self-published authors talking, helping each other and newbies like myself. They are discussing cozy mysteries, not a genre I have heard of.

"It's like Scooby Doo for adults," one writer explains. "There's no blood and gore and any sex happens behind closed doors. The focus is on the mystery to be solved." I make a mental note to look up cozy mysteries for Dad. They sound right up his street.

As I stick the spuds in the ground, I am satisfied that Dad will have potatoes when he arrives, and maybe I can surprise him with a small library of cozy mysteries to read.

The cats jump around my feet, sitting on the pile of earth I am just about to dig, then attacking the string on my hoody as I bend to push them off. One chases after a butterfly while the other bounces around after a lizard she's just lost.

Looney is always by my feet. She misses her pal Asha. I have never heard a dog sigh so much and look depressed. I look towards the pile of earth where Asha now lies. I miss her too. Ronan has been admiring dogs online. Big bloody dogs. Neither of us are ready for a new arrival and I am definitely sticking my heels in about not getting a big dog again. Especially not a German Shepherd. We've had two in a row. They are great dogs, but they need walking, and Ronan is not a dog walker. I am, but I can't relax walking a muscly German Shepherd who loves me so much they feel they have to guard me against any approaching dog.

I also want nice furniture. I want a blue velvet sofa without dog paws on it and dog hair floating around. I've had several arguments in my head with Ronan about it already. We are not ready yet, but I know the day will come when we both feel ready to share our patched-up hearts with another four-legged family member, and when it does, there will be war. Ronan usually gets his way, but not this time.

"We'll need to clear out the ground-floor apartment. Mam and Dad are coming in the autumn," I say gleefully, putting our differences aside in the argument I just had in my head with Ronan, which he is completely oblivious to.

"They are?" He's surprised, happy, but a little hesitant. He loves my parents, but I am sure he perhaps feels a little sense of anxiety about invasion and how it will change the setup that we have not yet set up. We've never had that blissful time together where we just feel 'here we are, we've made it, life is easy and contented'. There has always been something. But now the 'we've made it' feeling seems closer than ever.

Although, having my dad to watch football and rugby with would add to Ronan's feeling of bliss immediately. His two brothers, who he lived with in bachelorhood before I arrived on the scene twenty-five years ago, died within six months of each other the year before we moved to Italy. They were his football and rugby watching mates. Now he just has me who, at the last rugby match between Italy and Wales, thought the commentator said that one Welsh player had more cats than the full Italian squad combined. I thought it was an unusual comment considering Italy's love of cats and wondered who had actually taken the time to work out this statistic and surprising fact.

"He said caps, Rosie, not cats," corrected Ronan with an eye roll.

"Don't worry, Mam and Dad will be independent of us. They want their own space. We probably won't even see them every day." I understand Ronan's fears. We both like our own space too, even from each other. "We'll work on their apartment. They'll happily look after one another there and have us to call on if they need anything and join us in the garden for dinner or a cuppa each day. It will be great."

In Mam and Dad's apartment to be, the bathroom is done, but the rest of the rooms are just acting storerooms for clunky furniture, rubble and dust. Like all the rooms, they need to dry out. I try to make a start on the front room, which will be their sitting room. Tapping the bottom half of the front wall, the old, mouldy plaster falls off in large chunks, revealing the stonework beneath. I'm sandwiched between the Fascist-style sideboard and the even larger sideboard wall cupboard nicknamed the coffin. I hit the wall several more times with the mallet, each time a slab falls and crumbles.

My energy is already depleting to a ridiculously low level, having dug the garden. The billow of more plaster dust rises. I look up at the cobweb-strewn, swollen window frames with minimal light filtering through the mud and cement matted glass, the mould in the corners, the roughly filled sections where the new electric cables run, the ancient door that refuses to be clean no matter what product we use.

As the whiff of the damp old mortar that has fallen across my slippers tingles my nose, I quickly and involuntarily suck in another deep, shaky lung-full of air as if I just got a shock. I am not sure if that is what's making my eyes water or the feeling of pure overwhelm at the enormous amount of work that still needs to be done to make this into the house we imagined. For the first time, I am having doubts. Huge doubts.

18

TO RAISE: SOLLEVARE

I t's Good Friday, the sun is shining; the temperature is perfect, so we pull out a table and chairs from the small kitchen and have breakfast outside.

"I am going to work on that today," Ronan nods towards the long red brick shack that runs along part of the garden border that gives perfect privacy from our neighbours on that side. It has a flat tiled roof and is divided into two sheds by a red brick wall in the centre.

Two heavy wooden light blue chipped doors have guarded the inside mess of rubbish bags, broken suitcases and crumbling oddments dumped when someone decided to attempt a clear out one of the apartments. In Italian, there are two words for blue; blu and azzuro. Azzuro is the colour of the sky, sky blue. So the doors are azzuro, not blu, and it's the colour I am planning to paint the sixty-six shutters.

My vision is to have the shack open at the front as an outdoor living room, a shaded seating area for writing, chatting, lazing, during the hottest summer months and shelter during warm rainy days at the crossover points in the seasons. I want to get the builders in to do it, as I am afraid if we attempt it; we are going to be left with a heap of bricks and a caved-in roof and it won't look like the Pinterest image in my head.

I am biting my tongue as I am trying to learn to control my bossy control freak self, so instead of saying, "Ronan don't you dare touch that, leave it to the professionals," I say, "Oh what's your work plan of action?" But before I have even finished the sentence, Ronan has leapt across to the shack and already unhinged and removed both doors.

I take a deep breath and go in to put the kettle on. By the time I have returned with my cup of tea, he has a sledgehammer in hand and is whacking the centre wall. The mortar has long since turned to the consistency of apple crumble topping and bricks are flying out like chocolate bars off a high-speed conveyer belt.

"Wait Ronan! There's no beam. That's the wall supporting the roof." This is not 'control freak me' shouting, but 'stop or you will be crushed to death freak me.'

He steps back and looks. "Oh, yeah... I'll get a beam."

"What?"

"One of those beams, from the old roof that the lads left in the garden." He is speed walking over to the other side of the to-be courtyard, disappearing behind the falling down garage to the pile of wood taken from the old roof the builders dumped for removal but never came back to remove. I had asked them to leave just the big beams for Jim to carve when he is over or to use as surrounds for raised beds. But instead they dumped and left all the wood there, including about thirty old rotten garden posts that were not even from our garden but from a different job they were doing. The pile looks like the eve of a 12th of July bonfire in Northern Ireland.

As we still are not in a position to pay the builders the outstanding debt, I can't yet hold it as a carrot for them to come back and clear up the large stack of wood, the pallets of bricks and bags of now hardened cement they left in the front garden.

Antonio had also promised to take the caved roof of the garage to the dump and leave the whole place, including the inside of the house, pristine. We rushed them out before Christmas, so I forgive them for their cement blobs and inches of dust inside, but I still intend for him to clear the garden before payment is completed.

"Here, I'll use this one. It looks about right." Ronan is throwing wood off the top of the pile the longest beam is buried under. "Ronan, that's at least 12 feet long and will weigh a tonne. How are you going to get that across the garden, never mind into place?"

"You'll help me, here grab the end."

"Are you bloody mad? NO! Wait until there are a couple of guys here to help you."

"Who?" He stands up and takes a couple of breaths, looking at me.

He's challenging what we have both felt from time to time but have not voiced. If we were in Ireland, we would have called on Jim or some friends to help out.

We have no support network here. No one to call on other than Lucia for support of any kind. There were no welcome notes or cards dropped in, no housewarming bags of home-grown vegetables or bottles of wine from the neighbours like we had read about from other people's experiences. No friendly nods or waves from passing neighbours. Covid was perhaps responsible. Everyone needed to keep their distance, especially from strangers. Perhaps we were resented; the foreigners who had come in and taken over one of the nicest houses on the road.

At times, my mind has raced to all the negatives the neighbours may be thinking of us. How dare they come here and buy such a big house when we are struggling to pay our taxes.

Other than the elderly couple next door, I didn't even know what the other neighbours looked like, never mind what they thought of us.

Ronan is pulling at the beam.

"Don't attempt to move that by yourself. Anyway, even if you got it over there, how are you going to get it in place? We'll find a few lads and ladders. Just leave it for now...Please."

He's ignoring me. I can feel my lips getting tighter. I've gone from logical, to pleading, to now getting angry at his obstinance. It's time to walk away. I have more tea to be made.

I make my tea and think about what I need to get for Sunday. It is Easter after all, so we should do something to mark the day. If back in Ireland, we would be going to Jim's for a big family dinner. Christmas at mine and Easter at his, that's how it usually fell each year since our kids were weeny tots.

At this point I would be blowing out eggs, dipping them in food colouring and making a centrepiece for the dinner table. This effort would be abandoned halfway through due to lack of time or missing food colouring and some half-assed arrangement would be created with an explanation of what it should have looked like.

But the Easter dinner of leg of lamb, roast potatoes, Yorkshire pudding, and Jim's meticulously made homemade gravy would go down a treat. We'd gather with Mam and Dad, all our now nearly grown kids, and talk about the weather, gardens and my upcoming trips to Italy for weddings during the summer.

But now I am in Italy, living the dream that we talked about during previous Easter dinners. Living the eventual dream... but without family. I hadn't really taken that into account too much. I think I just expected them all to visit a lot.

However, even if they did all live here, Covid regulations this year would have stopped us gathering together, as the region is going Red for the weekend, meaning don't leave your home and whatever you do don't visit loved ones or celebrate Easter with family. We had given up on the idea of Izzy being able to get here for Easter, but I buy her an Easter egg anyway and keep it along with the Christmas tree to celebrate when she can get to us.

The house is at last becoming physically warm, but emotionally it is cold. I feel no attachment. It is still sleeping, empty of any memories. Full of dusty remnants of the past, memories that are not ours and that I have no attachment to. It has the potential to be beautiful, but people are still taken aback when they see the state of the place we are living in.

There is a void, a hollowness that only family can fill. However, I console myself with the thought that when Covid is over they will come, and they will come often for long lingering stays and we will have big family meals again not just at Christmas or Easter but continuously, and these meals will be even better as they will be outside in our beautiful courtyard under the stars, and we will all feel complete again.

I amble back out to the garden. Ronan is doing his own re-enactment of the Passion of Christ, dragging the beam across the garden on his shoulder, knees bent, head down. All he needs to complete the image is a crown of thorns.

"Bloody hell, Ronan, you have pins in your shoulder and you are not supposed to be lifting heavy weights." He's not listening to my concern, which he would call nagging.

"I can't watch this. I'm going in for a shower." I needed to leave him to realise it couldn't be done rather than argue with the stubborn mule.

I'm only out of the shower when he is calling, "Rosie, come look."

I knew he was calling me to help him work out the impossible – how to lift the 6-inch square, 13 foot beam, seven feet up in the air to slot it into place.

I walk out to the garden to let my hair dry in the sun, ready to say "I told you so" but stop in my tracks.

There it was, the beam perfectly in place. It's a Good Friday miracle. "How the hell did you do that?"

"Like a weightlifter," he says proudly. "I rested it across the back of my neck and then hoisted it up arm's length above my head... it was touch and go at one point, didn't think I'd make it, but it slotted in perfectly."

The ancient wooden beam is perfectly in place, as if made to measure. I'm shocked and amazed all at the same time. I'm also very glad I wasn't in the garden to witness it.

With the beam in place, Ronan knocks down the centre post and wall, most of which he just pushes down with his hand as the disintegrated mortar is weak between the bricks.

By the end of the day, the building that had been two sheds earlier that morning, is now taking the shape of the open fronted outdoor living space I had imagined. And the beam, I have to admit, even after all my nagging, looks amazing. Plus, its story has made our first garden creation memory.

19

TO HURRY: AFFRETTARE

The good thing about a region being designated a red zone for the weekend is that there are very few cars on the road, so you can drive at high speed when you need to get to the emergency room at the hospital.

That was my experience with Ronan gripping onto the handle above the door with his leg sporadically going up on to the dashboard every now and then. I wasn't too sure if it was my driving that was making him act so or that the severe pain that he had been in for nearly ten hours now was getting worse.

He awoke suddenly, sat bolt upright and groaned, gripping his belly. A pain like a leg muscle spasm was wrapping itself across the top of his abdomen.

"Perhaps it's wind and you just need a good fart? ...Perhaps it's a contraction and you didn't know you were pregnant?" These are all the suggestions I offered, that's how helpful I am if you wake me at five in the morning.

I sprinkled it with, "You probably tore a muscle lifting that bloody beam, I told you not to do it."

I am sure my 'I told you so' nagging helped, as the pain eased a little from about eight and he slept a couple of hours.

When he woke again it was not so bad but he was still quite bent over walking around the house and didn't feel like eating. That was the first sign I knew that Ronan was really sick. I suggested we go to the hospital and he didn't protest, I then knew that this was really serious. If Ronan sliced his hand open, he'd stitch it himself or stick it together with superglue rather than go to the hospital. I am speaking from experience.

So here we were driving at high speed to the small hospital in a neighbouring town. The building's facade is in need of a paint job as is the inside. It is a faded version of that wonderful Italian ochre yellow with large arched windows and an orange roof.

If there was a prize for hospitals with the best view, this one would win. Perched on the edge of the highest corner on the hilltop town, it gazes over the lake where murmurations of starlings twist and billow.

"I've heard they save the rooms with the lake view for the people they think will die," I say out loud and then regret as Ronan squirms in pain.

I'm not allowed into the hospital because of Covid, but I'm quite pleased with myself as the woman at the entrance knew what I was saying and I understood most of her questions. Okay... I had prepared my speech using Google translate and glanced at it twice while saying it to her. Maybe she thought I couldn't keep my eyes off Facebook and that is why she was a little abrupt with me.

I've learnt that to speak Italian with an affective accent I need to talk like I am doing stand-up comedy and trying to imitate a stereotypical Italian. I practically sing the words as they go up and down on a roller coaster ride out of my mouth, and I use my hands.

I understood when she asked, "where is your husband?" and I could answer "in the car."

I also understood when she said, "Pain and vomiting can be a sign of Covid. He will need to go into the tent and wait for the nurse to come and test him."

The Covid testing tent outside the entrance is similar in shape and colour to the tent we used when all seven of our family and a granny would go camping.

A nurse shorter than me, came out dressed in baggy green PA gear, a mask and eye goggles covered by a visor. I'd seen them dressed like this on news reports. It must have looked scary to patients when this all started out.

She had two zip-lock bags in her gloved hands, each with what looked like test tubes inside. I can hear Ronan do a weird involuntary high pitch gag several times as swab cultures are taken from the back of his throat and back of his nasal passage.

Why did she have two, was I next? I am doing a translation of how to say, "Let us wait until we see what his result comes back as first."

I could go and be with him in the tent while we wait for the result, but instead I stay outside. It's a Covid testing facility after all, people go in there who think they have Covid and some will have it, I'm not taking any chances even if Ronan is in there. He has no choice but I do and we have Luca at home.

I'm standing outside on the grass verge under the spruce trees and thinking if circumstances were different, the tent would be a great place to have a camping holiday. Great view of the lake, nice shaded area for a BBQ under the tree, close to a town... and a hospital in case of emergency.

We hadn't considered Covid as a reason for Ronan's symptoms. We've been super careful. The only places we have been in the last few weeks are the big airy DIY store and two supermarkets with a limited amount of people allowed in them.

What if the hot flash I currently have is a fever building? What if all the hot flashes I've had are intermittent Covid fevers? Does fever last six months?

We had arrived at about 3.45pm, Ronan had his Covid test at 4pm, and by 4.30pm, the negative result is back. He could proceed into the hospital, but alone. I point out he can't speak Italian hoping my efforts might qualify me as a tag along expert translator but no, Covid rules.

I'll go for a walk down the main street while I wait. We would normally come here often to eat in one of the restaurants or for a stroll around the shops. It was definitely somewhere we would come when we had visiting family and friends to explore the fabulous castle and follow the secret passage to the open-air cinema. But we haven't been here in over a year now, we haven't had visitors in over a year. I take a few steps into the main street. It is completely deserted, except for one man in the distance.

The town is on a peninsula that juts out into the lake, so it has lake views from both sides. On a warm sunnier holiday week-end, this street would normally buzz with people enjoying a coffee or an apéritif at Caffe Latino or a pizza in the wisteria-dripping courtyard of one of our favourite pizzerias.

The only man on the street in the distance is walking close to the wall, stopping, and I think, looking at me. I am a stranger in the no-go red zone unless urgent. Going to the hospital was urgent. But me taking a walk down his street is not urgent. I stop and sadly turn back.

It's a quiet day at the hospital. The entire time I am here, only one other car arrives– a man older than me, bringing his mum, who gets out of his car and walks in by herself. It mustn't be too urgent.

I go sit in the car, so I can charge my dying phone. A wind picks up, it gets suddenly stronger, showering my car with dry leaves from the tree I am parked under.

Some emergency responder guys carry a box between them full of bright yellow tissue paper wrapped chocolate eggs to the door of the hospital's reception. Two nurses, one dressed in bright orange and one in bright green scrubs, coyly come out of the emergency entrances and go around to the reception. They are called into a photoshoot with the guys delivering the chocolate eggs.

Ronan texts me, "They have done all the tests, bloods, x-rays, ultrasound, just waiting on the results now."

"Jeez, you've had a full MOT and all within thirty minutes. Shouldn't be too long waiting. It seems very quiet."

"Yeah, I think they were delighted to have a patient."

The wind has got stronger and has brought a brief rain cloud that has relieved itself on the hilltop town.

An hour passes.

"Any sign of the results?" I text.

"They've done another ultrasound, so just waiting on that to come back."

This worries me. From getting ultrasounds when pregnant, I know things can be seen instantly. So the only reason they'd have to wait on results is because they found something. Best not to think about it. Live in the moment, I tell myself, and at this moment nothing is known.

After some more waiting, I see Ronan coming across the grass of the small park outside the hospital gates, sucking on a longed-for cigarette. He still looks in pain. I start the engine, so we're ready to go. The storm is getting stronger. Ronan opens the passenger door and sits into the car out of the rain. It's light but still wet.

"They want to keep me in for a few days. My pancreas is inflamed. The doctor said it's my choice, but they would prefer if I stayed."

"How do you feel about that?" I ask, knowing Ronan hates hospitals more than morgues.

"I think it would be stupid of me not to."

Ronan would usually argue against such a decision and try to find some sort of compromise. He's obviously in a lot of pain and worried.

"It sounds like the best thing to do, so they can get you sorted and get the pain under control." I've put on my logical rather than emotional head.

"you'll need to bring me a few things like... Pyjamas."

"Do you have pyjamas?"

"There are pyjamas somewhere in case of emergency."

I didn't tell him I think I used them as dusters two years ago.

"And a dressing gown."

"Do you have a dressing gown?"

"There is one somewhere. Your mother got me it for Christmas one year and we kept in case of emergency."

"Okay, leave it to me. You'll want your cigarettes too and medication. I'll be back in an hour."

I walk him back to the door where a woman in navy scrubs, who speaks some English comes out from behind a computer in the reception area. "I'll need to bring him personal items, pyjamas and stuff. What will I do?"

"Okay, you can bring it later and leave it at the desk next door. You cannot visit because of Covid. "

"Bloody hell, I hadn't thought of that, bloody Covid."

"Okay..." I look at Ronan standing on the other side of the threshold. The invisible barrier. I won't be able to touch him for another week so we both lean across and go to kiss goodbye forgetting our masks and then pulling them down. The emergency woman is smiling. She probably thinks "ahh isn't that nice, two grey-haired people still loving each other after all this time."

Back in the car, I am like a robot. I'm thinking of all the things I need to do – stop at the shop and get some supplies, get dog food, cat food, gin, wine. There's nothing like a Dunnes Stores or Primark here. Well, in Corciano, thirty minutes away, there is a shopping mall, but nothing around here. The supermarket has a small section with some clothes items. Maybe they will have pyjamas, so I'll try that.

Halfway to the shop my eyes prick. I'm going to be without Ronan for the first time since we moved into the house, since we moved to Italy. I had spent nights away from him staying over at friends or going back to Ireland, but he had never left me to go anywhere.

I run around the supermarket. It's quite busy considering it's Easter eve, one of Italy's many national holidays. I am grabbing random items such as men's socks 'Ageless in Design' is on the front label, with an old man's hand pulling on a sock. He'll need toiletries, razors, shaving foam, toothbrush. I'll get him snacks. Rice crackers, biscuits, fizzy water, a bag of small dark chocolate. There are no pyjamas.

Ronan messages me just as I get back into the car.

"The doctor has said that I will be here about seven or eight days... No food whatsoever for three days... Unfortunately he said my pancreas is pretty bad and it's very serious. He said it was good that I came in. If not looked after, it could be fatal..."

20

TO WORRY: PREOCCUPARE

"Have you got a room with a view of the lake?" I ask, trying to be casual but digging my fingernail into the soft part of the car's dashboard while I hang waiting for the answer.

"No, my window faces the castle wall."

"Well, that is a big relief. They don't think you'll die then."

Back home, my brain's autopilot switch has been flicked on again. "Luca, Dad has to stay in hospital for a few days and I need to bring him in supplies. Go over to the shop and buy cat food and dog food."

"Bloody hell, is that what they feed them in hospital here?"

"Noooo I bought him snacks and socks and gin and wine for me, but while running around the supermarket I forgot the pet food."

He must have overheard the story of my Aunt Rita telling my mother she was mad to consider moving to Italy. "They don't feed you in hospitals there, you have to bring in your own food." This was a concern my mother voiced to me immediately upon hearing. "Rita said they don't feed you in hospitals in Italy, you have to bring in your own food. If I went to the hospital, I'd have to rely on your cooking, which would probably finish me. Maybe I shouldn't move to Italy."

From what Karen has told me, I know the hospital food is good in Italy. She's been to hospital many times with her accident-prone kids and has told me about the nonnas. These are old dears who have time on their hands, so they volunteer at the hospital.

When Karen's son, Charlie, had pneumonia a few years back, she stayed over in the hospital with him. Karen is coeliac, and the grannies used to bring her in special homemade gluten-free dinners and when John, her husband, arrived, the nonnas told them to go down and have dinner together in the hospital restaurant and they would keep an eye on Charlie. The restaurant had lovely food, and they even had wine with their dinner.

I'm thinking of the nonnas. They must be lost without being able to do their volunteer work. I hope Covid hasn't wiped them all out and the tradition can start again when this pandemic is over.

Ronan is texting the things he needs; "earphones as they are as noisy as hell here. I don't have Wi-Fi so messages will be slow."

Luca is throwing in an entire library of books he thinks Ronan will enjoy. As all our clothes and possessions are in black refuse sacks dispersed in various parts of the house, I hadn't a clue where to even start looking for the mysterious pieces of clothing.

I'm emptying all the bags of clothes, searching at high speed for the elusive dressing gown and pyjamas. It's getting dark and stormy. I need to leave within the next ten minutes to get there and back before the 10pm curfew hits. I can't find the PJs, so tracksuit bottoms splattered in paint would have to do and an old matching hoody can act as a dressing gown.

"Luca, you are coming with me for company." I don't give him a choice. I need his company to stop me crying and in case the car breaks down or something, at least we will be together rather than me worrying about him as well.

By the time we reach the hospital, the trees on the top of the hill are bending in the stormy wind and even though it is dark, I can see dots of white surf on the choppy lake water below. I walk through the hospital doors where the girl had told me to go to leave the bag at reception. There is no one around. It's like an abandoned movie set. The florescent light bulbs cast an antique yellow hue on everything that is not in shadow strengthens the creepy atmosphere.

I walk down the corridor. It's completely empty. We're in the middle of a pandemic, but it seems no one is sick or in need of hospital care. I'm looking for the reception desk, then realise I have walked past it. It's a small temporary desk at the entrance, abandoned. I want to get out of this eerie place as quickly as possible before the zombies arrive.

I bring the bag around to the front desk of the emergency entrance. The abrupt woman sees me and smiles with her eyes. She hurries over and takes the bag from me. She is much friendlier this time. Perhaps she now knows Ronan, the friendly giant, is genuinely sick and not wasting their time, I suppose. Either that or her shift is ending soon.

I call Ronan from the reception to tell him the bag is on its way. "I have hidden some rice cakes in the bag just in case you are starving."

"Rosie, the doctor said this is serious, as serious as a heart attack. I need to follow orders." His speech is a little slurred and distant.

"Ronan, the doctor hasn't mentioned cancer, has he?"

"They don't know what is causing it. When the inflammation goes down in a few days, they can run some tests."

Back home, I shove a frozen pizza in the oven. I'm not hungry but I haven't eaten since lunch so I think I should.

I'm about to open the bottle of wine but stop myself. What if I am needed at the hospital? I need to drive. So I make myself tea instead.

With Luca gone to his room, I'm left looking at the snacks on the counter I bought for Ronan. My eyes are pricking, not because of the money I have wasted on all the snacks he is now not allowed to have, nor of the impending possible loneliness, but with the thought of this loneliness lasting forever without Ronan. I know we are both thinking the same. What if it's cancer? My heart hurts. I am without Asha for comfort and now without Ronan.

The following day is Easter Sunday and dinner for Luca and me is an 'inventful' event. The fact that I have left the cooking and grocery shopping as Ronan's responsibility for the last twenty years has made me more than inept/useless when it comes to meal planning.

Our home cooking since moving to Italy has been suffering due to the small kitchen where Ronan found a new love for the speediness of a frying pan, which probably didn't help his pancreas.

Along with us usually being both too tired from renovations to do anything more elaborate than a simple pasta meal.

I haven't told my parents or family at home that Ronan is in hospital, they are sending me photos of them all in Jim's garden safely distancing having dinner together for the first time in a year. I send them a picture of a very nicely cooked leg of lamb I have found on the internet and pretend I cooked it instead of the pot noodles we are having.

I have told Izzy about Ronan and she, of course, wants to come home. But travelling from the UK is still not possible. We can just hope the rumours about travel being possible in May are true and she can get over before she starts work again.

"They have done more tests... I have acute pancreatitis," texts Ronan.

Before texting him back, I take a deep breath and Google... 'Acute Pancreatitis'.

I'm ready for all the disclaimers where the pages tell you the worst-case scenario; that you should visit your doctor or just skip that and book your day at the mortuary.

Acute pancreatitis is a condition where the pancreas becomes inflamed over a short period of time... Most people with acute pancreatitis start to feel better within about a week and have no further problems.

There is no mention of death or impending catastrophes.

Causes are a lot of alcohol – well, that is not an issue since Ronan has been sober fourteen years – gallstones or a trauma to the area.

I text Ronan and copy and paste what I found and 'you might have gallstones.' He immediately calls.

"Oh, thank god you Googled it, I have no Wi-Fi so haven't been able to. So it doesn't sound too bad?"

"No, it sounds great, well great in the sense that is not saying the usual when you consult Doctor Google with a symptom, and it tells you to start writing your will. It sounds like with hydration and antibiotics by IV you will be right as rain in a few days."

"Phew. The doctor said it could be a virus."

Italians say everything is a virus. I think our equivalent is saying it's an infection.

"They want me to stay in eight days."

"You heal fast. You might be out in a few days. Let's wait and see."

Later that day I am listening to the Indie authors on Clubhouse again. There are women talking who are making five figures a month from writing fiction, some have six-figure months, some have been writing a book a month for years and now have a huge back catalogue of books to their name. They are living my dream, being full-time authors, self-publishing and being their own boss, running their writing like a business and making bloody good money. I never knew writing fiction and self-publishing could be so profitable.

"Listen, you will need to get a bag of pellets for the fire. You can get them across the road." With his anxiety down, boredom from lying on his back in hospital sets in and Ronan starts thinking practical thoughts and is telling me how to organise myself.

"I'll be here for a few more nights so you'll be able to fall asleep in front of the telly without me nagging you to stay awake."

I'm more relaxed too and enjoying having complete silence and time to myself. With no emails or work to do, I plot out two cozy mysteries and I begin to write non-stop.

"I'm not going to be watching TV," I respond. "I'm going to write. I have decided what my new business will be. I am going to do what I always dreamed of doing someday. I am going to be an author."

21

TO EAT: MANGIARE

The average height of an Italian male in the north of Italy is 176.9cm (5'9.7") whereas in the South of Italy the average is 174.2cm (5'8"). The average Irish male is 178.9cm and Irish women stand at an average of 165.1cm.

Ronan texts me during the night, as he is finding it hard to sleep. The beds are too short for his 6'2" frame. Perhaps they are specially built for Italians who tend to be shorter.

Maybe all that marching on roads to Rome affected Italians' legs and made them genetically shorter. As they are more than an inch shorter in the south, it proves my theory. Their legs got worn down by the time they reached Rome and beyond. Same for the women, the average height up north is 163.2cm (5'4.2") whereas down south it is 160.8cm (5'3.3"). I rest my case.

I definitely feel less of a hobbit over here.

On Monday morning I open the fridge hungry. We are out of milk and eggs. I have nothing in for breakfast, so I grab a bag and go over to the supermarket, which is closed.

I had forgotten the day after Easter is another holiday day for all of Italy. So I jump into the car and do a tour of the supermarkets which would normally be open on Sunday morning. My logic is that they would be open on a bank holiday Monday too, but none of them are open.

I pull into the car park of the last attempted supermarket and text Lucia. "Do you have any eggs? Ronan normally does the shopping for the basics, all the shops are closed and now I have nothing in for breakfast. I am such a bad mother! Anyway let me know, I'll be passing your place soon."

Ronan rings. "I slept until about 3am and then all hell broke loose with the guy across the hall screaming "Mortina". That went on until about ten minutes ago when all six staff arrived together and talked at once to him. The poor guy is either in terrible pain or he's a total wanker."

He continues, "Then there is an elderly woman, she sounds English, who comes out of her room now and then and says, 'please tell the management I don't approve of the room'."

"Ronan are you sure they said pancreatic? Cause it sounds like they have you in the psychiatric rather than pancreatic wing?"

He ignores me and continues about his plight. "I was just drifting back to sleep this morning when a nurse arrived in all light and breezy at 5.45am, all lights blazing and took nine blood tests, weighed me and told me he needs a 'pee pee' test. I can't count the times they have taken bloods from me at this point but instead of leaving a tube in my arm to draw blood from, they spend ages each time prodding my arm with a needle to find a blood vessel again. My arm looks like it belongs to a heroin addict."

"I'm in a ward by myself, lying flat on my back. I'm not allowed to sit up and I'm hooked up to two drips. Antibiotics in one and other they call 'gator aid' with the essential salts and minerals. I have to call the nurse and ask her to turn out the light."

He's hangry, I can hear it – Ronan likes his food, and he's now on day three of no food and is just being given ice to suck on.

"There must be a light switch beside your bed?"

"There is, but it just turns on another light."

Ronan is still angry. "No one has given me a new mask so I've been wearing the same one for three days which cannot be healthy."

"Ask for one?"

"How? No one speaks English."

"Although I managed to ask for a walk around stand for the drips so I can go out to the bathroom a bit easier than trying to juggle the drip bags in my hands while trying to keep them above my head.

"The doctors are not telling me anything. They come in each day, look at my chart and say 'Bene', then leave, except two that seem to run their office from the table in my room sometimes. They won't even share the Wi-Fi code with me so I can at least watch something on my phone. 'No, no, not for patients,' he said."

Lucia still has not replied by the time Ronan has to hang up as someone has come into his room to do another blood test. So I drive to her place and leave her a new voice message. "Okay, I am outside your place now, so I'm going to raid your chickens' asses for eggs and hopefully you have not got there before me."

I grab a spare mask from the car; a perfect egg carrying hammock. As I walk past the farmhouse, Lucia comes out from the top balcony. "What are you doing here?"

"I'm here to steal eggs. Did you not get my message? I'll trade you for dinner tomorrow night at our place with Luca and me."

The chickens supply me with six eggs.

Ronan is back on the phone. "A guy came to my door with a tea trolley, asking me if I wanted tea or coffee, I asked for coffee and then he laughed, 'Ah no nothing for you Signore' They have a sign on my door no food or drink. It's like something you would see on the bear pit in the zoo.

"I'm still trying to figure out what caused this. I think it was the rich food I ate the night before. That chickpea curry you made. Or it could have been the rice crackers I ate. They're supposedly sneakily lethal, perhaps it was them?"

"Or it could have been your Jesus Christ Good Friday impersonation the day before? Or it could be your diabetic medication? They are both things I've read can cause it on the internet."

Later that evening, a doctor that can speak some English confirms what we thought.

"It was most likely my medication."

It looks like his Type 2 Diabetes may have reversed and he no longer needs the medication he was taking which overstimulated his pancreas and caused it to inflame.

"I'm supposed to get my diabetes checked regularly and I can't remember the last time I was able to get that done. They have taken me off that medication completely. One doctor said I can throw it away. It's the Mediterranean diet. It has cured my diabetes."

"Ronan, living in Italy doesn't mean you can just eat anything and call it a Mediterranean diet. You don't just absorb the goodness of it. Spag bol three or four times a week, steak and chips and burger and chips are not exactly Mediterranean diet specialities. It's more fish and salads. And the only fish you eat are a pack of twelve fish fingers thrown in a pan."

"I fry them in olive oil. Olive oil is good for you."

"Yes, supposedly red wine is good for your health too, but not a whole bottle in one sitting, like I did last night. You are eating fried food every day and that is not good for you."

By day four, Ronan has had enough. After three days and three nights of lying on his back in a room on his own, no TV, no Wi-Fi, no food and no visitors due to Covid, just lots of drips and blood tests.

"I am going to leave the hospital tomorrow. Ask Lucia if I can legally sign myself out. This is ridiculous. No one is giving me any information. I don't know if they're considering Saturday as one day of fasting as I didn't eat that day or is it from Sunday which will mean tomorrow is day five to me but day four to them. I haven't slept in days."

As he continues his litany of misery about how he has not been able to shower since arriving in the hospital as no one has shown him where it is or helped him understand how to wash with two drips hanging out of him, I turn on the tap in the kitchen to fill the kettle and a sparse trickle comes out.

As soon as Ronan is off the phone, I'm on to Danny Boy and Antonio, but they can't help. They say it must be the water company. Lucia contacts them for me and they say it is because the bill has not been paid.

"What bill, we have not received one?"

"It was sent to your old address."

"Why would they do that when it is for this house?"

The guy is helpful on the phone. He changes the address, takes payment over the phone and assures me the water will be on in 24 hours.

The following day, Ronan's drips are removed. It's day four of not eating, but really day five. He's been shown where the shower is and sounds in much better form when he calls.

However, that all changes an hour later when they move him into the ward with the mad old man that shouts constantly.

"I'm sorry Rosie, I've signed myself out. There was no way I was staying in that room just for observation for another three days. I need to sleep. And there are different nurses and doctors every day coming in from outside and dealing with dozens of patients. It could turn into a Covid fest."

They had brushed off Ronan's statements about leaving until he was dressed in his paint-covered tracksuit and was heading for the door. All five doctors met with him in the chief doctor's office. Two acted as translators as Ronan thanked him for their care, but he knew his own body and it needed sleep and food.

The head doctor laughed at his notion of knowing his own body's needs. They were happy with his progress. The inflammation had gone, but he needed to be observed for another two days of introducing foods slowly.

"At home I will be safer from Covid, I will be able to sleep and I can introduce foods slowly at home. Thank you again for your care."

The younger doctors understood where he was coming from, but the older one was still astounded that he was signing himself out.

I sat outside in the getaway car. After being infused with vitamins and losing several kilos of weight, he looked well-toned, fresh and healthy.

"Jeez, I might check myself in there for a week. You look fabulous."

"I know! I've now got a six-pack."

"Wow, you developed stomach muscles in there?"

"No, the six-pack of rice crackers you got me. They are still in my bag."

22

TO PREPARE: PREPARARE

I t's the end of April. Through her job on TV, Shelly hears the inside rumours first about travel restrictions. "I think if Izzy books a ticket for after mid-May, she will get through if she gets a negative PCR test the day before and has her vaccine certificate. The UK is not policing the airports and there are flights between the UK and Italy daily. She can travel for work reasons, so if you give her a letter of employment as a backup that might work."

Izzy goes for it and buys her ticket and I arm her with a letter of employment as my PA as back up. If I have to follow through and employ her for the summer officially, I will do it, anything to get her back safely to us, for a hug and some mothering.

"Is it okay if Dave comes too? He'll follow me over after the first week so that we have family time together before he arrives." I didn't care who she brought as long as she gets home to us.

I will not allow myself to get excited until she is actually here. I have turned into a Doubting Thomas. But it doesn't stop me from getting a new energy boost of panic to get the house in a more presentable order.

The days that follow are a sprint in home decor like one of those programs on the telly when someone leaves for a day and comes back to a made over house. They always make me bristle, as I think; that gloss paint must still be wet or at least tacky and they have put furniture against it and hung pictures on the must-still-be-wet walls.

We whitewash a room that will be her bedroom. I can't stomach tiling ever again as it triggers a form of PTSD from the pre-Christmas passport debacle, so I leave Ronan to do the second bathroom. I don't care what it looks like as long as we have a second working toilet and handbasin before they arrive.

Our current bedroom is still in the downstairs box room beside the guest kitchen and near the loo. It's the room that will be my parents' bedroom within the next year hopefully. So Izzy and her boyfriend and Luca will have the second floor to themselves, including the half-finished bathroom. Ronan has done a great job but like me, he now never wants to cut another tile in his life.

"Bloody hell, we still don't have a dining table."

"Well, it's the beginning of summer. We are in Italy, so we'll eat outside on that pastry table."

"The one we use as a workbench and has been left outside all winter?"

"Yeah, I'll power wash it and with a tablecloth we won't know the difference."

I get lost in the detail and start painting the chipped ironwork of the banisters a dark matt grey. They look fantastic, but one section for eight steps has taken the best part of three days. So I abandon that and focus on dust busting, rubble removing and whitewashing dried-in mould stains in the hallway and second floor.

Time is running out, so with a week to go, my focus becomes even more focused on the areas they will walk through; from the sitting room and kitchen to the bathroom and to their bedroom and to outside.

"I'm just making them look reasonable and leave the rest," I say dabbing paint over the dark splodges.

"Do you really think Izzy will be that bothered?"

"She won't be, but it's the first time we're meeting 'him' and we should try to make some sort of decent impression, for Izzy's sake."

It's the day before Izzy arrives and we are doing a rush job of finalising her bedroom, finding suitable furniture from the stuffed storage rooms. "Oh bloody hell, we don't have a double bed base for her mattress? How come we are short a bed base?"

"Because we didn't bring one from Ireland and Giovanni's house came with bed bases provided," Ronan responds, pulling out a chest of drawers.

"We need to go get one. How have we not realised this until now?... I've seen them at the furniture shop. Let's hope they have them in stock and it's not something we have to wait twenty days for."

Thankfully, the shop has the base for a double bed in stock, and it is only €70. In Ireland, we are used to beds being divan beds – sold as a covered base and headboard with a neatly fitted mattress on top. Drawers in the base are an optional storage extra which ups the cost of the said beds. Here, it is more common to buy a base of black metal and wooden slats, then you buy your decorative bed with headboard sides and base to go around the base, both freestanding single units in their own right. Then you buy your mattress.

We pick the base we want in the showroom, which is not difficult. There is only one type. We pay for it at the cash desk, take our receipt and a docket and drive down to the 'magazino', the warehouse. It's a quarter to eight on a Saturday evening. We are the last customers and they are not open the next day. There are still last-minute buyers trailing out of the grocery shop with which the furniture shop shares a car park.

We're delighted with our successful purchase until we try to fit it in the back of the van. No matter which angle we try, the double bed base will not slide past the wooden bench seats we built when converting the van to a camper van.

We consider tying it to the roof, but the potential of velocity turning it into a flying bed and causing mayhem on the motorway changes our mind.

"Ronan, it's no use. It won't fit," I say as I watch him trying to fit a square peg into a round hole. But who am I to doubt Ronan?

"Oh yes it will," he says with determination as he angles himself against one side of the van's interior, like he is sliding off a seat under a table, lifts his workboot-clad foot and kicks the camper van bench we so lovingly built five years ago to smithereens. "We were going to do up the camper van anyway this summer, so we might as well get a head start now. Get me a hammer would you Love?"

The van rocks with each smashing heel kick. I laugh hysterically at the lengths he is going to, to get the bloody bed into the van at the last minute.

"Oh Dio, Mamma Mia!" exclaims the guy from the warehouse who has come out after hearing the commotion and is looking at the actions of my madman.

"Un martello?" I say to him. The word for a hammer comes to me like other needed words in an emergency.

Within seconds, he is back with a sledgehammer.

He's laughing giddily watching Ronan demolish the inside of our van, a small crowd have gathered to watch the destruction.

I just keep on laughing. One, because I can't help it and two, to make sure people know I am okay with this man wrecking the inside of our car.

Considering Italians would never even eat inside their cars and that there is a queue every Sunday at the carwash and the most popular colour for cars here seems to be gleaming white, I'm not sure what they make of our 20-year-old van that, if ever washed, would probably fall apart.

"Now it will fit," says Ronan clambering out the back of the van awkwardly like a giant getting out of a clown car. The crack of splintering wood accompanies his every step. I'm picking up the bits that have fallen out and throwing them back into the van as Ronan and the guy from the warehouse slide the bed base in with ease.

"There, that did it," says Ronan, brushing his hands off each other like he had just finished a masterpiece for the Uffizi.

He hands the hammer back to the guy who has been asking Ronan a dozen questions about where we are from and what we are doing here and telling Ronan about his life like it's a therapy session, while he helped destroy our van's interior.

"Nice guy," is the only words Ronan says as he pulls on his seatbelt and we drive out of the carpark to the small crowd. Two are still clapping.

The house is as ready as we can make it in the short space of time. We have rearranged and got rid of a lot of stuff by emptying and refilling rooms of furniture and our belongings.

I've painted patches in a multitude of rooms with different tones of paint to make it look like we are doing colour swatches to choose the perfect colour for each room. They look like they are purposely placed to catch the different light throughout the day... not to cover mould patches underneath.

I pull the toilet that has yet to be fitted in from the hallway. It's still-boxed lid on top. Covered with a throw, no one will be any the wiser of what is underneath. This move achieves two things: it gets the new toilet that has been sitting on the landing like an ornament out of the way and fulfils the need of a bedside table.

The six-month-old hoover gives up. I've told Ronan repeatedly that if he force feeds it too much fine dust, it will die. But he hasn't listened and has continued to use it to cut through the thick carpets of powdered cement dust sprinkled with rubble here and there that continue to appear from the heavens covering every surface and corner and embedding into every crevice.

He, of course, does not acknowledge that the issue was his misuse of the hoover – it's because it is an Italian brand he is not familiar with, of course. So he will do the same to the next hoover, no doubt.

I go to bed exhausted but have my alarm set for early. Tomorrow I get to hug my girl for the first time in a long year.

23

TO CELEBRATE: CELEBRARE

Pulling into Fiumicino Airport, the first airport I've been to in fifteen months, and it feels like all its missing are bales of tumbleweed rolling down the road. The usually busy airport has abundant empty car spaces, a few taxis at a rank in the far distance and just one person in sight in a high-viz jacket.

Just as we park, I get the long-awaited text from Izzy. "I just got my bag and I'm waiting outside the arrivals door."

"She's here!" I leap out of the car before Ronan has switched off the engine in the parking spot, overlooking the arrivals terminal portico, and scan the large black glass sliding doors with the large numbers of each terminal above.

I call her. "Which arrival door? There are lots. Can you see a man in a high-viz jacket?"

"No."

"Can you see taxis?"

"Yes. There's a rank to my right."

"Okay, turn left and walk down the archway. I am at terminal door number three."

"Ah, now I see a number. I am at number one."

I've crossed the road without waiting on the boys and I'm speed walking down the archway.

We stay on the phone to each other. "I can't see you."

There is still no sign of life. I still have doubts I'm in the right place. A flight has arrived, but there are no people. Then I see a figure in the distance, at the other end of this long walkway. I'd know her bouncy walk anywhere, trundling along with a big suitcase. It's her. There is no one else.

"Ah, there you are!"

"Where?"

"I'm in front of you. I'm waving."

"I see you!"

We both start to run. Why the hell did I wear flip-flops? I haven't run in months, possibly years. I feel like I am going at snail's pace. My legs feel heavy, my feet clumsy. All I need now is to go head over heels, bang my head and go unconscious for five years. The way my life has gone, it would be a typical ending to this episode.

Honestly, why can I not run fast? This is ridiculous. And how long is this bloody walkway? Izzy isn't going much faster, slowed down by her case. As soon as we are no longer a blur, as soon as we can see one another's eyes, she lets the case go. I kick off my sandals and run barefoot. Both our arms are outstretched, screaming. In my peripheral vision I see the guy in the high-viz vest, leaning against the barrier between the walkway and road. He's laughing happily at us. The mock screaming and laughing stop. My face buried in her hair and hers in mine, there is just silence as we grip together like a tightened vice.

"You smell nice," we both say simultaneously. We pull our heads up from the comfort of the neck tucking and laugh while we rub the tears from each other's faces.

"Have you got a tissue? I think I have snotted in your hair."

"I don't care."

We're laughing again as I reach into my pocket with one hand to hurriedly give her a tissue so I can go back to giving her another bear hug.

I glimpse the guy in the high-viz jacket. He's wiping tears from his face. I smile at him as my face squelches up again.

"Your shoes!"

"Your bag."

I just about feel safe enough that she will not disappear like a beautiful mirage before I loosen my grip. "Come on, Dad and Luca are waiting. Let's go home."

She wears her mask all the way home in the car, talking nonstop. The four corners of my world are complete again. I think back on the last time she was here nearly a year ago and the precautions we took wearing homemade hazmat hug suits made from garbage bags. Covid is still flying about the place and is more prevalent than the year before, but at least vaccines have taken away the severity of fear and mandatory pre-flight Covid tests have given some level of confidence.

Although only in her early twenties, Izzy has already had her first vaccine shot in the UK, while we still patiently wait for ours. Italy has administered nearly thirty million vaccine doses, and the country has nearly ten million people vaccinated with a double dose, but even though Ronan is considered vulnerable and is in the age bracket being vaccinated at the moment, he still cannot get it because he doesn't have a health card number and there is no way around the system.

But we don't care about that at the moment. We are all together and don't plan on going anywhere outside our own house.

We have a week of just us time, talking a lot but then also sitting together writing, planning the year ahead, watching Bake-Offs and foreign movies.

Then the day arrives that 'he' arrives. I'm cautious or perhaps jealous. What human being is good enough to have absorbed so much of her love and attention? Ronan drives to the station with Izzy to collect him from the train while I stay at home to try and clean up the new layer of thick dust that has settled on everything.

As soon as I hear the car pull in I run to the kitchen and pretend I have been busy preparing dinner. Looney is ecstatic at a new being arriving, I can hear her yaps getting louder and the deep Scottish accent talking to her getting closer.

He's at the kitchen door, his big bold smile is wider than it is in photos. I had always expected Izzy to go for a tall, dark guy but he is more average height with sandy tight curly hair and a reddish stubble. "Ah Rosè," he greets like I am a pink shade of wine. "So lovely to meet ye' at last," he holds out his arms and goes to do the Italian thing of kissing me on both cheeks. I haven't been physically touched by anyone other than close family in so long due to Covid, that I happily respond and of course go for the wrong cheek which means, just as Izzy is walking in behind him, I'm giving her boyfriend a smacker on the lips.

"MAM!"

"Jezuz,"I yelp.

David is laughing and pulls me in for a hug.

By day three, I can see he is good for her. He's fun, he cooks well and is quick to laugh. Over our al fresco dinner a small spider lands on top of Izzy's head, I am about to reach to brush it off before she notices and does a screaming dance, but, because he finds it difficult to take his eyes off her, his hand gets there before mine and tenderly brushes a strand of hair from her cheek to disguise his action.

He'll do.

So I let down my guard, it's time for him to see the type of family he is getting into. While they are out at the beach, I take boxes out of one of our flea-market-style rooms. The boxes are exceptionally dusty after only five months in storage. Dust blankets everything.

I carry the boxes to the garden, pull the Christmas tree I have nurtured and kept alive onto the flagstones and open the box of tinsel and baubles.

"What the hell are you doing?" It's Luca, up early for once.

"This weekend we'll have Christmas. Want to help?"

He jumps to the challenge, pulls the table over and arranges the chairs.

By the time Izzy and Dave get back sun-kissed and relaxed, I have Christmas carols playing, the place smelling of turkey and the tinselled tree as a backdrop to our Christmas table decorated with ivy from the garden and thick church candles left over from previous weddings. The candles are soft from the summer heat, but they do what they are supposed to do and give the Christmas atmosphere.

A few days later we celebrate Easter with the chocolate Easter eggs I stashed a month ago. The day after that there is cake and candles for Luca's 18th birthday that happened quietly three months ago. Another day, Dave volunteers to make dinner and has mastered the art of making the perfect Aperol Spritz and bruschetta, there is more cake to mark the birthdays we have missed together and everyone has a turn of waving out the candles with a hand fan rather than blowing because of Covid. Sporadic catch-up celebrations all have the Christmas tree baubles glistening in the sun as the backdrop.

Three weeks go by fast. We haven't had time to say all the words, all the feelings, all the conversations that we have both planned over the last year. It wasn't from lack of trying. Some-times sitting in silence in the garden stroking Izzy's arm, or her head on my lap as I played with her hair, was enough to say more.

On the last evening we go to a local fish restaurant and have dinner with Lucia under the stars. The wooden tables and chairs line the alleyway between the restaurant and the church, with string lights draped between the ochre and stone facades. Candles flicker on the tables draped in red gingham cloth. We feast on fish from the lake, local cheeses, bruschetta and wine while talking about all the places we are going to travel when the pandemic is finally over.

But the perfect evening does not end well. As we pull into the driveway, my eyes shoot to the pavement across the road. I know instantly it's one of ours. I wait until everyone is inside and pull Ronan back and lead him across the road with me to be sure. Someone has taken the time to place her body in against the wall. She has a tail, so it is Moonface. The busy road had claimed her little life.

Dave takes it upon himself to be the one to break the sad news to Izzy, I watch from afar as he tenderly hugs her and wipes away her tears.

This time we dig a beloved pets final resting together as a family, including Dave. The emotions we feel seem somewhat easier to bare with us all supporting each other through the shock and sadness.

Within the space of living here for five months we have already got an established family pet cemetery.

We are all up and out early the following day to drive two hours to the airport in Rome. With a traffic jam delay, getting Izzy and Dave and their luggage out of the car is a rush with only thirty minutes until the flight leaves. No time for prolonged goodbyes, a quick hug and off they dash, disappearing through the departure doors with cases dragging behind them at high speed.

It's not like the last time she visited. The last time she left, we let her go knowing there was despair to come. And there was a lot of despair. Covid was severe and fickle. Countries were opening and closing borders like drafty doors, and restrictions were on and off like light switches. We were completely in the dark as to what lay in store. All we knew was because of her work, we definitely would not see her for the next six months - until Christmas, and who knew what lay ahead then.

We knew it would be bad, but it turned to worse than bad, a nightmare of passports and flights being missed. Any coloured hair I had left in my head went grey. It saved me a fortune on getting my hair a consistent silver.

This time it is different. I am not leaving the same girl who, a year ago, had bought three 10-foot rolls of bubble wrap and thirty boxes to move from a tiny apartment she had been living in for six months. I was leaving a woman. A very beautiful woman inside and out who now had a loving partner to give her emotional support, make her laugh and love her like she deserves to be loved.

The start of the trip back home from the airport was in silence. Thunder rumbled and big globules of rain, made silver from the sun and exaggerated by the soft dark grey ahead of us, burst like water balloons on our windshield.

Ronan knew better than to try to overtake the trucks on the motorway. He could see those who did were being blinded by the halo of tsunami waves, created by the speeding cars on the other side of the barrier going towards Rome. The sheets of puddles thrown over the cars ahead caused them to jam on their brakes and wobble.

Hail stones as big as marbles bounced off the windshield and bonnet. There was a flyover ahead, cars were pulling in to shelter under it, and we joined them. We were in the queue behind the ones that got to the underpass for shelter so we, like a bunch of other cars, were not sheltered but at least together in numbers we felt somewhat protected from the heavenly onslaught.

The hail stones got bigger, big marbles, half the size of golf balls bashed our car. We put our hands on the windshield, hoping to absorb some of the impact to stop it from breaking. The pounding noise was so loud we had to shout over it to hear ourselves. "Rome in May? Unbelievable! Who doesn't believe in global warming? This is mental!"

Within a half an hour, it had eased into a shower. We took our chances and, with others, we eased away from the sheltering herd. The sky ahead was still a dirty grey, but there were gaps where the sun had squeezed through, sprinkling the hills and valleys around with small rainbows. This time I chose not to look at the darkness, but at the rainbows.

She's happy, and she'll be back.

24

TO PAY: PAGARE

L ucia calls up with a half dozen eggs from her chickens. I
think she is afraid I cannot feed Ronan.

"The town hall called the notary who called me saying that
they understand you are not Italian so you probably do not
understand the taxes that need to be paid on the house, but they
see you have paid no taxes on the house like the IMU that is
due to be paid by June and the garbage tax TARI.

"They want to explain to you the taxes you have to pay as an
owner, but of course nobody there speaks English. I didn't
want to fight with them but I was so angry and I said 'is there
not one person who speaks English in the town hall, in a town
where a lot of English speakers come to live?' It is ridiculous.
Anyway, this is urgent."

Lucia automatically starts cleaning my kitchen. "I am sorry. I
am fighting with Alessandro, so I need to clean. It's what we
Italian women do to get rid of stress and I have nothing left to
clean in my house."

I am perfectly okay with her using my house as her stress ball. She has done this before. Everyone should have a stressed Lucia in their lives. I put on the kettle and get back to the urgent matter she has called in about. "We are living in Italy. It is perfectly okay if they don't speak English. But I am confused about their message. I tried to get bins, and they said I can't as we are not resident. And we never got a property tax bill. I do not know why they don't email me like they have done before about an issue?"

"She did not contact you directly as she is embarrassed she can't speak English. Anyway, the first appointment available is on Wednesday at 9am, so on Wednesday we have to go to the town hall. It is very important, she says it is very urgent. I think they are nice as they give you no fine. If it was the other town, they would have sent you a lawsuit by now and a fine.

"But, in your town, they understand that you have to learn the taxes. But I am sincerely shocked that your commercialista has not done this. This person has to take care of your taxes. I will fire him if I were you."

"I can't fire my commercialista, as I don't have one."

"Then get one. It is important, so they help you with your taxes."

By asking around the yogis, as Ronan calls my yoga group, Shelly recommends a commercialista who is English but has worked here for thirty years. I call and book a consultation with her to try to figure out what taxes we need to pay and how to go forward with my business if I do become a resident.

Wednesday arrives. Lucia calls me, "I cannot go, my baby goose is ill and I need to bring her to the emergency room, but my father will go with you to the commune for the tax meeting."

At the town hall, we go up to the first floor. There is a woman behind a desk. Even though there is a large window behind her, the room still seems dark.

She explains I need to pay property tax on my four properties. "Has the architect not submitted the paperwork to make it one property yet?" She flicks through the cardboard file.

"No, it is registered as four apartments and a garage."

I make a note to contact Mick Kelly about this oversight.

"How much will it be?"

"She cannot tell you. Your commercialista will work that out for you using a formula."

"Will they send me a bill?"

"No, it is up to you to pay your property tax twice per year. By December and by June. But if it is just one house, and it is your home, your primary residence, then you don't have to pay property tax."

"But it is one house, and it is our only home?"

"Yes, but it is not registered as one. It needs to be registered. And you pay on the square meters of the part you live in."

"Ah okay, so we have only been there since-"

"Yes, you have been there since before Christmas."

"Only the day before Christmas."

"Yes, the registrar lives close and passes your house every day. She saw you moving in."

"But we don't use the top floor, so we don't pay property tax on that?"

"If there is electric and water there, then you must."

"But there is not."

"You may have to prove that."

"How? By not having lights on when the woman is passing and looking into our house?"

"Yes."

"You are paying for the six months ahead, so if you get electric and water on the top floor in the next six months, then you pay the tax. Your commercialista will explain."

I ask her about getting bins. And she hands me the form for the TARI.

Great, I am looking forward to getting bins. I start to fill it out. It asks for my Tessera Sanitaria number. I tell her I don't have one because I am not a resident.

"Oh, you are not a resident. Then this doesn't apply to you. You can't have bins, so you don't pay the TARI."

She whips away the form from under my pen so quick it leaves a line of ink running down the centre. Without hesitance she tears the form up in four and throws it in her already over-flowing bin.

"I can't get bins? What are non-residents supposed to do with their rubbish?"

She looks at me as if I have just asked her what her bra size is.

After the meeting, I call into Mick Kelly.

"Mick, it looks like I am going to get a whopper of a property tax bill because the house is still registered as four properties. Why haven't you registered as one yet?"

"You want me to do that now?"

"It was part of the sale agreement with the notary that we would register the property as one before December 2021. I thought you had already done it?"

He doesn't answer this question directly. "Okay, I will do it. It is a quick process."

The following week we have a meeting with the commercial-ista who confirms what we already know about running our Irish business in Italy and how complicated our lives will be.

"Your property tax bill for the year is.... €1,310. Have you paid your TARI?"

"No. They have told me once that we should, and twice that we can't have bins because we are not resident."

"But you need to pay it even if you are not resident and own a house as it pays for other things like street cleaning too. If it's not paid, they will fine you."

"I can argue that it is not from lack of trying. And they haven't sent me a bill for the TARI or the property tax."

"There is no holding hands in Italy. It is up to you to pay your taxes and if you don't, they just fine you without question and there's no comeback. There is no one to argue with. I advise you to get back on to the woman in the Commune who contacted your friend about you not paying the TARI and ask her to register for your TARI bill. "

But there is no need for me to contact her. A few days later Lucia sends me a message;

"The town hall has been on to me again to say you have to pay the garbage taxes soon. They were worried about where you put the garbage as you don't have the bins. I did not tell them you use mine.

"They need a document filled out and they need the square meterage of the house and number of people living there."

When people asked me what the square meterage of the house is, I looked blankly at them. They might as well be asking me what the population of over 45-year-olds in Outer Mongolia is.

"She said normally they have an architect approval of the size, so for this I emailed Mick Kelly because he has to do it and then you need to print out the form and complete it. She needs it back before this evening. Otherwise, they need to send you a fine."

25

TO ACCOMPLISH: RIUSCIRE

I have received my TARI bill. At last, we will get bins. I go to the commune to pay it. It takes summoning up courage, as I know no one there speaks English.

I go to the reception window and say my pre-prepared Google translate line, "Pagato TARI qui?" I pat myself on the back for understanding the Italian answer, "yes, the second floor." I go up one flight of stairs and wonder if the second floor is what I would call the third floor or is it this floor?

There are two bells with labels on the panel beside the locked door with a top half of bumpy yellow blur glass.

I don't understand what is written on either label. Neither say TARI. So I buzz one. There is no answer. So I buzz the other. I say in my well-rehearsed line. "I need to pay my TARI bill."

"TARI il campanello sopra."

I freeze and start to sweat. Flight or fight has kicked in and I am about to turn and abort the rubbish mission when my brain orders me to think, think, think. I know these words. I have learned them. Sopra is above and Campanello is... just as my brain cogs are clicking in, a friendly-faced woman partially opens the door, juts half her body out and points to the buzzers I just pressed.

In Italian she explains: "I am social services." She points to the lower bell, the bell above "Campanello sopra for TARI." Now campanello and sopra are imbedded in my brain. This is what I need – Italians to communicate with me with a little patience and simplicity.

"Prego" she says, opening the door wider and inviting me into the corridor that runs the length of the building with mid-century gloss painted panelled walls dividing same size offices on the other side of the corridor. A glass panel on the top half of the panel allows you to see into each office.

"TARI is here," she points to the office in front of us behind the photocopier machine, and walks off. There is no one in the office, there is no one in the corridor, so I stand there, wondering what to do, until a woman with an eighties style perm comes out of one of the offices to use the dated photo-copier. I feel like I've entered a time warp to my youth.

"I need to pay my TARI bill. Where do I go?"

"In there." She points to the empty office.

"I enter and wait?" I say, not wanting to go into somewhere I am not supposed to. Again, fight or flight has triggered all my Italian word knowledge.

"Sì," she says, not understanding my hesitancy.

All the offices in this building seemed to be built north facing, making the light in the office dull and gloomy. It was the same in the office where I dealt with my property tax. There's the now mandatory glass 'Covid protection' screen running just the length of the desk, crudely put up with a large gap underneath for document exchanges. The desk is long, with an even longer one forming an L stretching along the dividing wall.

They are old-style chunky hardwood desks, well I think they are, I am just going from the bits I can see underneath as every surface is piled with massive over-stuffed ring binders, and piles of papers and cardboard divider files with reams of well-thumbed documents in each.

 Each pile, some probably a foot high, is held down with a shiny rock; the type I am familiar with seeing around the lake.

I wonder if the office manager jogs across to the lake and plucks one out every time a file pile is reaching its unruly peak. I also wonder if the twenty or so large filing cabinets jammed along the full length of the other dividing wall, are all so full of similar files that she has run out of space or has she just emptied the contents of them all onto her desk to look busy. The idea of the paperless office seems to be lost on Italy.

I wait patiently for five minutes. There is no noise coming from the other offices. But then I hear footsteps coming down the hall and a woman, probably a bit older than myself with short black hair, enters briskly carrying a cardboard file of documents.

She greets me with a bouncy 'giorno' and briskly takes her place in the Charles Dickens scene, adding the file to the one on her right, making it as high as her smiling head on her now seated body.

"I want to pay my TARI bill, please." I lift the bill up to illustrate.

"You don't pay it here, you pay it at the post office or bank."

"Oh. Not here?"

"No." She smiles.

"Ok thank you" and I get up and leave.

Why the other three people in the small enough building could not have told me, when asked, that I don't pay my TARI bill there but at a post office, is beyond me.

I had come to the Comune with the intention of also tackling a request for a roadside mirror, so we can drive out of our driveway on the bad bend without fear of being mashed, and also getting the hole filled in our garden.

Mick Kelly has told me the appropriate office is on the second floor, which I think means the third floor.

I have no idea what the name of the appropriate office would be and I don't know how to word simply what I want to ask, even in English. I am feeling drained of will power. As there are no lights in the stairwell to the third floor, I decide I will leave these requests for another day. Maybe in about four years when my Italian is a bit better.

So I leave and go to the post office. I queue for a half an hour and eventually, after a full morning is lost, I get to pay the bloody TARI bill.

Back at home, I email the woman who contacted Lucia about our TARI initially.

"I have paid our TARI bill today, so how do I get the bins?"

"You can collect your bins on Thursday morning."

"Where do I collect them from?"

"Here at the Comune before 11am on Thursday."

This seems odder than no one telling me I don't pay my bill at the Comune. I am not sure what to expect as I know they divide the garbage into card and paper, organic waste, plastic and then other non-recyclable waste. This would mean there will be four solid bins to collect.

At Giovanni's we had similar wheelie bins to the ones we had in Ireland – large black hard plastic bins that you could fit two or three full black plastic bags of rubbish into.

"Maybe we should bring the van?" suggests Ronan.

"I think we'll just go in the car and figure it out first. You can run back up with the van later if necessary. I mean, what are people supposed to do if they don't have a van, or even a car? Do they drag the wheelie bins all the way home one at a time?"

"Well, I've never seen anyone dragging a wheelie bin through the town. "

"Have you ever been in the town on Thursday mornings? Perhaps there are marauds of locals looking like zombies dragging bins home behind them and we just haven't been up early enough to experience the sight?"

"I wonder where they keep them? The bins, I mean, not the zombies. Maybe there's a warehouse or an underground basement. I just can't imagine where they would keep stacks of bins in that small building."

On Thursday we arrive at 10.30am. There is no sign of bins being ready for collection outside, so I go into the reception desk. I hand in my well-stamped TARI bill showing payment.

"I collect bins here?" I ask with interpretation.

"Yes," he answers. "But now we have none left. Come back next week. But you should come earlier. They go fast."

I am imagining I have just missed scenes of hordes of people fighting over wheelie bins, grabbing the ones they can, pushing each other out of the way for the last blue topped one.

So we are without bins for another week.

The following Thursday we are there earlier, at 9.30am. I've somehow left the house without my payment receipt. All I have is the bill. There is a different person at the reception. "I'm here to collect bins." I wave the bill in front of the glass screen. He doesn't even check it.

"Sì." He smiles. "Come this way," he says in English. He walks out of the reception office and opens the door into the hallway. There, stacked neatly inside each other against the wall, are three different bins. They are tiny compared to the wheelie bins we are used to.

"This one is for carta," he takes a shiny blue one from the top of the pile. The bin is square and is barely up to my knee. Then he takes a grey one that fits neatly inside the Carta one. "This one is for non-recyclable garbage."

There's no way even one black bag full of rubbish will fit into it.

"And this one," he says, lifting a small brown bin the size of a bucket, "is for organic waste." He places inside the other two.

"And these are for plastic." He lifts two large rolls of yellow plastic bags and sticks them in the blue lidded bin. "When you run out of these, come back here and I give you more."

He then gives me a colourfully illustrated, accordion folded leaflet and talks me through it in a mix of pidgin English and Italian, pointing to what I am not to put into the bins and the collection day's schedule. There is a collection every day except Wednesday and Sunday. The organic waste is collected twice per week, naturally as the Italians do a lot of cooking at home with fresh vegetables, so there are more offcuts to be collected.

I text Ronan. "We have bins!"

He is leaning up against our car having a cigarette and is busy texting, "Will I come and help wheel them out or should I go get the van?" when he spots me walking towards him, swinging my blue bin like a picnic basket.

"Don't tell me that's all they gave you?"

"No, there are other bins inside it. Like a babushka doll of bins." He's out of the car and looking inside the blue bin as I go through the explanation, "the brown is for organic waste collected twice per week, the blue is for 'carta' and the grey is for all the other crap we produce. Oh, and the plastic bags are for plastic."

"Are they serious? We will never be able to fit all our rubbish into that grey bin."

"Maybe it's time we took a look at the waste we produce." Within weeks we have surprised ourselves, carefully dividing the waste we produce into the assigned bins, flattening cardboard packaging and washed plastic containers, and we can indeed fit our waste into the assigned bins, which are collected promptly around lunchtime each day.

I never thought I would feel so accomplished over rubbish.

26

TO SHOUT: GRIDARE

I t's the first week of June. Both Antonio and Danny Boy have been texting to ensure the payments will be made as planned. I have emailed Veronica, the contact at the bank, several times in the last few weeks, but she has never responded.

So I email the bank exactly at 9am eight weeks from the date of application, copying in Marco, the bank manager who gave me his card with a wink the first time I met him.

"Hi Veronica, I hope you are well. It's been eight weeks since our application was approved for the 50/50. Can you let me know which day this week the money will be in the account as I am waiting on it for payments?"

She doesn't respond.

There is only one thing for it. I need to go to the bank even though I will find it difficult to communicate. It's thirty-three degrees and I queue for twenty minutes to get in, only to discover Veronica was not at her desk this morning. The temperature tester installed because of Covid shows my temp as abnormally high, but no one does anything when it beeps. Once in the cool, my temperature goes back down to a normal level after two minutes while waiting for my turn at the cash desk.

I ask the woman with glasses and smooth black hair for a balance statement on my account, hoping the money has gone in.

"Io tr tata qual ti so blah blah," the woman shouts at me from the other side of the perspex screen with her mask on.

In Italian I say "Excuse me, I am sorry but my Italian is not good, can you talk slowly?"

She says the same thing at the same fast speed but louder. Her shouting it doesn't make it any clearer. So I skip the need for the statement and ask in Italian, "Veronica not working today?"

"No," she shouts.

"When will she be back?"

"In five days she will return," Shouty Woman shouts in Italian.

That will be the 13th of June. The day both invoices are due to be paid. My eyes are getting stingy. I want to ask if anyone else is doing Veronica's job while she is away, if someone can check the status of the payment. I try to piece together the words but Shouty Woman is unmerciful and just says she doesn't understand me and throws her hands up in the air at her colleague walking by to the photocopier who greets me in English.

"Speak Italian to her if she wants to live here." She clearly says to him in Italian in her lowest voice yet, but it's way more understandable than her shouty voice. "She is English, and she needs to speak Italian."

"I am learning," I say loudly in Italian. "And I am Irish, not English."

She's not embarrassed that I understood but talks rapidly explaining herself and says she doesn't understand me. Veronica will be back in five days... "I need to deal with the next customer," and waves me away from her.

Well, that is what I think she has said. More than ever, I feel the need to be able to speak Italian. My eyes sting some more. I wish Roberta was still here and not Shouty Woman with the severe eyes behind her glasses.

I wait the five days and email Veronica again. She doesn't respond, so I ask Mick Kelly to call her. He calls me back, "Are you waiting on a loan?"

"No."

"Veronica said she thought you were waiting for a loan?"

"A loan from where? And what has that got to do with the 50/50?"

He calls her back and then I receive an email from her in response to the twenty I have sent her.

"I'm sorry for the misunderstanding, but I understood we would first enter the loan request and only after that the credit transfer. If you want to proceed with the insertion of the assignment, I will proceed immediately. It is understood that in this case you will first have to finish the payment of all the works and then carry out the assignment."

"WHAT? Oh, no no no."

I'm on the phone to Mick Kelly, "We need to go to the bank NOW. I'll be at your office in ten minutes."

He obliges. He has no choice. On the way from his office to the bank, I'm venting like mad. "She's saying she hasn't sent in the application because she is waiting for me to apply for a loan? She knows damn well I can't apply for a loan because I am not a resident. What is she talking about? I am relying on that payment to pay Anto and Danny."

"I don't understand the delay with the bank. I applied for the work at my house after your application was approved and I got the money back last week. You have no other money to pay the bills for Anto and Danny with?"

"NO. I am not made of money. I am careful with money, but a surprise bill of nearly €30k on Christmas Day when the agreed work had been paid up to date was a shock and not budgeted for. And I am still questioning the bills that Anto gave me. I don't care what they say together, but Danny clearly said they would put the walls back the way they were. And Anto had none of that work pre-approved. It's absolute bullshit. I understand the work had to be done, but the agreement was that all works had to be pre-approved and priced. Where does he expect me to pull thirty grand from?"

At last I have got it all off my chest and Mick Kelly is not sure where to look.

Veronica is in her mid-twenties and with her acrylic nails, she pushes her Hello Kitty mouse and matching mouse mat to the side. There are eight stamps hanging from a rack in front of her. Italians love stamping things. Veronica is all sweetness. She leans forward towards Mick Kelly, her forearms on the desk, elbows pushing her breasts together.

"The works need to be finished and paid for first," she says, thick false eyelashes beating so fast they are nearly taking flight. Clearly she's into Mick Kelly.

"Yes, they are finished, and they have been paid for. That is what the approval by Deloitte was for."

"But they need to be signed off as complete."

"Yes, that is what I have done on the application."

"But she said she needed the reimbursement to pay for invoices of work done, so she needs a loan. She can't apply just for part of the work."

I am surprised I can understand enough of what she is saying to piece together the meaning.

"Yes, it is possible," says Mick Kelly. "It is stated in the application. Call head office and they will tell you."

She calls head office but not a private line between banks, it's the same number Jo Soap could use. She has it on speakerphone. A series of 'Press one if you are calling about X, press two if you are calling about Y.' It goes up to eight options before Veronica makes her choice. She obviously hasn't done this before.

There is crackly hold music. Depeche Mode are singing 'Words are very unnecessary'.

Mick Kelly steps out to make a call. Veronica is staring at her screen, demolishing a paperclip. Her email screen is open. All the emails are red, meaning not opened, with only a Zara sale email as white. I spot my name several times in the reds.

As we go through a third bout of Depeche Mode, head office answers and basically confirms within two minutes what Mick Kelly has just told her.

"Okay, so now I can send it off."

"Okay now she will send it off," Mick Kelly says, relieved.

"Only now?" I say. "Ask her how long will it take."

"About one or two months?" She says hesitantly and sweetly to Mick Kelly.

I understand her response, and I am spitting venom.

"Did she just say-"

"She said-" Mick interrupts me.

"I know what she bloody just said. It's going to take another one or two months because she messed up and didn't do her job."

She can see I am annoyed. She clicks her pen intently.

I leave without saying goodbye. My anger is turning into upset. "I am not going to be able to pay the invoices on time."

"I will call Antonio, don't worry. No one pays their bills on time in Italy."

But I am not no one. I hate being in debt. I need to think of something else.

By the following week, I have been approved for a loan of €25k in Ireland. The same week, Mick Kelly sends me a form to sign. It's saying I have already paid out €75,972 in renovation costs. This doesn't include the money we have paid out for tiles, paint, the kitchen and DIY stuff we have bought ourselves. So we could safely say we have spent €90k on the house so far and it still looks like a complete mess, but at least we have a good roof and new wiring and plumbing. The body is good, the rest is mostly now cosmetic.

Our savings are dwindling and with no work coming in for the second year in a row, the pot of gold is not being replenished. Now that I can cover the payments with the loan, that means when the €26k reimbursement comes through, we need to be careful how we spend it. It needs to get the house in a finished state. There is no more money after that.

At least we save a fortune on laundry soap during the summer as Ronan goes around topless the entire time we are inside our gates. He's bought a lawn mower and our grass is staying surprisingly green compared to the dried out hay the grass would turn into up the road at Giovanni's.

Being near the lake has its advantages. The sounds of summer are different here too. There are fewer cicadas, so their clicking is not so loud and there are more songbirds. There's an owl that hoots at night in the trees near the lake. When she stops to sleep, it's the songbirds' turn to take over, welcoming the day with the morning chorus starting at 5am.

It's also great to be able to walk along the lake into town and have a coffee or drink with someone from my yoga class. I've been attending weekly sessions by Zoom over the winter but as summer is back and restrictions have been loosened, yoga classes are back to being held outside on the terrace of a local hotel, beside the lake.

I have my favourite warm spot under the giant umbrella pine and when I lie back in savasana at the end of our session; I stare up at the intricate crossed over branches filtering the azure sky and sun beams. Listening to the birds above with the low lapping of the water on the shore, Ruth doesn't have to tell me to take deep relaxing breaths as they happen naturally. I couldn't do outdoor yoga in Ireland. The slightest fresh breeze would give me goosebumps. This is where my body likes to be.

After our weekly yoga session, a few of us usually go for coffee by the lake.

Today it is just me and Daisy. We are sitting chatting about her life as an actress on a soap I used to watch as a kid, when a friendly-looking dog walks by. Medium-sized and hairy, he's having a sniff around and visibly smiling. He's the personification of my perfect dog. But it is not his smile that makes me stare. It is the blue watch he is wearing on his front ankle. A proper Swatch wristwatch. "What the heck, is that dog wearing a watch?"

"Ah yes, that is Francesco," says the waitress at our table. "It was his birthday yesterday and someone gave it to him."

"He is like a dog at the rescue centre I volunteer in," says Daisy.

"I didn't know you volunteered at a dog rescue? And there's a dog like that looking for a home?"

"Yes Brigette."

"Oh, don't tell me her name, it's too soon. We're not ready yet."

"Well when you are, just let me know."

Later that day, I get notification that the money from my bank in Ireland will be through on the last day of June. It was easy to get. I can't imagine what applying for a loan here would entail. With the financial problem solved, I lie back in my hammock with pen and paper to figure out what we need to do next. There is so much.

I give Anto and Danny an update of when to expect payment. Danny responds. "Okay, but it must be paid on that day, otherwise it will cause terrible problems with my accounts."

"Okay, I will. I will also have the money to complete the project, so can you please schedule us in to finish the top floor and solar panel in July or August?"

"Yes. Tomaso is back from Thailand, so we can meet with him to do a plan."

So I text Tomo about coming to the house to figure out what the rest of the work is going to cost, so we can finish the house before the bad weather starts again.

"What day would suit you?"

As usual he doesn't respond.

It seemed too easy... I was right.

27

TO LEARN: IMPARARE

It's mid-July and Italy has reached sixty million administered vaccine doses. Ronan's age group have all been vaccinated, in fact any adult citizen in Italy who wants the vaccination has at least got one dose at this stage except our category – non-residents.

Without the Tessera Sanitaria, we still can't get past the page to register for a vaccine on the Italian computer system and neither pharmacies nor anyone else seem to be able to help.

The glitch has even been reported as a main story in The New York Times and the prime minister of Italy seems oblivious, as he is reported as saying anyone who wants a vaccine can get one in Italy now. But no matter what avenue I take, including the Irish embassy, I can't get us a booking.

One pharmacy tells me I needed to go back to my own country to get it. But without a vaccine, it's dangerous to travel? She shrugs.

Having been so careful for a year and a half now, for Ronan to travel without a vaccine would be foolish and if I travel alone to Ireland without residency in Italy and there was another lockdown, we could get stuck in two different countries.

I want to get home and assess the needs of my parents face to face before I decide to apply for residency in Italy, to see if staying here full time is still practical.

Without the vaccine we can't travel, we can't go into restaurants and, more to the point, we are vulnerable.

Lucia's doctor suggests we apply for temporary residency due to health, so we try that, but as we are self-employed we are refused.

Open days for vaccines are starting to happen in Rome. But the days coincide with days we are not allowed to travel outside our region. I go back to social media expat groups which I haven't been on since my Christmas Witches experience, and share our problem.

It turns out, there are many of us in the same predicament. An English woman called Jo who works in a health centre in Liguria, agrees that as we are EU citizens we should automatically be entitled to the vaccine as it is an EU-bought vaccine and EU law, in matters such as this, overrules a country's individual rulings. But Italy hasn't ruled we can't get it, it's just their bloody system, their stupid bureaucracy that is making this and everything so bloody difficult.

Jo, who I speak with on the phone, has a very thick Liverpool accent and is a child speech therapist. I'm imagining lots of little Italian kids in Liguria going around talking Italian with a Liverpool accent. She manages to get us into the system with the assistance of a very helpful pharmacist in a place called 'Sunflowers' but he can't book us a vaccine, so Jo will keep trying.

We're thinking if we can find an open day anywhere in Italy we could travel there.

I am trying every region as they all have different websites and application pages. For one region I get a message that they are looking at my application for a vaccine and will get back to me in 48 hours. I get excited but then realise it is Abruzzo which is way down on the Achilles heel of Italy and not Arezzo as I thought, which is less than an hour away. But it doesn't matter as they never get back to me anyway.

By the fifth region I've given up hope. My head is boggled trying to understand the Italian and find my way through the maze of forms only to meet the TS requirement on the final page.

Jo talks with the helpline in Umbria on our behalf, "unless something changes you do not fit a category and will not be included in any vaccine drive. If a pharmacy can't book us a vaccine no one will be able to."

I'm feeling exasperated. Danny and Antonio seem to be taking it in turns at texting me every day for the past two weeks about payment in different ways without asking.

Even though I have told them it will be with them by the first of the month they are still finding ways to pressure me by just telling me how urgent it is, how it needs to be paid as soon as possible, how they need to pay workers, pay for materials, if the invoices are not paid by that date they need to create new invoices and it will cause all sorts of hideous malfunctions in their accounting office that might just trigger World War 3, apparently. It's like they are having a moaning conversation between themselves and I am in the middle of it.

So on the same day I am feeling my lowest about the vaccine I get notice that my loan has arrived in my Italian bank account. At least I will have the pressure of the guys off my back and no longer have guilt over the debt, even though it was unexpected and in the space of six months I have miraculously sourced €25k from nowhere to cover it.

So I go to the bank with the invoices in hand and brace myself for Shouty Woman. There are four customers allowed in the bank at any one time. I stand in line and wait for the first customer to stop giving out to Shouty Woman about something. She takes ages. Next there is an elderly man who has been sitting on the seat beside me. He takes ages. I stand beside the water cooler preparing what to say, rehearsing it in my head. I can sense the man about ten years older than me standing a bit too close behind me and sighing impatiently at the length of time the old guy is taking.

The old guy gets up, and out of graciousness and out of respect for the social distancing rules, I let him move out of the way before I take a step towards the counter. Mr Impatient behind me cuts ahead of me. I look around, there are only two of us in the bank.

He stands in front of the counter and asks something to Shouty Woman, she has changed her hair a bit. Shouty Woman is responding yes to him. Sì sì sì. I give him a moment, maybe he is just confirming an appointment or asking if someone is there. But then he takes the seat in front of her.

I am sure he can see me eyeballing him in his peripheral vision. If he can't see me, he can surely feel my glaring stare. He is taking advantage of the fact that I am not Italian.

An Italian middle-aged women would not stand for this, they are not timid. In the same situation they would attack and not give him the benefit of the doubt that perhaps he just misunderstood and thought I was standing there to admire the paintwork or I had nothing better to do. For the first time I feel like an Italian middle-aged woman. I am becoming furious. I continue to glare, waiting to catch his eye.

He has to look slightly to his left to talk to the teller and I am in line with his slightly left peripheral vision. If he didn't feel in the wrong he would have glanced back to see what I was looking at. So I move forward more so he can't but see me.

Shouty woman is starting to tap the keyboard for his details and as soon as there is a break in their lighthearted conversation I say? "Scusi... SCUSI ..." They both look. "Io sono prossimo?" "I am next?" Is what I think I have spat at him my hands waving around in perfect Italian signalling. As least I have mastered that part.

"Aww I am sorry," he says in Italian. He's all hands and gestures. "I thought you were with the gentleman."

If I could speak Italian I would have said "My ass you did! If I was with the gentleman I would have left with him and wouldn't be standing here like an ornament."

You don't have to know a language to know when someone is completely lying. He makes big gestures to Shouty Woman and to me about stepping aside mid-transaction to let me go before him.

Normally I would say 'it's okay, finish what you are doing' but my heart is beating like the drum of an over wound Duracell bunny.

So I step forward, take the seat and he steps back to where he was before. Shouty Woman is pissed off as she will have to input all his details again when it comes to his turn.

I give her the two invoices and at this stage I know how to answer the questions she fires at me.

She grudgingly gets up and gets a form from the cupboard. She is talking rapidly and loudly the whole time. I don't know what she is saying, whether she is asking me questions, telling me off, telling me what she wants for Christmas, who knows. I don't think even an Italian could make out what she is squawking about as her loud voice is muffled by the mask and she is standing about three feet away from me behind Perspex with her back to me.

She starts to fill the form out, reading aloud everything she is writing. "Con nome, Mel...o...d... nome.... Rosa....mar...eee...aa...Codice Fiscale, R M sette, due, zero..." and she continues imparting my information around the building for all to hear and emphasising how much work she has to do to fill out the form.

But she has found a problem. She starts to talk rapidly, pointing at Danny's invoice and pointing at the form.

"I'm sorry I don't understand, slower please," I ask. But instead she shouts louder and faster the exact same words. She mentions Mick Kelly's name.

"Wait," I say and I dial Mick Kelly's number, it rings out.

I send him a text "Urgent I'm in the bank and they need to talk to you."

But he does not respond. I try to figure out what she is repeatedly saying. She just sounds like she is telling me off.

I look at her pleadingly for help but she just pushes the paperwork back to me. I don't understand. There is thirty minutes left before the bank closes for the rest of the day. Italy is breaking me.

"Wait" I shout back but can't find the rest of the Italian words to explain I will go to Mick Kelly's office across the street. Instead, I just run. As I leave the bank he calls me. I don't wait for greetings, "I have money in my account and the invoices for payment. The invoices are the very same as previous ones paid without an issue. I am running to your office now."

Mick Kelly meets me outside the door, I realise I am trembling.

"Rosie, what is the matter?"

I burst into tears. "I can't get the vaccine, I can't go home to see my parents and I can't understand that horrible woman, I am trying to learn Italian but it's just not sticking, I just want to pay the bloody bill and she is making so bloody difficult."

Now that my outburst is over I feel a bit stupid, but he is kind and calls Danny and Antonio and explains I am trying to pay the bills today but there is some issue with the invoices, he will find out what it is but payment may not reach them today. And they both respond... "no problem!"

We create a plan. I am to go back to Shouty Woman before the bank closes and call him when I am being served. He will then discuss the problems with Shouty Woman.

"Ok I am next at the desk." I text. "I will call you now."

I call him and he does not answer. My heart starts to race again. I call him again. Shouty Woman is staring at me. "Pronto?"

With that Mick Kelly picks up and I push my phone across the table, he is on speaker and asks her in a very long-winded way what the issue is.

And she responds by asking him very clearly if it is for the 50/50 benefit. If she had said it like that to me I could have easily answered 'Si' but she never asked me anything as clearly as she just said to Mick Kelly. He asks her is anything else an issue and she says no!

Ten minutes later she has completed the paperwork, completed the transaction and both payments have gone through.

The bald guy, who seems to deal with commercial loans, recognises me from before as he heads towards the photo-copier beside Shouty Woman and greets me in English just as I get up to leave. She scowls at him and throws him a cutting line in muffled Italian, but I understand her, "She lives here she needs to speak Italian."

"IMPARARO... you rude, horrible woman," I say to her clear enough for her to understand me. I have never been so direct.

I am not sure if I like the person that Italy is turning me into.

28

TO RETURN: RITORNARE

I resign myself to the fact that the only hope of getting back to Ireland is for me to apply for residency and deal with the consequences afterwards. At least I know I will be able to get to my parents, get the vaccine in Ireland, and get back to Ronan in the event of another lockdown.

But then, just as I give up hope, someone on an expat group posts about an open day for vaccines in Umbria and it is not just for citizens, it is for tourists too. I go through the participating pharmacists and find one that will book Ronan in for a one jab of Johnson and Johnson on Saturday. It turns out, by coincidence, that out of all the pharmacies in Italy, it is the same pharmacist that helped Jo get us in to the system.

We go the day before and fill out the forms. The smiley pharmacist speaks some English and the following day we turn up for Ronan's vaccine. "You are the first foreigner I have done. I honeymooned in Ireland. I am so sorry it has been so difficult for you to get the vaccine. It is the Italian system, it is so stupid. For me to give you a vaccine, we have to create a temporary Codice Fiscale for you, even though you already have a Codice Fiscale. "

I ask if he can jab me too. "Ah no, you are too young." It's a long time since someone told me I was too young to participate in something, but the open day for Johnson and Johnson is only for over sixties.

He and his team seem to be whizzes at finding their way around the system. "Can you try to book a vaccine appointment for me?"

"Yes, it should not be a problem. We need to do the same for you, create a temporary Codice Fiscale." Within ten minutes of tapping on the keyboard and entering my details and about five people in white coats standing around the computer helping at some point, he announces, "there you go, you have appointments for you and your son for your first shot of Moderna. It is at the centre in the town beside you on the 10th of August."

"Really? You've done it? If it wasn't for Covid, I'd kiss you." My eyes fill. He has restored my faith in Italian kindness.

I can go back to Ireland... I can see Mam and Dad.

29

TO SING: CANTARE

I bought the tickets for Ronan as a Christmas present in 2019; Andrea Bocelli in the Theatre of Silence near his home in Tuscany. The concert was originally to take place in July 2021, the weekend of our 24th wedding anniversary but, of course, because of Covid, it was postponed to the following year to the date of our 25th anniversary, which would make it even more special.

We stopped off for a quick lunch in a hilltop town on the way. It was 2.15pm, so we had to find somewhere quick. As everyone in Italy knows, restaurants open at 12.30pm for lunch and usually close by 2.30pm. They don't open again until 7pm for dinner. There are a few 'in-between' time dining places. And you'll never see an Italian walking along eating a sandwich or snack like a bar of chocolate or a bag of crisps. That just does not happen in Italy. Food is to be savoured.

This takes a bit of getting used to, especially if you are a tourist... You have a leisurely breakfast at your hotel, set off to visit a small town, do some sightseeing and want to sit to eat at 3pm or have a drink. Not possible.

"No! You are in Italy," I heard one waitress roar at a German tourist last week who had enquired about having a snack and some beers at 3pm just as the restaurant was closing.

So you can't eat between three and seven in the evening. Not only that, but you can't shop between 12.30 and 4pm, because all the shops close 'for lunch'. So even if you time it right and go to visit a town in time for lunch at 1pm and finish by 2.30pm, you are left wandering the streets salivating at the things in windows you would like to buy, but can't, because they are not open until 4pm.

I've asked Lucia what we are supposed to do during this 'lull'.

"You are supposed to be having a siesta. To digest your lunch."

"But if a tourist is visiting a town an hour or two from their accommodation, what are they supposed to do? Go sit in their car?"

"I don't know, but the Italians need to digest their lunch."

The concert was due to start at 8.30pm. Seating was open from 5.30pm. Refreshment and food stalls would be available. So we plan to arrive by 7pm and get something to eat at one of the food stalls. Nothing major, just something to fill us up.

There is traffic entering the area from all roads but it's all well organised with lots of staff to direct and keep the traffic flowing.

We park in the assigned field out in the middle of nowhere and follow the crowd walking through the fields winding up the hill to the outdoor theatre, coloured orange with the summer sunset. Some people are carrying picnic baskets. I had considered bringing food and drinks, but thought it would be like previous concerts I had attended back in Ireland, where this was forbidden. This event is much more casual. More of a Sunday picnic feel.

I had thought the amphitheatre would be bigger and more sloped, like some of the many amphitheatres I've visited throughout Italy and that we would sit on stone shelved seating, but this is flat enough for plastic chairs to be placed on the different levels. So it gives more of a feeling of a field than an amphitheatre.

There are no food stalls. There's a gelato cart with a long queue of people and there are drink stalls. These also sell panini. We queue and then notice it says 'no bancomat. Cash only.' So we queue at another, but that is the same. We panic. Neither of us had considered bringing cash. We usually have some tucked into a pocket or in the back of our wallets. But not today. We are searching in our pockets and end of our wallets and scrape together €16 in coins. "That's enough for a panino, €6, two bottles of water, €2 each and one glass of wine €6 or a second panino."

"I'm still okay from lunch, so I'll have the wine and no panini," I say, sacrificing myself.

"Do you think Bocelli is going to come galloping in on his horse?" says Ronan jokingly. "Like he was on the cover photo of the magazine you worked on a couple of years ago. He lives nearby. Why not?"

"Don't be ridiculous Ronan... that's him there." I point to the helicopter, making a dip over the crowd before flying off to the other side of a hill. "Although it would be pretty cool to see him coming across the hills on his horse. I'd love to meet his horse more than Bocelli himself. From the photos, he looked amazing."

An hour after the scheduled start time, church bells toll over the speakers and the orchestra makes their way to their seats. I feel quite excited. Just as they sit, a large drop of water lands on my lap. I feel like someone has spat on me. Not a good feeling during Covid. Within seconds, others around me are looking up to the sky at the large dark cloud that has parked above us. I'm wondering what they will do if it starts to rain. There must be a cover that goes over the stage to protect the classical instruments.

They do a warm up song and I remember how good a live orchestra sounds and pulls at your emotions. In walks Andrea. I settle in to be amazed. The gods spit on us again throughout his warm up. He then performs an operatic piece with another guy. Then another with a soprano woman. There's a song in between by another excellent soprano who was one of his scholarship students.

They are all great, but I am not an opera fan. I want to hear Andrea Bocelli classics. The other soprano woman does a solo and the skies open just as she finishes. The orchestra makes a run for it with their very expensive instruments.

The conductor announces, "we'll just wait a few minutes until the rain passes". The rain stops after ten minutes and the orchestra returns. They set up, and it starts to rain again. So they run off with their precious instruments.

After five minutes, Andrea comes on and someone brings him a guitar. He sings 'Yesterday' and 'Che Sera'. Obviously, it was not part of the planned repertoire, but at least it's Andrea Bocelli and not opera.

The rain is spitting on and off, but too much for instruments. They announce they will have an early interval. It stops raining immediately. When the interval time is up, the orchestra makes their way to their places again. As soon as they are ready, it starts to lightly rain. The musicians make a run for it. We wait. It stops they make their way out again cautiously. The wind is picking up. It's 11.15pm. My back is hurting from sitting in the seat for three hours now, my stomach is growling and I'm not in the 'overcome with emotion' state I expected to be in by this time. I'm just a bit damp from the rain. "If it happens again, will we go?" I say to Ronan.

He has been enjoying watching the bright orange fork lightening bouncing around the hills. It's getting very close. "I don't think this concert is going to happen. It's weird they don't have a backup plan, even a recording of the orchestra which he can sing to. I know it wouldn't be the full experience, but Andrea doing karaoke would do me just fine."

We wait. The rain stops. The orchestra returns. I feel sorry for them. I'm sure they need to get into the feel of things more than I do to do their best and they can't be happy participating in the Olympic style sprints off the stage as the gods tease us under dark skies. I see some stars above. A break in the clouds, that's hopeful.

As soon as they are seated, it spits again. I see the stage manager arguing with someone. They all look demoralised as they walk off again.

"Come on, let's go," I say. "This is just frustrating." It's the event planner coming out in me. I plan outdoor events and there always has to be a backup plan. I wouldn't mind getting wet sitting in the audience, but I would expect a backup plan to keep valuable instruments safe and able to continue the performance.

It's close to midnight and we're not the only ones who are leaving disappointed. We join a large crowd of mask wearers as we stream out of the theatre space and make our way down the beaten track towards the car park, passing a cluster of vehicles shielded by a temporary wall built of straw bales. People are leaning on one side chatting. I divert our walk to the other side of the bales and there before me is a beautiful chestnut stallion with a long, black mane. On his back, there is a man with a fantastic face, chiselled and lined.

The horse is frisky, a bit freaked out by the lightning and distant thunder. We come close to being eye to eye. But I know by the man's face he is in complete control.

"Oh my God, it's Sir Cesar. I recognise him from the cover of the magazine," I say to Ronan at the surreal scene in front of me. The snorting, frisky beauty dances as another flash of lightning strikes the hill behind.

"You know that guy?"

"No, the horse. It's Andrea Bocelli's. You were right. He must have arrived on horseback!"

It's too late to get food anywhere, but we find a shop open on the way home and we buy two bags of crisps for dinner.

It wasn't exactly the romantic, memorable night I was expecting for our 25th anniversary celebration, but at least I got to be eye to eye with Andrea Bocelli's horse.

30

TO THINK: PENSARE

"I've been thinking while working in the garden," says Ronan, covered in cobwebs from the old shed. "It's a shame not to have a dog out there to enjoy it with. I still miss Asha every day, but maybe it is time?"

"Oh, not yet Ronan." I can feel panic rising and don't quite know why. "I need to get back to Ireland first and see if everything is okay. I have a feeling someone is not telling me something. Having another dog would just give us another obstacle to think 'is something not alright' about and I have to stay longer."

"Do you think we should move back?"

"To where? To my parents' tiny two bedroomed cottage?"

"Well, no... but back to Ireland, we'd figure something out we always do."

"And leave all this?"

I wave towards our mould ridden dilapidated mansion and think about the absolute ridiculous hoops we have had to jump through to get the basics such as bins and the vaccine, Shouty Woman, the abysmal loneliness and destroyed plans Covid restrictions had brought and my inability to still grasp the basics of the language after four years.

"It's just a thought," he says. I'm not sure if he is referring to the dog or moving back to Ireland, but I know Ronan, whichever or both, it was not just a thought. He'd have been thinking about it for a long time and would have been just waiting for the right moment to suggest it.

Even with this flea in my ear of returning to Ireland that Ronan has planted, I still needed to apply for residency to avoid having to pay higher property purchase taxes. I take a determined stroll down the town the following morning. There is a separate entrance to the office where I am to apply for residency. It is the same office that I use for registering marriages for my clients, so I know what the guy looks like even though we have had a two-year lull in weddings. I know he won't recognise me as I have one of those faces people forget immediately after meeting, apparently. No one ever remembers me. I'd make a great criminal.

However, the office is closed. On Thursdays it opens after 3pm, on Fridays it doesn't open at all and on Monday to Wednesday it has a variety of opening and closing times all between 8am and 12 noon. I make a mental note that the safest time to come to the office will be 10.30 to 11am early the following week.

So on Monday I arrive. But it's closed. It's an Italian holiday I didn't know about. On Wednesday I try again and bingo it's open. I say in my prepared Italian that I want to apply for residency. He remembers who I am. I suppose there are not that many Irish wedding planners around.

He presents me with an A4 page with a list and reads through it with me.

"Contract of work." He crosses this out after reading.

"Receipt of employment recruitment." He crosses this out.

"Last paycheck." He crosses this out.

But he puts an asterisk beside a long paragraph...

"Translation and legalisation of the certificate certifying that I possess sufficient economic resources for me and my family or a precise statement of source of origin of these resources specifying the origin..." blah blah blah. It goes on for three more lines.

This sounds very official and difficult.

Leonardo writes €5,749 beside the paragraph. This is the amount you need in your bank account. You can prove this with just a letter from the bank. You don't need to give a revealing statement.

"But a bank statement will do?"

"Yes," he shrugs. "Or just a letter to say you have more than this in your account."

"Communication receipt of sale of building (Atto Casa)" he writes beside it in brackets.

I print off the first three pages of the fifty-five page document the notary sent me. I still have not received the deeds of the house. They are in her office, but they are safer there than in our dust bag of a house.

"Health insurance covering all eventualities."

I knew about this and had emailed the woman who had arranged our house insurance. The broker said a two-month policy would do for the residency process - that is what she normally does. It cost €290. It's a bit ridiculous, having to get insurance for just for the period that the application is being processed, having been here three years without any. Our EU health insurance covers us during any emergencies, such as Ronan's Easter trip. So I have my health insurance deed ready.

"Marriage certificate translated and legalised." I don't need this as I am only applying for myself.

"Codice Fiscale." Yes, I have this.

"Passport." Check. Got it.

"VAT number." He circles this.

'Two Marche da bollo (da €16)' he writes in brackets. "You get these in the tobacco shop," he explains.

My fascination with Italy's pokey tobacco shops grows some more, they are now not only establishments where you can buy cigarettes, which you need to pay cash for, but also the only place you can buy stamps.

Most have a few gambling machines in a dark shifty looking corner of the shop sometimes closed off with a curtain. I'm not sure if this is just so you can't see which neighbour has a gambling addiction or to give a casino type atmosphere. They also sell trinkets - matchbox cars, bouncy balls, marbles, fancy paper stationery kits, bubbles. Stocking filler type stuff. Perhaps it's part of their long-term marketing plan; to lure kids in, who, perhaps, when older, find themselves addicted to nicotine or gambling, will have fond memories of the shop as a child and become loyal customers?

On the way home I stop off at the tobacco shop and get my two silver-coated stamps that are needed.

The bank is closed, so I can't get a statement. I am feeling relieved that I don't have to go in there and face Shouty Woman. Instead, I will give him a statement from my Irish bank that has enough funds to show I can keep myself going and not be a burden on the Italian State. Although I am not sure how anyone can live on less than €6k a year but that is the bar that they have set.

I stride home feeling accomplished.

Ronan's in the creepy shed. "We'd forgotten about these," he says, carrying out two massive green glass demijohns.

"Oh wow," I join him pulling out eight more of the bulbous jars of different sizes and two ancient wooden handmade ladders that were once used for olive picking.

He drags out the power washer and blasts the demijohns inside and out while I secure the olive ladders against the wall beside the French doors leading into the sitting room. I replant the jasmine into the large terracotta urn we treated ourselves to for our anniversary and twirl it into place in front of the ladders, entwining the jasmine through the ladder rungs.

We dot the demijohns around the courtyard and they are instant beauty.

The July sun is hot, but in the dappled light of the persimmon tree and shade from the bay and hazelnut trees, the courtyard stays an enjoyable temperature.

I sit back on the olive wood bench Ronan pulled his back out moving from Giovanni's and admire the developing courtyard that now looks nearly complete when my mam calls.

"I think I have nearly everything that is needed to apply for residency, just need to get the vaccine and I can get back to Ireland."

"That's great news, but bring your wellies. It's like winter here, stormy and raining."

"You should be here. It's a gorgeous thirty-four degrees."

"Thirty-four? Oh, no, no, that would be far too hot for me. I wouldn't be able to stick that heat at all."

"I would!" shouts my father from the background. "I might go without your mother," he jokes, which makes me laugh as they haven't been anywhere without each other in the sixty-six years they have been together.

I sit back and am thankful for the Italian sun on my face and not the Irish rain. Soon I'll be able to travel back home and see all the people I love and feel whole again.

31

TO RESPOND: RISPONDERE

W ith residency applied for and my building bills up to date, life in Italy feels on track again.

The day after I made the payment, Antonio texted to ask when he and Tomo can visit to do the next stage of works, even though my earlier requests of visits to plan and schedule were met with brush-offs and the conversation brought back around to when the payment will be completed.

With so much building work going on around the country, we had little choice of builders who were available. But whoever we got, this next stage was going to be done on our terms.

"You can come this week. But let's be clear, any further work will need to be priced and agreed in advance with a time schedule."

"Most of my crew are working on a different building project, but Tomaso has two guys that can work with Omaroberto and Joseph on your house."

I trust Omaroberto and Joseph, so I agree.

We soon have a day and time agreed.

The walk around the house with Antonio and Tomo is heartening. The work before was all stuff we couldn't see, this stage will turn the shell into a home. Luca acts as translator, but I understand enough building terms now that Luca is just helping me confirm my understanding is correct.

"You need to finish the drainpipes both out the front and the back."

"Certo, certo."

"And build a concrete dam across the front gateway to stop the water from flowing in from the road. These are the most important things before winter."

"Certo, certo."

"But enough outside. Let's move on to what needs to be done inside to start making this house beautiful."

There is still some construction work to be done. "We need to put lintels here, here and here." Anto points to three-bedroom doorways. "For the main bathroom, we need to reinforce the floor and the roof, especially if you want to eventually make it as a terrace. We will put down waterproofing and we can tile it nice. It will need a layer of concrete."

"Not more bloody concrete."

"Yes, we must."

"Most of all, I want a bedroom finished, and another room finished I can use as an office. And the main bathroom with a bath. That needs to be done. I don't want to go another winter without a bath. They are the main things that must be finished."

"Certo, certo."

We go to the door of what will be our bedroom. We can only go as far as the door as it is full of stuff. Old dusty stuff. The next room beside it is not much better. They are identical rooms, both decent size with two windows each and scalloped ceilings.

"You want to keep the ceilings like this or plasterboard?"

"NO, not plasterboard in here. The ceilings are beautiful, they are part of the character of the house."

"Yes, I agree," says Antonio and we all stare at the ceiling with two big chunks of plaster missing from when the rain poured in. The remaining plaster is acned with black mould. The lengths of flat iron between each of the five scallops is rusted and the walls, while now dry, are decorated with large mould stains from ceiling to floor.

I'm not even sure how this room got so bad, as it is under the smaller roof that still remains to be done. But I am now hopeful I will have a beautiful bedroom and bathroom before winter. We also want the top floor finished so that Luca can move into his room and we can get the heating on so that the rooms there can dry out completely too.

We discuss the flat roofed big bathroom which is currently a cobwebbed brick structure that murderers would store their victims in. It is like an added-on extension on stilts to the back of the house, where the Star Trek pipe system is now housed underneath. From outside you can see there is a bricked-up doorway leading onto the flat roof. It will make a perfect terrace on the second floor.

"Danny will need to come to do the plumbing and electrics for the top floor and for the big bathroom before we can work on it," states Anto.

"I tried to contact him, but he is not responding. I'll try again tonight," I say in the hope Tomo can wave his magic wand and get his mate Danny to come along to play ball.

I'm still determined that this time things will be done on our terms. "You'll need to tell me which rooms you want to work on first so that I can clear the rooms for you as we go."

"Certo."

"So, when can you start?"

Tomo scratches his head and rocks on his heels a little. "Soon it will be Ferragosto, so not this month."

"But it's only the 3rd of August, Ferragosto is on the 15th?"

"Yes, but it is August," he says as if I am ridiculous to think that he or anyone in Italy will be working during August.

"Not bloody Ferragosto again," Ronan sighs. "It's like deja vu from last year."

That evening, I text Danny again. "Can you please respond? Tomo was here today and is working on a schedule of work and we will need your input."

As if by some miracle he does respond.

"We are currently messed up for work and we have some work to close before Ferragosto. If we want to meet, we have to do after 25th August... Let me know."

"But when can you work on the house again? I really want to have some things finished before the end of September."

"I honestly don't know what to tell you. I have to close some works before the end of August. Let's talk towards the end of the month. Ok?"

"Okay, I understand you are busy. However, I asked to be booked for work to start over in July and this was agreed. So be sure to plan for early September."

"Ok, I find a way and let you know as soon as possible."

There's nothing for it but for us to blend into the Italian way and write off August. It's too hot to do anything anyway, so I sit on the end of the diarrhoea sofa with fans blasting and my laptop open, looking up flights to Ireland. My residency application hasn't come through yet and I know it won't until at least September as the Comune staff will also probably take most of August off because of Ferragosto.

I'm not prepared to wait any longer. Tomorrow I will get the vaccine and I'll take my chances of being stranded in Ireland and go without residency. Within ten minutes, I am booked on a one-way flight for myself and Luca. Ronan will stay in Italy and take care of the pets, but I'll be home to Ireland in two weeks' time and hugging my parents.

32

TO FLY: VOLARE

A t last, after eighteen long months, I am flying 38,000 feet over Turin and Milan, over the Alps, Paris, London and into Dublin with Luca.

We're getting the bus to Belfast first to visit my brother Tony who has had a pandemic baby, conceived and born during the Covid years, who none of the family have been able to meet yet due to travel restrictions.

"Show us your wee tickets," says the cheery bus driver in his Northern Irish accent.

"Hmm, we don't have tickets. Can we pay by cash?"

"Surely you can. Or you can take a seat and go on the app there and buy them online."

"Okay, how does that work?"

"I don't know, I've never had to pay for a bus in me life! If you have the cash it would be easier."

"Okay, let's pay by cash then."

"You're staring," he states.

I'm slightly embarrassed and confused, "I'm sorry, I didn't realise I was... staring?"

"What? Nooo." He slaps the steering wheel and roars laughing.

"I asked you Euro or Sterling?... You've been away too long, you don't understand your own language anymore."

My new nephew is already nine months old and gorgeous. I'm sad I've missed the new baby cuddles, but lots of nine-month-old cuddles make up for it. I sit playing Lego with the three other little ones and for dinner I insist on a Chinese takeaway. All the things I have missed, trying to make up for lost time in a few hours before I take the morning train to see my parents and other brother Jim in the south.

Dad is waiting at the train station. It's lashing rain so there is no running down the platform into his arms scene. It's more a scurry out of the station and spot his car illegally parked nearly on the platform, waiting for us. I swing open his door and grab him tightly. "What are you doing? Enough of that. Will you ever get into the car out of the rain," He's not one for sentiment.

"We just need to stop off and get some milk and your mother a bottle of whiskey," Dad says as we pull into a small car park of a local shop. Luca runs in and gets the 'messages' Dad needs.

That's what we call a few groceries in Ireland, "I'm going to get the messages" means "I am going to get a few things at the supermarket." I never thought it odd until someone foreign asked what the hell I was talking about and realised we all probably sound like secret agents.

Luca is back in the car. He met an old school friend in the shop and they've arranged to meet up later on. He's only in the country five minutes and his social life has kicked back into gear already.

Dad reverses out of his space and bumps off a parked van. He glances around and pulls off quick, "No one saw me." Luca is laughing, but I am shocked, it's very out of character for my dad to pull away after doing something like that and being at fault. It makes me think it's not the first time.

I can't get out of the car quick enough when we arrive at their little cottage. Partially because of my dad's driving but mostly as I can't wait to see her. "My Mam!" I have her wrapped in my arms. "My Daughter!" She says back laughing. Giving me a tight squeeze. "I think you are getting fatter!" She's still laughing.

"Jez Mam, thanks. You really know how to make me feel good about not seeing you all this time."

Now that Dad is in the house out of the rain, I can give him a proper hug too. He hugs me back for a long moment. It's out of character for him but these are extraordinary times. "Will you stop out of that and go put on the kettle?"

Mam has shrunk. Dad has got thinner. But they are both looking well.

Unpacking, I find the gift I've brought. "Here Dad, I've a surprise for you."

He unwraps the tissue paper and holds the book, staring at the cover. "A Nun-Holy Murder... Rosie Meleady... Did you write this?!" He looks up with his mouth open.

"Yes, I wrote it with a criss-cross of the books in mind that you and Mam like to read. It's a genre called a cozy mystery, described as Scooby Doo for adults."

"And you got it published?"

"Yes... well, it's self-published. Lots of writers self-publish now and make a good living out of it. That book and 'A Rosie Life In Italy', the book I published last year, are selling quite well."

"And you're writing another one?"

"I'm working on two at the moment. I write one thousand words per day no matter what happens. It's the first thing I do in the morning and I don't do anything else until they are done."

"That's amazing." He has that held back smile twitching across his face that tells me he's bursting with pride.

"I'll give this one a read and let you know what I think."

By the afternoon the traveling and emotion have all caught up with me and blanket tiredness makes my eyelids too heavy to stay open. I awake after an hour to all the familiar sounds of home.

Mam is clanking around pots in the kitchen singing her repertoire of song lines, 'I wish I was a monkey in a tree', followed by a few lines of 'There's no business like show business' and 'You are my hearts delight'.

The warm sun is beaming through the chinks in the net curtain, so I creep outside to the garden where my dad is adding a contraption to his already weighed down tree of bird feeders. He's singing 'Daisy Daisy', the only song he knows all the words to and his party piece. He sang it at our weddings and has sung it at every party we ever had.

"I'm making this for your mother to see if it will attract more gold finches. We sit in there and watch them," he says, pointing at the Perspex room he built on to the back of the sitting room with a flat roof Jim helped him put on.

The inside of the ceiling is lined with election posters. Only we know they are politician election posters, visitors can only see the back of them, which is plain white, but the corrugated plastic they are made from has a cushion between them where small pockets of air sit. They are perfect insulation boards for their less than €200 DIY extension.

They were left on the telegraph poles after the election, so Dad went out with his ladder one dark evening and removed the offending faces. "At least the useless bunch are of some use now," was his justification.

The floor of the Perspex sunroom is suspended on bricks and pallets. Again, Jim did the engineering, ensuring Dad's crazy idea was safe for them to walk on. Once Dad gets an idea in his head, he is like a dog with a bone and won't let it go. He'll ask Jim around for his opinion and before poor Jim knows it, he is stepping in to fulfil Dad's vision, and doing all the slog work.

"Come on, let's go in and see does it work," as he grabs me by the hand and leads me to their sunroom.

"Mary, come out here. It's time for our cruise." He shouts towards the kitchen.

"I can't," she shouts back. "I'm making the dinner. I've no time for you and your cruising today." So I take Mam's seat.

"This is what we do. We sit here and we pretend we are on a cruise. Not that I'd ever go on a blasted cruise, bloody waste of money, but so many people do it and here we are doing the same thing. Sitting back in our chairs with our eyes closed and the warmth of the sun through the glass.

"It's just like being on a cruise. Except we don't get seasick and we have nice birds to look at rather than silly ol' ones and ol' fellas. I mean, what more do you want? This is what we've done through Covid lockdown... a cruise every day here in the comfort of our own home. Then we'll go in and play Scrabble. Mary will have a few drinks and I'll watch the telly."

Mam comes out with a glass of whiskey. "The dinner will be ready in about half an hour. I'll have a little sit down while I'm waiting."

"Are you ready for the cruise, Mary?"

"I am, Tony."

"Slainte!" she says, lifting her glass as she flops down in her seat I have just vacated.

"Now what type of birds do you get in Italy?" Dad starts off.

"Well, there are similar birds to here, but I also get a lot of long-tailed tits."

"Oh, the punk rocker ones with the mohawk?"

"They are the ones. There's also an owl I hear at night. And woodpeckers, white egrets and cuckoos."

"God, that sounds fascinating. Mary, are you on for going to live in Italy? We'll bring the binoculars." Dad finds everything fascinating. Jim and I are a bit like that, too.

"I'm not going anywhere until this Covid is finished." She quickly changes the subject.

"I saw a dolly wobble bird in the garden a couple of months ago."

"Do you mean a warbler?"

"Well whatever they are called. You don't get them here. I looked it up in the book and it was definitely a dolly wobbler bird. They are from New Zealand. He must have been blown off course when migrating."

"Mam, birds don't migrate here from New Zealand."

"It was definitely one of them. He must have been blown up here on a wind or something."

"A Jazuz, Mary," slags Dad. "Next you'll be saying you saw a Dodo in the garden. Will you ever stop."

"I'm telling you, it was a dolly wobbler. For sure... Oh, isn't that beautiful," she says, pointing with her glass to the sky.

I see a black rain clouded sky ahead, but she sees the distant rainbow.

33

TO LOVE: AMARE

Mam is constantly cooking like crazy. It's not just me and Luca who have come home, but my brother Peter is coming to visit from New York too.

After the first day of rain, the weather becomes idyllic.

Cousins, who I haven't seen in years, come to visit. We have coffee and lunch and laughs about old times. Friends come, nieces and nephews gather in the garden, it's a perfect storm of love and relief that we can all see each other again after the shit-show of Covid restrictions.

Every morning, I am up and out the door for a long walk down to the beach.

Waves crash and lap around my bare feet on sand as soft as talc powder.

For the first time since arriving in Ireland, I am having decent alone time. Time to think. I sit on the sand dunes and watch the water, the horizon, I hear the familiar lilt of Irish voices and inhale the fresh salty air. Maybe I was giving Ireland a bad rap. This is beautiful.

There's something very comforting about familiarity.

Driving without having to think about directions, speaking without having to struggle to translate. Shops with products in English and for everything you could want, even out of season.

Sometimes on the way to the beach I meet Laura, my friend and previous neighbour, who fills me in on the local gossip. The headmaster has left his wife and four kids and moved in with the cleaner. I miss banter and gossip. Do these things happen in Italy? I am sure they do, but I am not part of the community or in on the gossip, not even by eavesdropping, as my language skills are abysmal.

Ronan calls, "We finally have a quote from Anto. He seems keen to start work soon. The quote is five pages long and comes to just under €25k, but we can cut it back for sure. It details filling holes and making holes a lot. I don't understand the making holes bit. I used Google translate, and it is making three holes in the bathroom and he wants to charge us €3,045 for the pleasure."

"Did you ask him what they are?"

"Yes, and he said it is too difficult to explain. And to ask Mick Kelly."

"So did you ask Mick Kelly?"

"Of course. I sent him a snapshot with, 'what is this?' and he said 'I don't know ask Anto'."

This trip has been everything I could want it to be. Mam and Dad are okay. They have each other and there was nothing mysterious they weren't telling me about. I've had time with friends and family. I've got a lot of writing done. Everything is okay. Ireland is home, as it is where my parents are.

I'm not sure if I will ever feel quite as at home in Italy. Perhaps if my parents moved over and perhaps if the language ever takes up residence in my head, I might feel less of an intruder. Whatever the future holds, what I need to do is get back to Italy to get the house finished before the winter.

"I started reading your book last night," Dad says over lunch. "I like it so far. Your ma and I were fighting over it. You should have brought two. Where do you get your ideas for all those words every morning?"

"I just sit and they come to me. You'll like the second one in the cozy mysteries. I remember you telling me a story about Hitler robbing art and that triggered the idea for this book."

"That's fascinating."

I want more undistracted time with him. "Dad, do you want to go for a pint?"

"Not at all. I'm perfectly happy to stay away from those places. They'll rob you for a price of a pint. I've cans of Guinness in the fridge. Have one of them."

"It's not the same. It doesn't get the same head from a can."

"Ah you are not doing it right. Get me a glass and I'll show you how."

With a can from the fridge in one hand, he pulls open the tab and turns the whole can upside down in the glass, lets go and then lifts it up high as the level of black stuff rises.

"It doesn't look bad, but I'll stick to the draught." I say, laughing at his bizarre but effective technique.

My brothers are happy to take me up on my suggestion of an afternoon pint and we spend an idyllic hour in a sunny beer garden courtyard, Luca having his first pint of Guinness.

Peter stays a week before heading back to his home in New York. I hadn't booked a return ticket for me or Luca.

"I think I'll go back via London and stop off for a visit with Izzy. What do you think?" I ask Luca.

"Can I stay on here longer?"

"Sure."

After a year and a half of not being with people his own age, Luca was making up for lost time with his old school friends. Maybe he'd be happier if we moved back to Ireland too. Both the lads would probably go along with whatever I wanted to do. The problem was I didn't know what I wanted to do... Should I stay or should I go?

The following day over breakfast I let my parents know what I'm thinking, "I think I'll book a flight back to Italy for this weekend..."

Dad takes a gulp of his tea.

"I loved the flight over to Italy that time we went. Do you remember seeing God, Mary?" I vaguely remember the story but don't have to strain my brain cells as Dad is already recounting it.

"We were above the clouds and I looked out the window and a young kid about three or four, who looked like you when you were little, was standing in the seat in front of me and she says matter-of-factly, pointing out the window "There's holy God in Heaven." And I looked and there was a perfectly round rainbow, I never saw anything like it. Have you ever seen that in all your plane journeys?"

"No," I smile. "It was just an optical illusion, Dad." But he's not listening. He takes another gulp of his tea.

"Maybe we'll go back with you?"

"Would you?" I'm genuinely surprised.

"What do you think, Mar?"

Mam smiles, "I'd be happy to go. We've always said if something happens to one of us, the other would go, but why not go now? As long as it is not too hot."

I think back to the text Ronan sent me the day before. "You are the best thing that ever happened to me in real life. It's 40 degrees here today, too hot to do anything."

"Well, it's a different type of heat. You might be better waiting a few weeks, but if you were going to come, I'd wait here with you and bring you back with me. "

"What do you say Mary, will we go?"

"Yes, let's."

I'm ecstatic. Covid is still an issue and unpredictable, so having them in Italy with me where we can all be together would be such a relief. I spend the rest of the day putting plans into place, looking at dates and flights.

"I'll stay for another two weeks to help get everything sorted. We should be good to go by 1st September. I'm sure Jim would be happy to come over on the flight with us and help get you settled in. He would never say no to a free holiday and he's dying to see the house as he was with us when we first viewed it."

I have flights picked, worked out the logistics and have Jim confirmed as a voluntary travel companion. Luca has agreed to travel back at the same time, so we have lots of help with the travel wheelchairs and baggage through the airport.

I call Ronan from bed that night. It's the first opportunity I have had since my parents said yes and my head has been going a mile a minute of what has to be done in the short space of time.

"Mam and Dad are coming back with me!"

"Really? What? Oh."

"Are you not happy about it?"

"Well yeah, but Rosie, the house isn't ready. I mean, it's still a building site. We don't have a bed for them or rooms ready."

I know, but we have the downstairs bathroom finished and we just need to get a bedroom finished for them, the small one that we used to sleep in?"

"We have slept in nearly all of the twenty rooms so far. Which one are you talking about?"

"Twenty-two."

"Room twenty-two? I didn't know they had numbers."

"No, we have twenty-two rooms, not twenty. I am talking about the one downstairs. The middle one, beside the one that is going to be the small kitchen."

"Okay, I can do it up, but there are so many other things that need to be taken into account, they would be better waiting until Spring..."

There is a pause as I digest the truth of what he is saying before he talks again, "... but I know it's what you want and we'll make it work."

I go to sleep with my excitement tinged with a niggling undertone of concern which I can't put my finger on.

At 3.30am my eyes shoot open, my mind racing. What if they get sick? What if they need to go to a hospital and they can't speak the language and I can't go in with them because of Covid?

What if Mam can't stop sneezing because of the dust that she is so allergic to? What if they are too cold, too hot? What if there are mosquitoes? What if they hate it? What if the bedroom is too small and claustrophobic for them? Mam likes a window open and that window is not easy to open. How the hell am I going to have time to finish the downstairs, finish two books, do my work and think about everything that is involved with moving two elderly people to another country?

What was excitement has now turned into a massive ball of anxiety.

Before the sun rises, I get up to make a cup of tea, and I'm surprised to see Mam is already there before me. Her eyes are red.

"Are you okay Mam?"

"I haven't slept a wink, Rosie. I don't want to disappoint you but I can't go to Italy so soon. There's too much to think about, and your dad has not stopped talking about how he will need things the same there. He wants to get a car immediately, eat the same food... he has my head tormented. And there's my medicines and..."

It was like we were having the same thoughts through the dividing wall.

"Mam stop, it's okay. You are right, it would be great to have you come back with me, but it would be much more practical if you waited until Spring. I'll talk with Dad about the car issue, it's not something we have even explored and I think he would need to become a resident to do that and I'm not sure if getting insurance for an 87-year-old immigrant would be too easy."

"But he's adamant about getting a car, don't tell him he can't as he might not go at all then. I am not very confident in his driving ability anymore. He can't drive in the dark and he's driving in the centre of roads now and he clipped the wing mirror of another car last week."

Having experienced Dad's new style of reversing on the way home from the airport, I knew what she meant. I couldn't imagine him adapting to left-hand drive, new rules of the road and the speed of crazy Italian drivers. Things would be different, maybe too different.

"Go to bed and sleep, Mam. You don't have to come back with me. It's fine if you wait until the new year."

"You aren't too let down?"

"Not at all, actually I'm relieved, I think. I'd like the house more finished before you arrive and I'd like you to feel more ready. Don't worry, I'll book a flight to London for this weekend, see Izzy and then get back to the house to get it ready for you. But for now, sleep and don't worry, I'll talk to Dad, it will be fine."

"Don't say I mentioned about the car. I'm just telling him I am overwhelmed. Which I am."

Later that morning I meet Dad out in the garden. We both have our morning tea in hand.

"So your ma told you last night she isn't ready to go."

"Yeah, we both had racing heads. I think she is right Dad, I'd love yous to come now, but it's very hot at the moment and it would be better if you came in the spring so Mam would have time to get used to the heat and also the house will be more ready."

"I don't know what has got into her. She wanted to go but has suddenly changed her mind."

"She just feels overwhelmed."

Dad shakes his head slowly. He looks at his cup, sloshes around what's left in the end, and then breaks the silence that has fallen between us. "I wanted to get her settled there. It would be better for her bones, it would be better in every way. I'm so disappointed... I will miss you something terrible... And I mean that." He throws the remaining tea from the cup in the direction of the rambling rose outside their bedroom.

I'm speechless. Dad does not do sentiment. Dad doesn't say these things. We always just joke together, we never say serious things like this, we keep these thoughts undercover, never to be vocalised. But now he has and I don't know what to do with the words. So I swallow them and digest them in the pit of my stomach, where they morph into a deep ball of sadness. I know what missing someone terribly feels like. I have felt it in the last year being apart from them. And now that feeling is back, even though he is standing in front of me.

"Dad, you can come in Spring in time for my 50th birthday. It will be better then... We'll have the house finished. It won't be so hot. You can ease into summer and we'll have a big party."

"I better bring Mary in her breakfast." He goes and picks a rose from the tree. "Breakfast in bed every morning served with a flower. That's how your Ma likes it. Remember that."

34

TO COMPLICATE: COMPLICARE

S taying with Izzy was just the tonic I need. Laughs, cocktails, some shopping, and hugs. Just a couple of days and I'm on my way back to Italy alone. Ronan meets me at the airport and we take a route through the hills home.

White cows and white egrets amongst white tissue-like flowers splatter passing fields. We don't see many cows or sheep around where we live. Livestock farming seems to be more for the cooler mountain pasture areas of Italy. Sunlight sits on my lap all the way in the car. If there was an ant on my pants, it would be frizzled to death by now. My shoes are still damp from the puddles I had to traverse through from the airport bus to the terminal in Dublin.

Balls of olive trees dot the black soil and upside-down cypress cones line winding roads. Finally, we shoot out of the last tunnel and there is the emerald-green water of Lake Trasimeno glistening with little waves to welcome me back.

According to Dad, I had been spoilt with the best two weeks of the summer while in Ireland. Since I left, the weather there is back to its old tricks of four seasons in one day. "It's better for your Ma. She prefers the cooler weather."

This confirms in my head that waiting until Spring was the better decision. Arriving into this heat that has dropped just a few degrees below forty would have been a bit of a shock to her system.

As Luca has stayed on in Ireland, for the first time in twenty-four years Ronan and I are alone for a week without either of our kids. I'm thinking it's going to be lonely, but it is the complete opposite. We blast music, eat when we want, walk around naked, stay late in bed.

After a long leisurely lie in after a late breakfast in bed, wrapped in his arms, the windows open and the sound of cicadas doing bass to the birdsong, I find myself saying;

"Ronan, I think it's time. I feel ready for another one."

"What, a baby?"

"Bloody hell, no! Are you crazy?!… A dog."

"Oh thank God, I thought you were losing it."

"Great, I'll get on the case." And that was the end of our romantic morning. Ronan rolled out of bed and was on his laptop with a cup of coffee within minutes going through all the dog rescue sites of Italy that he had already been secretly looking at.

"There's a gorgeous German Shepherd..."

"No German Shepherds, we are not getting another big dog." I'm already regretting mentioning it.

"Why don't we contact Daisy from your yoga group and arrange a visit to the dog shelter she works at?"

"Excellent idea."

"Do they have a Facebook page?"

"I'm sure they do. I'll check with her."

I already had their Facebook page. She had sent it to me after we had coffee by the lake and saw Francesco the watch dog. Sharing it with Ronan at the time would have been lethal, as he would have had me pestered to death with dog suggestions. I send him the link as if I just found it.

The descriptions of the inmates keep him amused for hours as they write stories as if it is the dog is talking;

"I am a bouncy dog that needs lots of walks. I used to sleep on my owner's bed but then I woke up and found she was dead. So now I am alone and sad. I need your full attention. I cannot share you with other dogs or cats and definitely not children."

"Before I came to the kennels, I was alone and sad, I wandered the streets, eating from garbage cans or sometimes scraps from the plates of tourists. I see people come and take the younger dogs, but I am old and all I want to experience is a family of my own."

While Ronan is in full mission mode to finding us the perfect, giant four-legged addition to our family, I am back focusing on what I need to do to make money to get this house finished. I need to write, but I constantly have a guilty feeling that I should be painting a wall, hauling furniture around, clearing cobwebs.

Every time I do something to move the house forward, I feel my energy levels crash as nothing I can do seems to make a difference. The task ahead feels too great to know where to start.

There is no denying it any longer. To push on, we need some help getting at least some rooms finished so that we can see an end in sight and have some hope before it fades away completely.

I text Danny Boy the day I get back.

"Everything is fine. I have tried to call Tomaso many times to meet and discuss the times and jobs, but I have not received an answer." Tomo has lapsed into his old work etiquette of not responding. It's time to get around the object in our path.

"Ok Danny. Anto was at the house and has sent us a detailed list of what needs to be done. We can meet without Tomo. My son now understands Italian and I am improving." The last bit is a lie. Luca is still away and my Italian has got worse if anything, but I don't want to miss the opportunity of a meeting.

"Tomo, can you please respond to this text and let me know if you can meet with Danny? More importantly, we need to meet urgently to go through the quote that Antonio sent. Please get back to me."

I get a response. "I am on holiday this week."

I feel like responding "Still??" Bloody hell, he's been on holiday nearly a month already.

I'm back onto Danny with a solution. "Tomo is on holiday. If you prefer, I can send you a list of the work that remains to be done and you can cost it that way? Maybe you don't need to come to the house. Please let me know when the guys can get started."

He doesn't respond, so I send the list anyway.

A week later, after many texts from me, the annoying Irish woman I am sure I am known as, I get an answer. "Rosie, I spoke to Tomo, so tomorrow I'll put together all the work to be done with the list you gave me and send you a quote. And then I will see you when Antonio returns from vacation in two weeks."

"What the hell? Antonio is also on vacation? Again?"

"No. Not again. He just has not finished his first one."

I have things on my mind other than building work and vacation rotas. While we have patiently waited and despaired and finally got our vaccines, we have a new issue to deal with – Italy has announced a Green Pass will soon be mandatory to get on trains, eat inside restaurants, access colleges and museums.

We try to follow the instructions online to get our Green Passes, but again we are faced with a 'Do Not Pass Go' impasse. To get a Green Pass, a Tessera Sanitaria is required.

We go back to the nice pharmacist who calls several Government departments and helplines on our behalf. There is a 'glitch'.

For the people without Tessera Sanitaria health cards in Italy, the government created a way around the system by giving out temporary codes that would be used instead of our real Codice Fiscales to get the vaccine. But now the system doesn't recognise the temporary codes for Green Passes.

So all the temporary codes of the people without the Tessera Sanitaria have to be manually entered into the system by the government offices before we can get our Green Passes. The problem is, there are one million of us.

"It's like a million people were born overnight in Italy," explains the pharmacist.

"I wonder why they didn't set it up so that pharmacists could enter the codes on presentation of the valid certificates, considering they were the ones giving out the green passes?" I ask, completely deflated again at the Italian bureaucracy.

"Because this is Italy. They like to complicate things."

While it's an inconvenience to us, it is worse for Luca. Even though he is fully vaccinated with a recognised vaccination certificate from Italy, he can't get the train to college, and even if he got into Florence he couldn't get in past the college doors without a Green Pass QR code.

Life has all become like a Sci-Fi movie and Italian bureaucracy has done it again and left us unable to fully function.

35

TO DRIVE: GUIDARE

"We need to decide what to do about the car. The car insurance is up soon and to get it renewed we need the car tax up to date and to get car tax we need to have the road worthy test thingy done which means we would need to drive back to Ireland." I'm talking as I take out the road map of Europe from a large dusty pile of stuff that hasn't been moved in a long time. Planning a road trip with paper maps excites me.

"When you say it like that, Ireland sounds nearly as bad as Italy for bureaucracy." Ronan is not so excited by road maps; he would happily punch in Ireland and let the GPS take him on the fastest, most boring route.

Looking at the map, I'm not feeling the tingly sensation I used to. The prospect of a road trip like this was exciting in reverse, when we were leaving Ireland for new adventures. I'm already tired just looking at it. Three days of constant driving away from the Mediterranean sun to the cold dreary weather of northern Europe and Ireland, across three Covid-ridden countries, all with different Covid regulations.

Calum and Helga had driven seventeen hours in one day, coming over from Scotland, as Covid regulations didn't allow them to stop in France, not even for a pee-break. Driving with a potential full bladder for twelve hours across France would make it an endurance test rather than our usual adventurous road trip.

It would also be expensive. Two ferries back and forth could be €200 each way, three overnights there and back, Covid tests galore, food, dog sitter, petrol, it was all clocking up to over €1,500 in my head.

"It would be cheaper scrapping the car here or changing the plates. Scrapping would cost about €900, but cheaper than driving back. But it would be such a shame to get rid of it. Even though the car is old it has never given us any trouble," says Ronan, looking at my rough costings. "The only problem with our car model is the boot, it is made of some type of plastic."

I'm agreeing with him, "also, three days to get there, three days back and to make it worth our trip we would need to stay at least three to five days. So a big chunk of time too... Right, so what other alternatives do we have?"

"We could try trading the Prius in and buying a more up to date second-hand one." Ronan is trying to disguise his euphoria. I think this might be one of the happiest moments of his life in Italy so far. His two major joys in life have collided; searching for a new dog and now a new car.

But his joy is soon dampened. After visits to a local car dealer, he comes back saying second-hand cars are in short supply at the moment. Covid had slowed the production and shipping of new cars, which had a knock-on effect of second-hand being in short supply. People can't get new cars so were holding on to their old or had upgraded to a better second-hand car.

"Did the car dealer speak English?"

"No, not a word... he also said we couldn't trade in our own car as it was right-hand drive and anyway a 13-year-old car was of no value. I think our only remaining avenue without driving back to Ireland is to change the plates to Italian. To make our car an Italian citizen."

I'm not really listening to what Ronan is saying, I'm still in awe of his communication skills without a common language and my entrepreneurial brain is trying to think of how I could package his method to make us some money.

"Why don't you ask the people at your yoga group tomorrow? I'm sure someone there has changed their plates or might know a loophole. Let's just explore it as an option."

We had never considered changing the plates until now as so many people in online expat social media groups had said it was crazy expensive to do. The bureaucracy attached is ridiculous, and it wasn't worth it. But they also reminded me that once my residency comes through, we have thirty days to get rid of our car and replaced it with an Italian one or change the plates.

As if by magic, as soon as I mention it, Daisy says her husband did it for his car he brought over from the UK and changing the registration into Italian was a straightforward procedure. He did it through an agency that is just twenty minutes away.

So off we go with all the documents needed – car registration, IDs, Codice Fiscale, my residency certificate, driver's licence, insurance that was soon to expire.

The agency is a small shopfront with fogged glass. Inside is a surrounding counter with two computers behind Perspex. Next to the photocopier sits a small thin woman in her sixties, with her hair pinned up on top of her head and silvery blue eye liner. She has a kind face. Her son, who is about twenty, is a good-looking chap with soft brown eyes and light brown hair and ready to be helpful.

He acts as a translator for us with his pidgin English and my wren-sized Italian.

She answers all our questions... the age of the car is not an issue, of course you can change the 13-year-old car...It will cost about €800 to €1,000 to do the changeover... And she would get working on it straight away... it will take a month to come through...

This suits perfectly as I have one month's grace with my Irish insurance company to get my motor tax certificate to them. By then, I would have my Italian plates and Italian insurance.

The woman creates a cardboard file for us with all our photocopied stuff in it: ID, Codice Fiscale, car registration, car insurance. She writes our names across it and Lucia's contact number, as we still have only Irish phone numbers.

"Everything is in order, but..." her son says, translating to Ronan what his mother needs from him.

"Your cock is missing. She needs your cock."

Ronan looks down at his trousers.

"What is a cock?" I tentatively ask, trying to stop my wobbling mouth by not looking at Ronan.

"It is the document that has all the specifics of the make of the car. The certified copy would have been given when the car was sold to you."

"We bought the car second-hand five years ago, and it was already eight years old then, so I think his cock may have disintegrated by now or been lost along the way."

"We can get you a new cock in Italian for €230 or you can order one online for less."

"Does it need to be in Italian?"

"No."

"Well then, we'll do it online. We'll be back."

We returned home and Ronan Googles car cocks and after some surprising results, he finds what he is looking for.

"We can order one online for €85, just like they said. But I got a brainwave to contact Toyota. They knew exactly what we were looking for and within minutes had taken details of the car and the document is now in the post free of charge."

The document arrives in the post within days and Ronan goes straight to the agency with it. The lady takes two photocopies of Ronan's cock, which he is very proud of as he got it for nothing, and adds them to our file.

Car insurance was the next thing I wanted to check before making a final decision. This is the other thing people had said would cost a fortune. Even though I had been driving thirty years without an incident, they said my no claims bonus from Ireland would not be recognised in Italy, so it would be like starting off again as a first-time driver. In Ireland, insurance for a first-time driver can cost thousands.

"They have to recognise your no claims bonus. It's EU law." Ronan surprises me sometimes with his random knowledge of law and regulations.

"Well, tell that to the Italian government, I dare you." Orientating our way around legal stuff and bureaucracy is something we both became quite skilled at in Ireland but in a country with an alien language we don't have a hope in hell of knowing where to argue this point.

So I braced myself and sent an email off to the woman who organised our house insurance to give me a rough estimate. Once we had this quote, we could weigh up the costs of every option again and make an informed decision.

"Ronan, you are not going to believe the car insurance estimate they just sent. Go on guess?" Ronan is PC (pre coffee) and not in the mood for guessing games.

"I dunno, fifty thousand, two thousand, what?"

"No, €450! But she would need the full details of the car, a road worthiness certificate and it needs to be Italian registered before going ahead. I couldn't believe it. All this time I thought it was going to be ridiculously expensive, but it is costing the same, actually a bit less than our insurance in Ireland."

"Wow," even PC Ronan was impressed. "So decision made, it's full steam ahead with making our car an Italian citizen."

The following day Ronan is closing the plastic boot of the car and a whole section cracks off in his hand. He superglues it back together and hopes for the best. It's then I notice the small print on the insurance quote. It is for six months, not per year. So it is, in fact, double the cost of my Irish insurance.

36

TO WALK: CAMMINARE

"We're not getting a big dog. We're not getting a guard dog breed and that includes German Shepherds." I'm reiterating what I have said a thousand times in my head and several times to Ronan as we follow Daisy's directions scrawled on the back of an envelope to the dog rescue centre.

"The right dog will find us," responds Ronan confidently. This worried me as inevitably the biggest, sloppiest, hairiest dog would 'find' us in Ronan's eyes.

"We probably won't find a dog here. It's the first time we have looked and don't let them bully us into taking the saddest dog."

I get out of the car and there are about fifteen dogs standing at the fence, some barking, some just wagging their tails smiling. And there she was, Brigette, making her way between the other dogs, minding her own business with a red teddy in her mouth. A medium-sized terrier like Sandy in the original Annie film... However, I get distracted, looking at a dog in a wheelchair.

"That's Bob," says Daisy, coming to the gate and following my line of vision. "They can't find anything wrong with him. He just decided not to walk anymore." It's coming up to lunchtime and Bob is being lifted from his doggy wheelchair in the shade to his private kennel apartment with a blanket outside for him to rest on.

He lies back in the arms of his carrier who is chauffeuring him across the yard, his back legs stretched out, his front legs sticking up in the air, relaxed at his wrists. And then settles down in the shade of his kennel, nibbles his lunch and has a drink before going back to snoozing. Bob is living his dolce vita.

A Rottweiler runs towards me with a pack of dogs at his heels. He's growling or grumbling. I'm trying not to be nervous. He's not the biggest dog in the place. There's a Great Dane beside him with droopy bloodshot eye-bags and greying hair. His giantness is amplified by the corgi at his ankle. But he's not the biggest dog in the place either.

There are several large pens with very tall fences. At the far end, I see a pony. "They have rescue horses here also?"

"No, that's Prince. He's an Anatolian Shepherd, one of the biggest dog breeds in the world, and he's a big version of one. He's been here for years. He is lovely though. Do you want him?"

"Let's have a look," Ronan says enthusiastically.

"What part of we are not getting a big dog do you not understand?" I'm trotting after Ronan, but not getting very far as I stupidly thought bringing dog biscuits in my pocket was a good idea. They have all got a whiff of them and I'm like an over popular version of Snow White with twenty dogs of various sizes wanting to be my best friend.

"I mean, he's not just a big dog, but a big version of the biggest dog breed in the world variety." I feel I'm like the corgi nipping at the Great Danes heels, as Ronan strides ahead, oblivious to my yapping.

Prince is massive, with a head the size of a boulder and legs that go up to my belly button. "The shepherds clip their ears like that," explains Daisy, pointing to his cauliflower ears as if he has been playing Rugby all his life. "It's so wolves don't grab them when they are fighting."

Ronan reaches towards the fence to pet his nose. "No don't do that," three of the volunteers say in two different languages but with equal fright. "He doesn't get on with other dogs or men. Only Cinzia and Gabby can go into his pound. It used to be just Jill, but then Jill died."

"Did he kill her?" Ronan asks with curiosity rather than sympathy.

"No, she was here when he arrived and worked here for years, but unfortunately cancer got her, not Prince. He still misses her, I think. He'll probably never be re-homed. He needs to stay by himself as he's quite territorial. Do you want him?"

In other countries, dogs like Prince and Bob would have probably been euthanised years ago but not here in Italy. Dogs don't get put down just because they don't have a home, instead the kennels become their forever home.

"I think Charlie would be a good fit for you," says Daisy.

"Where's Charlie?"

"Here he is now."

A tri-coloured pup about half the size of the biggest dog in the world bounds towards us and immediately starts smothering Ronan in licks. He's going to be huge. I need to move fast as Ronan bonds quick with builders, people he is buying second hand things off and most of all dogs.

It's then I spot him and my heart melts a bit. Curled up on the raised pallet in the sun under the shade of the tree where Bob had been previously sitting. His golden-haired, lanky long legs crossed at the paws, curled up like a baby deer in long grasses. His long floppy ears and bigger than normal black glistening nose on his protruding snout make him look like a cartoon character.

"What about that one over there?"

I go over to sit beside him. He rolls onto his back a little, revealing his belly for a scratch and thumps his long tail to the rhythm of a cheerful dog.

"That's Conan."

Ronan is petting Charlie like crazy, his young paws already on Ronan's shoulders. He'd flatten me now, never mind when he is fully grown.

Brigette comes over wagging her tail at Conan, his going in time with her plodding gait.

She gives him a sniff and then walks over to the Rottweiler and trots off with him and the gaggle of other dogs towards the fence as another car pulls up. Charlie leaves Ronan and is immediately over barking at the fence. Conan performs beautifully, rolling over to greet Ronan and putting his head on his lap as soon as he sits down, his tail thumping on the pallet.

"Would you like to bring him for a walk?" asks Daisy.

"Yes, let's do it. And can we bring her also?"

I point at the shaggy-haired dog.

"Ah Brigette, that is the dog I was telling you about, the one that looks like the watch dog we saw."

Conan doesn't like being on a lead. Cowering away from the harness that is coming towards him, he is all legs. He has rolled over on his back and it takes two of the dog carers to wrangle him into it. He really isn't keen but once it's on, he's happy to walk. Brigette doesn't put up a fight, she's a real hippy, happy to go for a walk.

We walk through the stub field along the dirt track beside the kennels. Neither are pulling on the leads and Conan is looking up for approval and commands. Brigette doesn't seem too bothered or interested that we are there as long as she can smell the smells left from earlier dog walks.

Conan looks like a half-sized Irish wolfhound. Same skinny hind body with the same textured hair except golden, same long spindly legs and long curved tail. He has a wolfhound face too but more like a Disney animal with his gorgeous brown eyes, whites showing on the sides when he looks around making them as expressive as a human, long floppy ears and long snout topped with a big black shiny nose.

"They are both so gorgeous. Which is your favourite?" I ask Ronan as we are walking back to the kennels, Brigette pulling me along, straining on the lead, keen to get back to her pals.

"I can't choose..."

"Would it be crazy to take both?"

"We have done far crazier things, Rosie."

Daisy and the manager Gabby open the gate. Gabby is tanned and well-toned and not one for small talk or unnecessary smiles. "Which one do you think you will adopt?" asks Daisy enthusiastically.

"Both. Is that okay?"

"Oh, that is wonderful, as they share a kennel together. They are good friends."

"So, what do we do now?"

"So one of us from here will need to inspect where you live, just to ensure it is safe and suitable. I can come on Friday? In the meantime, visit a few times, bring them for walks, get to know them and ensure they are the dogs for you. Gabby wants to know if you are sure you don't want Charlie?"

"He is beautiful, but we are in love with this pair," I say kindly, refusing Gabby's offer. I am feeling they want to get Charlie off their hands before he became the size of Prince when fully grown, and we seem a suitable target.

"Okay, so I can come visit on Friday to view your garden. It's just a formality and if you come to walk them later in the week so they get to know you."

The next time we go to visit, we bring Looney and Luca. Luca waits with Looney on her leash while we go in to get Conan and Brigette. Conan twists and turns, trying every which way not to get his harness on without protesting, while Brigette gladly obliges. Ronan takes off with Conan and I follow with Brigette. As soon as she sees Looney in the carpark, she digs in her heels and tries to turn back. "What's up Brigid?" (Of course we are going to Irishize her name).

There was no moving her in English or Italian as long as Looney was in sight. So Luca walks on with Looney up to the other end of the field and Brigid then walks on with me, encouraged by some dog biscuits I had retrieved from the car.

Brigid is not keen to make friends with Looney but Conan is smiling and happily flops around as they get to know each other's smells. Walking back, Brigid sprints towards the fence. She can't wait to get back in and be with her mates and red teddy.

"She has been re-homed three times, but always escapes and finds her way back to the kennels."

I'm looking at Brigid. She's delighted with herself carrying her teddy with a pack following her. "She seems very happy here. Maybe she doesn't want to leave?" I'm feeling a bit of a failure at not being the preferred choice to the kennels for Brigid.

"If we adopt them both, we'll need to change Conan's name. We can't have Conan and Ronan that would be too confusing." We are all looking at Conan circling on the pallet before he flumps down.

"He looks like an Irish wolfhound... how about... Paddy?"

"Brigid and Paddy. A good Irish pair of saints. Paddy it is."

37

TO DIG: SCAVARE

"I'm not sure if this will pass the kennels' requirements." We're standing with Daisy at the end of the garden, looking at the fence. Along the boarding sides, both neighbours have put up six foot high, green-coated diamond chain fencing, stretched between green-coated iron posts embedded in a low concrete wall.

They look good and must have cost a fortune. But the end fence between us and the hill up to the train track is old and rusted and sagging in spots. "Gabby will need to come out and have a look, as Brigid is an escape artist."

"Don't worry, I'll do a job on it before Gabby arrives," says Ronan and true to his word, he straightens the fence, cements in extra supports and patches up a hole or two before the kennel manager arrives the following week.

Gabby walks the perimeter, pulling at the bottom of our neighbour's fence with all her strength. This woman brings Rottweilers for walks. She's strong. Eventually she tuts and shakes her head. She has found a weakness that potentially a snake could get under if you squashed it in a mangle. "This won't do," she says. I gulp, she hasn't even got to the end fence.

At the end of the garden Gabby shakes her head some more and boots the fence in several places and then tries to pull one section off the newly-cemented post with all her might but fails, but she does manage to pull a section up from the ground that Ronan had spent hours pinning down.

She is talking in Italian and we can't understand her, but Daisy has kindly come along to help translate.

"It will need to be cemented down. And all the surrounding fenced pinned down better."

"But nothing could fit under them?"

"And it needs to be higher. When you have it done, call her and she'll come out to check it again."

The following week she's out again with Daisy and two others from the pound checking Ronan's new improved handy work. He found a roll of chain-link fencing in the shed and has patched, cemented, embedded and raised the end fence. He has also pinned any possible gaps that someone could shove a letter under between us and the neighbours.

But Gabby is shaking her head again.

"Chain-link won't do. They could get over it."

"I thought we were adopting dogs, not bloody kangaroos," says Ronan exasperated.

"They could use it like a ladder. Especially Brigid," explains Daisy. "Gabby is really not happy about the train track there."

"What? So she wants us to move the train track now? This is ridiculous!" If it was not for Ronan wanting the dogs so much, he'd be walking off, telling them all to take a running jump into the lake.

"And she says that they could chew through this fencing," adds Daisy, unaware of Ronan's boiling annoyance.

"It's bloody metal... bloody hell what type of dogs are these? They can chew through metal fencing?"

I'm now getting equally annoyed. "If they are going to want to leave us that much, then I'm not sure we should take them."

"I'm sorry, but Gabby really loves the dogs," Daisy says in an effort to console me.

"It sounds like she loves them so much that she wants to keep them all and not find homes for them at all," I say, unable to hold back any longer.

Daisy looks helpless. "I know a fencing place. I'll bring you there and we can send photos back to Gabby of the fencing before we buy it to see if suits."

So off we go to the fencing shop and end up spending €200 on sheets of wrought-iron mesh that are used for reinforcing concrete.

Ronan duly cements it in to the ground, wires it to the posts and sends photos to Gabby and Daisy.

Daisy calls by an hour later for a cup of tea. "Gabby is still concerned about the train line with Brigid."

Thankfully, Ronan is out, or he'd blow a gasket.

I'm staring out the window and regretfully come up with a solution. Time is ticking on and I want the dogs settled before winter. "How about we take Paddy first, get him settled in and then we'll see about Brigid?" I am reluctant to give up on Brigid but as she seems so determined to get back to the kennels every time she is rehoused, perhaps that is where she is happiest.

A few days later, we are there to collect Paddy. There's paperwork to be filled out in the office, home of the 24-year-old cat that is blind and struggles to do anything but breathe. Even that sounds like a struggle. Bob is sunning himself in the wheelchair, and Brigid is happily leading the pack around the yard, like an older sister who likes to boss her siblings around for their own good and her amusement.

Paddy won't get in the car. We have to lift him in. His limbs are going everywhere, like a cartoon. He's trembling, but we just have to go for it. Soon his head is out the window sniffing the air as we drive towards the lake, his long pink tongue flapping in the wind.

At home he wags his tail to greet Looney, who all too willingly gives him a tour of the garden. First stop, Asha's grave. Past the Alcatraz fence, which he doesn't give a second glance to, through the vines and over to the hazel bush where Paddy promptly collapses and rolls around on his back, getting all the aroma of fresh grass onto his hair. Spooky looks on, startled at the new thing in her garden. She still spends a lot of time sitting at the front gate, staring across the street at where we found her twin, waiting for her to return. I'm hoping Paddy, with all his bounciness and gentleness, will become a companion for her too.

We try throwing a ball for him, but he has no idea what that is about. Instead, he takes a gallop in the other direction, gets so excited about the grass under the hazel tree again that he tumbles head over heels, wiggles and then lies with his tail thumping off the ground until we give his exposed belly a rub.

As well as grass, being indoors seems an unfamiliar experience for him too. He wants to please and sits obediently on the bed we got him for when we all settle down to watch TV for the evening. There's a western on and Paddy is immediately on his feet, head going from side to side, watching the action on the screen. He stands with his front paws on the cabinet below and tries to sniff the cowboys, giving them a bark and a tail wag. The following morning he's back to the blank screen, sniffing it and checking behind it to find where the actors have gone.

He finds soft soil under the hazelnut tree and we watch him from the sitting room, digging and sniffing. Looney is in the line of fire of the flying clay.

"Maybe he's a truffle hunter?" I say hopefully, sipping my tea, thinking back to a few years ago when we could travel and I did a familiarisation work trip to Alba in Piemonte, the home of the most sought-after truffles in Italy. The organisers had brought our group on a truffle hunt. Accompanied by our very own truffle hunting expert, Marco and his dog Rocky, we arrived on the edge of a hillside lined with autumnal, rust-tinted vines. We traversed a carpet of fallen hazelnuts, another gem of the Piemonte hills, and headed into the darkness of the oak forest.

Truffle hunting is a competitive activity and normally under-taken in the dark of night or in the very early morning, before the sun has risen. This is so that the hunter's most coveted spots that spawn the best truffles won't be revealed to others. In the old days, they would carry candles shielded by heavy caps to light their hidden paths. Now, during truffle season, you just see occasional flashes from torches across the hills as the hunters momentarily turn on their lights to see part of their way. "That is why truffle hunting dogs are often white, so we can see them easier in the dark," Marco explained.

Rocky was on to something. He had gone ahead of us, had dashed back and sat staring at Marco's left pocket. "Ah, he has found a white truffle! When he finds white, I give him his favourite treat, some cheese which I keep in my left pocket. When he sniffs out a black truffle, I give him an ordinary dog snack, which I keep in my right pocket. So which ever pocket he sits at I know what type of truffle he has detected."

White truffles are the most prized (hence the cheese and not just an ordinary treat) and can fetch over €800 per 100 grams in the marketplace. "We are never short of buyers. Restaurant owners and chefs worldwide are always in need of fresh truf-fle. Private buyers for Michelin star restaurants fly in from Hong Kong and New York to buy prized truffles and leave the same day, as the truffle only stays fresh for about a week."

Once he had got his treat, Rocky led us through the dense wood to a clearing. His nose was frantically working overtime under an ancient oak tree and then he clawed the spot. Marco took out a well-worn trowel from his pocket and dug quite a hole. I could smell it before I saw it – a gnarled cream coloured lump that was the prized white truffle.

As my favourite autumn dish above all is a simple, softly poached egg with slivers of fresh truffle, I was excited that we might have adopted a truffle hunter.

"Or maybe he's just a diggy dog that is going to wreck our garden," says Ronan thoughtfully.

Paddy settles in well in no time. "There's no fear of him wanting to escape back to the kennels, he hasn't even gone near that bloody expensive fence we built," says Ronan being pulled along by Paddy straining on the lead to get back in our gate on return from our walk by the lake. It's the same every time; he can't wait to get home.

Seeing Paddy settle in so well and all the unnecessary drama about the fencing and him escaping, I'm tempted to suggest we go back to the kennels and fight for Brigid but something is holding me back. A feeling of something foreboding that is going to make life complicated.

For now, one rescue dog joining our crew is enough. I feel I need to keep my life as simple as possible to prepare for the unknown element ahead. I don't know what it is, but it's coming... and it's not going to be nice.

38

TO FILL: RIEMPIRE

Large, bronzed leaves from the magnolia tree outside blow in under the solid wooden front door with a swoosh. There is a visible reflection of the line of trees on the hall tiles under the door as the gap is so big. It's like an optical illusion, but I need a step there soon to stop the polar bears coming in.

It's mid-September before all members of the building trio are back from holidays and can meet at the house. But even then, Danny still can't make it, instead he sends a guy who has never been to the house before.

We have gone through Antonio's estimate using Google translate and we have eliminated things that aren't essential to bring the cost down. We still haven't got a straight answer about the three holes that are costing nearly €4k and a few other mysterious amounts of non-translatable work.

Danny has sent a quote for €16k with no breakdown as to what it covers.

This time, I definitely want to be sure I am not getting charged double for channelling out walls to install three light switches in every bedroom. One at the door and one on either side of where the bed might go. Even in the small rooms. A complete waste that I was blind to when they were doing the first set of work.

Antonio texts to announce that they will start work the first Monday of October. "But I am sorry I have to ask. Do we have to wait for payments like the last time?"

"Honestly this makes me a bit cross," I say to Ronan. "Of all ten invoices he and Danny had given us, all were paid within a week, which is unheard of in Italy. Except for the two unexpected bills they gave us at Christmas out of the blue."

"Ah relax Rosie, he's a good guy, he is just being cautious."

"He is just making sure the payments for that new sports car he has are being covered or his next month-long vacation." My rose-tinted glasses view of Antonio had been scratched, but trying to get any other builder was impossible as they were all booked up, now that Covid restrictions had eased.

On the assigned start day, I am up early and ready, but no one turns up. I am too busy getting my final edits done with my editor online to think about anything else. Book two in my 'A Rosie Life In Italy' series is just about done and the launch date is set for the 14th of November, a full year after book one. I'm not going to let any disappearing builders take away from that sense of achievement.

The following day I get a text from Antonio "Can we start work?"

"Yes," I text back, "but we still need to talk about some elements of your quote which we don't understand."

"Okay, Thursday afternoon we talk. If it is okay though, we get started today."

I do love his promptness. "Okay, so will they start in the room on the ground floor, first floor, or outside? As I need to know so I can get the rooms cleared."

"Roberto is coming with the workers shortly and then they will decide which rooms they do first and they can help clear them."

That afternoon, Joseph arrives with the two new guys I haven't seen before. The older one has a putty-like pock-marked face with a large bulbous nose and bald head. He's gruff. The other is the complete opposite. He's like a lanky weasel-human version of Goofy. They are busy getting things out of the back of the van while Joseph nearly runs us over to greet us.

Like me, with my lack of use of Italian in the last year, he has forgotten a lot of his English. But we communicate about his daughter and our daughter and how terrible things have been, but hopefully are now getting better.

There are no introductions to the new guys. They barely acknowledge us, they just follow Jo in, who shows them around the first and second floor.

I can hear the older guy taking charge. "Where will we eat?" he asks Joseph gruffly. He mentions the words for lintels and they carry extension leads up the stairs. They stay thirty minutes and then Joseph says they will come back tomorrow.

The following day Joseph smiles a "Good morning." The Gruffalo grunts and the Weasel scurries.

"Good morning," I say, happy that at least work on the house is starting again and we will soon be at the point of having rooms finished. Hopefully a bedroom without mould that's a pleasure to wake up in and an office where I can get organised and find things again before my wedding business starts to get busy now that Covid seems to be loosening its grip on the world.

"Omaroberto is not here?"

"No, he is on another job."

The drilling begins. Kanga-style. And it goes on until 12 o'clock when they stop promptly for lunch.

I'm busy working, under pressure to get a last few changes agreed on my manuscript, but I notice the lads are sitting on buckets eating their panini outside the front door. "There is a table and chairs in the back garden, use it," I say to Gruffalo in my broken Italian. He nods a 'grazie' and they begin to move their lunch bags.

"Would you like a coffee?"

He seems surprised at my offer.

"Sì, Grazie." His putty face softens a little.

I root out the mismatched espresso cups that were left in the house. I always feel I am setting up a teddy bears' picnic with a toy tea set when using espresso cups. The ones I have from the house are delicate white china with gold rim and inlays. They look like they belong to a posh toy tea set.

I spot Joseph rooting around in the shed and appearing with the two trestles which he and his crew left here nine months ago. I had since moved them into the shed and used a left behind scaffolding board to make a long bench for Ronan's eclectic tool collection, freeing the camper van of her duty as tool shed.

At the end of the day, we venture upstairs to see what they have done. I can see why they needed their trestles back. They have created a long platform in order to drill out above the doors. They have not just brought up the trestles but also some of Ronan's tools.

"They've finished putting in a lintel above one of the doors already," says Ronan, also joyful that at last work is being done again.

"Hang on," I say, noticing something. "That lintel is above one of the few doors that didn't need one. They have put it on the wrong door." I text Antonio with a photo and drawn in arrows pointing at the door, which it was supposed to go above.

"It's all okay," he texts back. "Gratis..." I look up Gratis... 'free of charge'.

I know that if Omaroberto was here, that wouldn't have happened. Or if Tomo had been here to supervise like he was supposed to, then it wouldn't have happened either.

The weather for the following day doesn't look great, so I clear the chair I'm working on upholstering out of the small kitchen to be, and haul it down the hall. Ronan and Luca help move the garden table and chairs into the room so the builders have somewhere to have their lunch in comfort. I show them the room and Gruffalo seems appreciative.

I clear away some more of my upholstery stuff. The Weasel lifts my staple gun. "What this is?"

"It's for upholstery." I demonstrate my amazing tool. "Ahh" he says in wonder. I leave it over with the foam on the mantle-piece, out of their way.

Gruffalo nods, "it is good for putting up cables on walls too," he tells the Weasel.

After lunch, Joseph calls me upstairs to ask if I have a hammer. They have pulled the wardrobe away from the wall in Luca's room and set up the trestles.

"What are you doing in here?"

"We fill the hole in the plaster," he points to the ceiling.

"No, this room is getting a new ceiling in plasterboard it is the scalloped ceilings that need new plaster. Has Tomo not given you a plan of works?"

"Mamma Mia," says Gruffalo and scorns at me as if I am the one to blame for him wasting all morning clearing all the furni-ture into the middle of the room and setting up the workstation for nothing. They spend the rest of the day moving the trestles to the other room, which will eventually be our bedroom, and then leave.

"Great, so tomorrow it looks like they will clear our room and do the ceiling," I say to Ronan, trying to be upbeat after their continued mistakes.

Later Luca comes down for dinner, having spent most of the day at Lucia's helping her build another chicken coup. "I hate to tell you this, but I think the house is haunted."

"Why?"

"All the furniture in my bedroom has been moved into the centre of the room."

We pretend we don't know how it got there, have dinner and forget to tell him the truth.

To this day Luca probably still believes a poltergeist rearranged his furniture that night, but he's so laid back he doesn't care.

39

PRENDERE IN PRESTITO: TO BORROW

M y second cozy mystery has been printed but there's no time to celebrate, the plan is to get a series of four or perhaps six out by finishing and publishing a mystery every two months, while writing the next 'A Rosie Life In Italy'; if I stay in Italy long enough without the bureaucracy beating me.

I have my corrections back from my editor on 'A Rosie Life In Italy 2' and have set the launch date. I am under pressure to get the edits done as I sit in my makeshift office at the end of the diarrhoea sofa where the foam has permanently flattened under my behind.

Enquiries for weddings are starting to come in for 2023, people are getting much more optimistic that all this Covid mess will be gone by then. So I am doubly busy, getting my book finished and answering enquiries.

The following day, Joseph arrives first and spends the first hour of his workday moving the trestles from the bedroom to the hallway. Instead of the bedroom ceiling, they are going to do the correct lintel. Dust and cement are flying in the air throughout the house.

Gruffalo arrives, his face squints up a little as he stands at the kitchen door. "Un Caffe?"

"Certo" I say. I'm glad he has relaxed enough to ask me for a coffee. It might help him work faster.

However, the gladness has worn off by day three when I have been interrupted at regular intervals by all three of them asking me to make coffee.

All take a heaped teaspoon of sugar in their puddle of coffee. I'm not an espresso drinker, but I don't think they are either. They are coffee flavoured sugar drinkers.

The kanga hammer starts up and is going nonstop for the next three days as they knock space in the foot-thick stone walls to put in the four lintels.

By the end of the week they have knocked off the internet several times and the Weasel short circuited the electricity by 'cleverly' pouring water over the heating thermostat on the second floor while dousing the new plaster above it with a bucket of water. None of them said anything until I detected where the problem was, and then he admitted it.

"That was me sorry," said the Weasel snort laughing. They don't say they will fix it. But thankfully Ronan is handy so when they leave for the evening he removes the blown up thermostat and joins the wires so that we can at least have electricity, but there is no way to turn on the heating and it's cold. It seems like a good enough reason to hassle Danny again.

"We have a problem. The builder put water in the thermostat," I text. "We can't turn on the heating. Please advise how we can do this. And please send through the quote."

"I am very sorry I still haven't had time to re-do the quote. I will do it this weekend. Tomorrow morning, Mario will come to fix the heating."

It takes Mario about two hours, and he asks how will we pay. I think it should be Anto paying but I just give him the €60 cash. We now have the heating on but only realise that night that it can't be turned off. So we message Danny.

"I bring a new one on Monday."

We are now leaving windows open as the rooms are too warm.

Mario arrives at lunchtime on Tuesday with the same simple thermostat they installed before. It is like something we would have in our house in Ireland thirty years ago. A dial that goes from five to thirty-five degrees with 'five' being off, apparently.

This time it's in the box with instructions, so I can translate the booklet on what the symbols are for and how to use it all it offers, as no one has explained it to us yet.

But there's no explanation of what the snowman, umbrella, sunshine and fire symbol are in the booklet.

We have stepped back and left the builders to do their work. They are taking regular visits to the shed in the garden.

"Do you have the charger for this?" Gruffalo asks, standing in the doorway holding up Ronan's prized drill, which he lost the charger for in the house move.

"No, we can't find it."

An hour later, we hear the drill going. Ronan finds an excuse to casually walk past them.

"That's my kanga and drill they are using."

"It's good that they found the charger for you. You've been looking for that for ages."

My positivity is challenged when Joseph asks me where our claw hammer has gone as he had it yesterday but can't find it now. We watch a little closer and realise the regular visits to the shed are to 'borrow' our tools.

They push it too far when we return from the supermarket and Ronan discovers they are using his hammer drill like a kanga to break the cement in the front garden for the pipe to connect the missing drainpipe to the rest of the system. "They are using it like an industrial drill. They'll burn out the motor."

He texts Anto, "the guys are using my tools. They cannot do this as they are not all mine. I am storing them for a friend." The last bit is not true as we have no friends here, really.

"I am sorry I did not realise. It will change tomorrow."

When tomorrow comes, instead of just helping themselves to the tools, they ask our permission. "Posso?" holding up a hammer, crowbar, or drill.

I am also getting tired of not being told which room they are going to work on next so we can clear it the evening before. Instead I am waiting until the drilling starts and then I run in with plastic sheets and try to cover as much as possible from the dust and flying cement.

But my efforts are useless. Everything we own is caked with cement dust again.

They are hopping from one partially finished job to the other. None of them seem to know what room they will be doing the following day, as they are still waiting on Omaroberto to join them and give them direction. It gets to a ridiculous point that Joseph asks me one morning, "what are we to work on today?"

"I don't know. Ask your boss." I say, but then I decide it's the perfect time to take control. "There are the scalloped ceilings still to be done. I want smooth ceilings in here and here." I walk him from the big bedroom to the room beside it.

"Sì, sì."

"But please move everything out before you start."

"Sì sì."

Gruffalo is sitting on a paint tin in the bathroom smoking a cigarette. My patience is running out, "Non fumare in la casa."

In the following two days, no one turns up. I message Anto. "I thought your guys would be here doing the ceilings or working on the terrace this week, as it is not raining? Are they doing a job somewhere else?"

"We need Danny to do some works for us to continue. When does he come?"

"I will ask him, but there is the bathroom roof that will be the terrace to be done and also the ceilings to be made smooth in the bedrooms."

"Tomorrow my guys come to you to fix the bathroom roof."

I'm relieved, annoyed, anxious all at the same time. I just want them finished and out of the way at this point so we can start cleaning up the rubble and dust and have somewhere to put clothes. I want our bed to be in a room that is a pleasure to go into rather than something out of a horror film.

I find Ronan making a cup of coffee in our one perfect room; the kitchen. "Okay, they are going to start work on the terrace tomorrow, so I think we will need to clear around it, as they will be putting up scaffolding."

"Is scaffolding really necessary? I feel this is something one guy could do. I could do if you'd let me."

"We talked about this. Anything outside needs to be done by a professional company and signed off by the architect, especially this, as we have to apply for permission for the doorway onto the terrace to be opened. But it will be good to have it waterproofed and tiled nice and ready for when we can get the opening made. It is the best place for sunset views over the lake."

I'm fired up again about getting the house finished, so I am back on to Danny.

"I am still waiting for your price breakdown. Anto is working on the house and he needs some plumbing and electric work done before they continue."

"Hi Rosie, I can't start the job before forty days. Thanks."

"Thanks!.... THANKS?" I yell at the phone.

"He can't start for another forty days," I yell at Ronan.

"That's nearly bloody Christmas! We booked him to start in July...."

I am texting like crazy.

"Telling me only now is a big problem. I asked you in early August to start work again. You said September and we've been discussing it for weeks. Telling me so late when I have builders here ready to do the job is mind-boggling. Can you do the electrical installation lights and sockets and the radiators attached on the second floor? I can wait for the two bathrooms to be done at a later date. It is important to get the electrical system installed on the second floor as soon as possible."

"I will try to organise myself to do the work. The problem is that I have to close some work because I am waiting for the materials and there is a shortage."

Ronan messages Anto about Danny's bombshell.

"I will talk with him," is his reply.

A cup of coffee later for Ronan and a stiff gin and tonic for me, Anto texts back.

 "I spoke with Danny, but he told me he can't do the work for another forty days."

"I bloody know that," Ronan is now the one shouting at the phone while reading the text. "And what the hell are the forty days about? Is he going off into a desert to do something biblical?"

Another text comes in from Anto.

"You need to find another plumber and electrician before we can do the work on the top floor."

Ronan and I have switched roles. I am now taking the calm approach. Shelly has posted a pic of their newly finished bathroom on social media done at record speed.

I text her, "Can I have your plumber's number?"

40

TO ASK: CHIEDERE

Alex the Albanian arrives. He has the look of a handsome garden gnome with a red beard, red hair and piercing Smurf-blue eyes. He is the same height as me, but appears taller and has already gained Brownie points as he can speak good English, having spent some years in America. Being able to explain and discuss what we want done is a big plus.

"We need two bathrooms plumbed." I like the word plumbed. It sounds as if we are asking him to make it soft and squishy and finished in a shade of aubergine.

I lead him up the stairs. "Why they do this?" he asks, pointing at the two black plastic holding tubes for electric wire casings traversing across the landing ceiling before we get to the bathroom.

"Because we needed electricity?" I reply, sounding like a quiz show contestant, wondering whether I've just given the right answer.

"Why they not put above? Who is this electrician? No, don't tell me. I don't want to know. Do you need a good electrician?" He speaks rapidly in English, not waiting for answers, the same way Italians talk Italian.

"You can do electrician work?"

"I can do everything. We are a company of four."

We have passed the black arteries, and we are now walking under one of the new lintels. "Why they do this and not finish?"

"I think they are still going to fin-"

"Why you do this?" Now it's getting personal.

He's pointing to the ceiling where the guys have just filled the holes in. "This is crap work. You pay them for this?"

"Not yet, I–"

"You don't pay your workers?"

"No I do, it's just, they are still-"

"Why they not fix this?" He is wobbling the stairs. Ronan joins in the wobbling.

"Stop it Ronan. You're making it worse."

"You like this?" He is tapping the yellowing varnished banister. "I can make you a nice iron handrail. This needs to be fixed. Why you not do this?"

"Well, we are not at that stage yet, we are still trying to-"

"Where is the plan for this bathroom?"

I'm chasing after him as he lands in the room he is here to work on – the big bathroom. It's not that big, it's just bigger than the three small ones.

"The toilet and bidet go here and the bath here."

"The bath in the centre of the room?"

"Yes, I have a nice freestanding bath. We have it stored in the van at the moment," I say, forgetting that not everyone uses their cars as storage units.

"It will not fit. Who told you it will fit? Where are your drawings from your architect?" says Alex, lapsing into an interrogation questioning method.

"I don't have drawings. I just took some measurements and want a bath. "

"You want to sit on the toilet with your head in the bath? Okay, if that is what you want," he says dismissively with a soft lilt.

"Well no, what would-"

"We put the bath somewhere else. Why not?"

"Because we don't have another -"

"We put the bath somewhere else and here we put a big walk-in shower. Something nice. It will be wonderful. Where's the other bathroom?" he says, ready to move on as he has now made up his mind what is best for us in this room.

I lead him to the top floor.

"What is the plan for here? Where are your drawings?"

I ignore the ongoing demand for drawings, realising how stupid I am not to have any.

"Well, the shower will go here and the toilet here and-"

"The shower in front of the window?" He laughs loudly. "Why you do that?"

I'm getting annoyed at his "why-ing". But Ronan is finding it hilarious.

"If you look at the size of the room, we don't have many options. And why not? It's fogged glass, so it's not like people can see in."

Ronan joins in, "It's so I can wave at people passing in the train while I'm in the shower," he says, demonstrating standing in front of the open window, mock-washing under his arms and waving out the window.

Alex is not laughing.

He's back out in the hallway and crossing to the other bedroom with the scalloped ceiling, tutting and shaking his head. Then he's back in the hallway again, looking at the tangled spaghetti wires.

"I don't do this job with the other builder. If I do this job I do everything, my own prep and finishing… They do this?" he asks pointing at splotches of fallen cement and plaster, lying hardened on the ground.

He doesn't wait for an answer. "Mamma Mia. I don't work like this. I work clean, do you understand? This is a mess. Did they give you a quote? Let me look at how much they are charging you."

I obediently go off to look for the original quote, while Ronan goes out to the garden with him.

"Why they bring all this here for this work?" He points at the pallet of cavity bricks and pallet of bags of cement which have been lying in our front garden since they finished the job last Christmas.

"It's been there since they finished the roof. I just presumed they would use it again for the second stage of the work."

"This cement is hard," he says, kicking one of the bags. "They are using you as garbage storage unit."

Next, Alex points to the scaffolding boards on the ground. They are bent and warped now because Ronan has been driving over them precariously.

"What is that?"

"It's our very own sink hole," I say proudly. "Like the ones that have popped up in Rome."

Without waiting for an invitation, he lifts one of the boards.

"It's the pipe carrying the rainwater from the road to the drain at the back that runs to the lake. But a section of the pipe broke and the clay above it caved in," I explain, pointing at the three-foot-deep hole, a questionable feature we noticed on our first viewing of the house.

"Why they not fix it for you?"

"Well, it's up to the Comune..."

"The Comune?! Ha, you will be waiting long time. We fix it for you."

It's not as if I hadn't asked Tomo about it. This is one of many of my holes that we discussed in the last year. But this one has always been brushed aside.

He looks at the prices. "You are happy to pay this? For plasterboard and for this and this? Why do you like to spend money like this? Tomorrow I come to you with a quote. You can pay me over time, no hurry. But if you work with me, I do not work with these people, but I make your house beautiful."

And he vanishes through the gate, leaving us in a whirlwind of whys.

Ronan and I stand for a few moments in silence as his van reverses out into the line of traffic coming around the dangerous bend. He pulls away, without a care for the pile-up he could have caused.

"What do you think?"

"God no, he's too aggressive. What the hell is it with all the why's?"

"I don't know... I kinda liked him," says Ronan, smiling.

"Really? I don't know, I think we're better off sticking with Anto and Tomo. Better the devil you know and all that jazz."

"Unless Tomo or Anto come up with an electrician and plumber in the next 24 hours, they are calling their workers off site. They have just sent those two stooges with Joseph to keep us quiet and because they are not good enough to work on the other project he's contracted to do."

All the whys of what Anto has done plays over and over in my head. We've trusted Anto one hundred percent and given him the benefit of the doubt, but by the following morning, my rose-tinted glasses of Anto and his gang are no longer just scratched, they have fallen off my nose and smashed at the bottom of a great chasm.

41

TO TAKE THE MICK: TO TAKE ADVANTAGE: APPROFITTARE

The following day I call Tomo. "We met with a guy yesterday that can do all the work for the second floor and can start in seven days. However, he wants to do all his own preparation and finishing. So we need to hand over that work to him," I say in mixed Italian English, which just makes him stare at me confused. So I give up trying and say it all in English.

"Anto can still finish what he has started, but the new guy will do the big bathroom and the top floor. I am sorry for Anto, but I need this place ready for my parents to come and stay in a few months."

The two stooges arrive with Joseph early the following morning and are drilling holes in the big bathroom wall. Perhaps it's the mysterious holes priced at nearly €4k on the original quote which we have never got an explanation for and definitely don't want.

"I don't think these guys should do the bathroom floors until the plumber makes a plan, as the pipes and water outlets need to be decided?" I text Anto as quickly as possible. "The new plumber is going to give me plans this weekend. So please tell them to finish the jobs they have started or do the concrete at the gate to stop the water coming from the street today instead of the big bathroom, please."

Within minutes, Joseph's phone is ringing. I am guessing it is Anto giving him distant instructions from his sports car – the one I still believe we are covering the instalments on by having these guys trashing our house.

I know the price for the concrete work outside is fairly low and it's something I really want them to do as it is now mid-October and although the day is warm and sunny the weather forecast for next week shows it is turning cold.

We leave the guys working and go to the car registration office in the hope our plates will be there for collection.

The woman smiles at us blankly, as if she has never seen us before. "We are the people with the Irish car?" I say in Italian.

"Ah sì sì."

She rifles through the wodge of files on her desk and then goes to another pile beside the photocopier where ours is sitting on top .

There is a posit stuck to the front of it. 'COC'.

"Ah yes, we need your cock."

"My husband already brought you his cock."

"Has put it here on the counter in front of you twice and you took a photo of it... Look there it is!" I shout in English as she flicks through the large amount of documents within the file. It's the first page, but she is flicking past all the documents to the end and then starting again, ignoring the front page.

"There it is! There's his cock," I shout in Italian when I finally find the words in the recesses of my brain as she flicks past the front page again putting it face down on the table followed by every other photocopied document we have given her.

"Ah yes. Okay, now I send all the documents off and I will call you when it arrives."

"How long will this take?"

"About one month."

"Again?"

Driving back home, I'm looking at the calendar. "Our insurance is up next week... We are going to have to rent a car for the month."

I start to Google long term car rental and it is coming up as over a thousand euro per month. This is not something we had budgeted for. "I'll talk to the yogis." My yoga group has become our go to solution for any issue we face in Italy. Except the Green Pass. That has stumped them all, which is not surprising as not even the Government knows what to do. We received an official message, acknowledging that there is a glitch in the system that stops us getting the Green Pass but they are working on it.

Back home I am up the stairs, just in time to see Weasel land on the bedroom balcony having jumped from the bathroom roof, laughing like a hyena at something some guy we have never seen before is shouting at him, following him down the stairs.

They are packing up a gas bottle and torch and some other tools they have miraculously brought with them.

"They must have been working on the bathroom roof for the terrace," I say to Ronan, satisfied that we caught them in time to stop creating the expensive holes in the big bathroom wall.

By the time we get to the back garden, they have reversed out of the driveway, leaving the gate open. I look towards the bathroom roof that will be our beautiful terrace someday.

"What the hell have they done?"

"Maybe it's just temporary to keep it waterproof?" says Ronan, sensing I am going to blow a gasket at the sight of the black torched on felt covering the roof stuck to the ochre stone facade with big dollops of black tar.

"I thought they were going to cement it and then use that paint-on waterproofing we were looking at for terraces before tiling it? How the hell are they going to do a neat tile job on that? It's bloody hideous."

The phone bings with a message from Anto and I read the translation aloud to Ronan; "We have finished the first floor and this week we finish the construction work, then we have to stop until the plumbing and electric installations are done. Without the plumbing and electrics done, I move my guys onto a different project next week."

"What? He thinks the first floor is in a state of being called finished? He hasn't even been out here, neither has bloody

Tomo," Ronan is shouting at my phone again. It's normally me spitting venom and Ronan been the laid back one.

I'm all over the place, now that they are claiming that they have officially finished the work assigned, I am walking from room to room trying to find a room that looks close to being finished, just one. But every room on the first floor needs something major done to it to make progress. With the added cement splashes and rubble, they look worse than when they started.

It's then I notice the big bathroom floor is swimming in wet screed.

"If that's anything to do with the expensive holes he can go get stuffed," roars Ronan up the stairs when he sees it.

I'm still walking from room to room, disillusioned. Nothing is finished, nothing seems capable of being finished, just patched. Like all our other houses before this; great potential in the right hands, but in our hands they just end up a mess.

"It's not like we were trying to do it all ourselves. We are paying good money to these guys to finish the house, not get a worse standard than we would do ourselves," my temper has subsided into sadness.

There are holes filled unevenly in a ceiling that was to be plaster boarded and even more uneven patches in the scalloped ceilings which still have large areas of mould. "I just want a smooth ceiling to wake up to. For my guests to wake up to."

"You can tell Tomo that those clowns are not to come back here tomorrow or ever again. It's a bloody mess." Ronan's dismay and disappointment hasn't turned to sadness but is brewing slowly into anger.

I pour myself a large glass of wine. This renovation is going to turn me into an alcoholic. I text Tomo, "Yesterday I said the guys can finish the work they had started and today they have started additional work and it is absolutely crap. We do not know what is happening and I need to work out a project management plan to get the house finished. This is a real mess, so the sooner we meet the better. Thanks."

Tomo texts back "okay, I am away this week. Next week I come with Anto."

For my mental health, I feel the need to finish something for the house, anything... I'll finish upholstering that chair I was working on.

I move the worker's lunch table to the side and pull the armchair back in.

"Ronan... have you seen my stapler?"

"No... well yes, the other day I was passing the room, and I saw Gruffalo showing the Weasel how it works. He put it back down on the mantelpiece."

"It's not here... the charger is gone from the box too."

"Are you sure you haven't moved it somewhere?"

"I am sure. I have not been in here since I set it up for their lunch and no one else has been in the house except them and us."

Ronan is in a fury. We walk from room to room.

"That's it. I'm hiding my tools and we should just cut our losses with them."

"I just want them to finish what they started so that we are not paying for something twice... I just want a smooth ceiling to look at when I wake up without any mould is that too much to ask?"

"They are not capable of finishing. Can't you see what has happened? Antonio has his best men or man, Omaroberto, on another job and he has left it to Tomo to send us Laurel and Hardy, managed by Joseph, who was the labourer's assistant, the gopher, the coffee boy, when he was here last. He's taking the mick." This does not mean Ronan is saying Anto is trying to have an affair with Mick Kelly. In Ireland, 'taking the mick,' means taking advantage.

"It's like we are their recreational therapy, something to keep them busy because they are on his payroll.... I think it's time to cut ties with Anto... It's time to call in Al the Albanian."

42

TO HOPE: SPERARE

In Italy, it is very precarious territory to accuse anyone of stealing. Unless you have video footage of them actually doing it. If you mention stealing, the accused can counter your accusation with a conviction of slandering their good name, which, to Italians, is a much more serious crime than theft.

"So let's be clear, we won't mention anything about the staple gun going missing. We know it was the two guys Tomo brought in and nothing to do with Anto or Joseph. They would be mortified and there's no point in causing trouble... but what are we saying to Anto when we meet him?" I ask Ronan, who seems to be more riled up after having 24 hours to think about it.

"We're finished with them. Anto needs to give us his final bill, and we are done. I don't want these guys in past the door. They're a mess and I don't trust them."

As if on cue, Anto's office emails his bill. A one page attachment with one line:

'Works done: €15,000.'

"... He's got to be kidding?"

My infuriated fingers can't write back quick enough. I need to fix this before I tell Ronan and he hunts him down with his sledgehammer... if the guys haven't taken it.

"We received the bill from your office. Can you send us a detailed bill with the list of jobs that are charged to us? Can you ask your office to send it today as we would like to complete this stage of the works this week."

It takes three days for the detailed bill to arrive. Listed on it were the three very expensive infamous holes we never got an explanation for, €1,500 for something else that was never explained, €499 for non-existing scaffolding to do the back terrace bathroom roof where they just slopped tar onto it. And to top it all, he was charging us for the missing down pipe that had been in our garden since before Christmas, before being moved to storage in his father Giovanni's garden along with all the other leftover stuff from our roof.

The detailed breakdown arrived just after I had opened a very nice bottle of chardonnay, which loosened my tongue and thumbs.

"Antonio, I am shocked by the detailed bill. There are clearly things we are being charged for that never happened or that were under question and were not agreed, such as the scaffolding. I am upset as I feel this is dishonest. I think we need to have an urgent meeting which cannot wait until next week. And I do not want your workers on site again until we have talked. Please arrange for Tomo to come tomorrow."

I copy in Ronan, who only reads it two hours later.

"Maybe don't send texts like that after a full bottle of wine. Calling someone dishonest is like calling them a thief in Italy."

"The full bottle hasn't kicked in yet and I wrote it when I was only halfway through the bottle. Bloody hell, can I not voice my annoyance without being accused of drunk texting? He sent an invoice with stuff that we did not get and if that is not dishonest, then what is? Look at it." I am no longer concerned if Ronan does decide to go after him with a sledgehammer.

A response has come in from Anto. "Tomo is on holiday."

"Again?" I shout at the phone.

"But I come with Mick Kelly tomorrow. He can translate."

***

"They should be here by now. It's 6.30pm. So bloody rude, being late all the time."

At 6.35pm my temper is rising. I text Mick Kelly. "Are you guys coming?"

No response. By 6.45pm I am at boiling point and decide it's best that they don't arrive now for their own safety. "We're having dinner now, so we'll arrange for another day."

Micko responds a minute later with a laughing emoji.

"What the hell is this supposed to mean?" I show my phone to Ronan. "Does he think this is funny?"

"Write to Anto," texts Micko, followed by an angry face cursing emoji.

I am speechless with fury. So I just respond with a question mark.

"I'm waiting him." Three minutes later he texts ,"Anto is already at your house. I'm at the office... if is fine, I'm coming."

"I'm starving," I text Mick Kelly.

I look out the window and I'm about to text. "And the lying bastard is not here," when Anto's black sports car swings into our driveway.

"Ok Rosie.. Sorry Anto is arrived now, so we can make another appointment in the next days. I am sorry, you are right, it is late."

"I'm going out to tell him to go home," says Ronan, turning off the oven and cooked pot of potatoes, before marching out the back door where Anto meets him head on.

Paddy follows Ronan out. I watch as Paddy lunges forward and goes for Anto's balls. Ronan pulls him off and Anto runs into the house. Followed by Ronan scolding Paddy. "God, that was very unusual. Paddy went for Anto."

Anto comes in as far as the doorway of the kitchen.

Before he arrived, Ronan has worked me up so much about how we don't want them past the door that I am fuming. I am ramming the masher into the potatoes. I can't even look at

Anto in case I kill him with the laser beams out of my eyes or the hot potato masher.

"We can't meet now. We are eating dinner," I say in Italian. Anger seems to be the emotion I need to make Italian words happen.

"Boh, I was waiting on Mick Kelly," he says, rolling his eyes. And giving a "I can't believe he is late" type shrug. I know it's a lie, Mick is always on time and Anto is always late. I am too hungry and angry to humour him. So I glare. He takes a little step back towards the sitting room. Paddy growls. Maybe he thinks I am going to throw my spuds at him and has weighed up being attacked by Paddy is the less painful option.

"He's here," I text Mick.

"Will I rearrange for tomorrow?" he texts back.

Ronan is in the kitchen now and trying to make small talk with Anto to cut the sharp silence. "So next week is a holiday. Are you doing anything?" He asks in broken, loud English. I try to translate and then I just say to Ronan, "What are you doing?"

"I'm just making small conversation."

"Conversation? You don't speak the same language as him and I'm fuming and trying to translate crap. I thought you were going to tell him to get lost?"

Ronan has softened while I seemed to have absorbed all his fury along with my own anger.

"Mick Kelly is suggesting we change to tomorrow."

"We can't do tomorrow, we have the appointment for Paddy with the vet. Tell him to come now and we'll get it over with."

"Can't do tomorrow, come now," I text back.

Ronan continues to try to have small talk with Anto, using just his father's name and the words for olives and house. And hand gestures.

Anto has eased back over the threshold of the kitchen but my h-anger is still boiling. Even so, Mick Kelly's response "Okay, set another two places for dinner" makes me burst out laughing, just as he taps on the kitchen window, his smiling eyes above his mask dissolve the feeling of wanting to kill someone.

Within a half an hour, we have the bill sliced down to €6k by eliminating the things the 'secretary' included by 'accident' such as the non-existing scaffolding. The tarred roof is only temporary apparently, just to keep it waterproof and they have supposedly cemented underneath it, but I can't imagine how they did that without a cement mixer in the two hours they were there.

The three holes were for iron bars to reinforce the floor. He has photos of them that the workers sent to his phone. But we are refusing to pay for them as they were not agreed, like we refuse to pay €350 for the three feet of copper drainpipe we have already paid for and has been stored in his Papa's garden. I've seen the same length of copper pipe at the DIY store for €17.

We agree to pay for the lintels and the extended drain, although I do argue over whether he had originally planned to leave that section out, and whether it was included in the surprise bill we already paid. We also agree to pay for some of the filled in ceiling plaster but only on the ceilings that were supposed to get it. It's bloody expensive, and the ceiling is still not smooth, but perhaps that has to be accepted as it is an old house. Plus, no one offered an alternative other than plaster boarding over it, which was not going to happen. I loved the scallop ceilings. It was just a shame they couldn't make them really beautiful again.

"Do we get a discount for tool hire?" Ronan says sarcastically. "And for all the washing powder we are going to have to buy to get the dust out of everything they couldn't be bothered moving?"

Mick Kelly does not translate, but I can see he feels awkward.

Anto leaves on good terms with the agreement to send us an amended detailed bill and to have all the building materials left in the garden for the last year removed by Saturday. This includes all the rubble and waste wood that is stacked behind the shed, some of which didn't even come from our house. I also add he needs to remove the shed roof, as that was part of last year's agreement.

We console ourselves that we can claim back forty percent, so it is only costing us about €3,500 and we have made some progress with essential lintels and drainage.

Before he leaves, Micko says hesitantly, "There is a problem with registering the house... They say it is too big to be one house."

I catch my reflection in the window and see my eyebrows have knitted into a cartoon style 'what the hell?' expression.

"Too big? There are houses much bigger than this around here, never mind in all of Italy. What do they want us to do, knock a piece off it?"

"They say it is too big to fit into the grade of a house. It is the grade of a luxury villa, which means higher taxes."

"Luxury villa?" I nearly screech the words. "Are they serious? Have they seen photos of the place?"

"That is what we are now trying. We have submitted photos of how terrible it is and a new plan and we hope this shows them it is not a luxury villa. We just need to wait."

It's mid-October, the house is still a mess and a building site. I can't help but still have a sinking feeling that this is all too much. However, by the end of the week we will be finished with Anto, have a clean garden and hope that our experience with Al the Albanian is a better one. He's our last hope.

43

TO TRANSLATE: TRADURRE

"The credit is on placement, please check it," emails Veronica.

"So the money is in the account?" I email her back excitedly. I was giving up hope about the refund and since the loan had come through, the pressure had been off to stay on Veronica's case.

She doesn't respond with a yes or no. "I need you to come into the bank. Can you come at 10 o'clock tomorrow?" And repeats what she wrote earlier, but this time in capital letters.

"Okay. Is it just a signature or do I need to take someone with me to translate?"

"No, my colleague can speak some English. See you tomorrow."

I rearrange everything I had planned for the morning to the afternoon. The bride I was to meet by Zoom, the Covid test

Luca was to get so that he could fly back to Ireland for midterm. I walk to the bank, mask up, disinfect hands, temperature check and in I go. Shouty Woman is standing talking with Veronica. They see me but continue their conversation together.

When they eventually finish their chat, I take a seat facing Veronica. She moves a large bundle of documents from the side to in front of her. Flicking through them, I see they are copies of the documents I signed over two months ago. "Allora." She flicks through each and sees everything is signed. This takes at least five minutes.

 I'm thinking, "Have you just got me here without checking to see if I really needed to be here to sign stuff?"

She gets to the last sheet and hands it to me to sign. It's a form that needs filling out.

I glance through it and try to recall the translation of the words 'assicurazione'.

I have no idea what this blank form is for, but like all the others before, I sign it anyway without understanding any of it. I think signing something you don't understand when I have asked her by text if I need a translator would stand up in court.

'Allora.'

Shouty Woman is still hovering, ready to take up the gossip train as soon as I leave. Veronica mutters through her mask behind the glass screen at Shouty Woman. I understand what she has asked her; "Do you speak in English?"

She's asking this to Shouty Woman who looks blankly at me when I say 'yes' instead of 'sì'?

Where's this colleague who can speak English she had mentioned earlier?

"Boh... a little."

Veronica asks Shouty Woman a question, again muttering through her mask behind the glass screen. Even Shouty Woman is having trouble making out what she's saying. She repeats what she's asking, and the meaning of the word assicuzazione has dusted itself off from the back of my brain and comes forward.

"So, for this house, do you have assicurazione?"

"Assicurazione? What is that? I don't understand what you are saying?"

I know exactly what she is asking. But she hasn't used the English word and if she can suddenly speak English now after months of putting me through hell, I'm going to play dumb because obviously I can't speak good enough Italian to her when I try and she makes me sweat for it, even though she can actually speak some English?

"Assicurazione, how do you say it in English?" She asks Veronica. I could translate for them, but I am not going to bother. They are both pulling on their school English memories and both come up with the word together 'insurance'.

"Insurance. Do you have insurance?"

"Yes, I have insurance with Generali."

"Ah, sì," Shouty Woman says and translates "she has insurance with Generali." I think even Veronica would have been able to make that out from what I said and my nodding.

"Okay." Veronica says something back to Shouty Woman who translates it to, "yes, because this bank can do house insurance."

"Yes, but I have house insurance in place for the last year."

Veronica could have asked me this in Italian. I would have understood. She has asked me much more complicated things in the past and I've found a way to understand it.

"Ah Allora," says Veronica, picking up the form I just signed and tearing it in two before putting it in the bin.

"Okay, all done," she says, gathering all the documents I had previously signed and putting them back into the folder.

I really wish I could speak the language so I could shout like an Italian, "Hold on.. Did you just get me to change all my morning meetings to come here so that you could ask me if I had house insurance?" The bloody Generali certificate of insurance is one of the documents she has just shuffled into the folder.

She could have just emailed me to ask, but what is really pissing me off is Shouty Woman can speak some English. If it wasn't for the relief of me having €26k in my account at last, I would be fuming.

I have my water bill with me, so I might as well pay it while here. I wave it in front of Veronica and say in my best Italian. "I want to pay this."

Shouty Woman isn't moving. She leans up against the door frame and waves me out towards the main area of the bank while she shouts a string of Italian words at me.

I take it I'm to go back out to the cash desk to pay it. The man ahead of me steps to the side to fill out a form and waves me on politely. Shouty Woman is behind the desk. I'm wondering how she got there so fast, although I thought she was wearing a cream top, not floral. She looks at me blankly. I push the bill towards her. She stares at me. She knows what I want to do. I just told her back in Veronica's office. "I want to pay this," I repeat, which comes out like a demand, but I don't care. If she wants to play silly buggers, so can I.

She strings off a litany of Italian. I say in Italian, "I don't speak Italian, but if you speak slower, I might understand."

"She is saying you can pay these online," interrupts the man who was before me in the queue, he looks familiar. He talks in a raised voice to Shouty Woman.

She snaps the bill from under my fingers and starts typing like crazy on the keyboard. They are now shouting at each other. Then I notice she is walking past me. Except it's not her, well it is, but she's also behind the desk. There are two of them. Two shouty women working in the bank with the same straight bobbed dark hair, same glasses and same shaped face.

I'm glancing from one to the other. Are they twins? I'm doubting it as usually one twin would at least have some redeeming personality qualities.

"I'm telling her," says the man, "that she should at least talk to you in standard Italian and slow down. She is speaking fast, but with her thick Tuscan accent and some dialect thrown in, you won't have a hope in hell of understanding her. I'm a fluent speaker and I found it difficult to follow the way she spoke to you."

I'm glaring at her. She is looking scornfully at me. I've found her out. I have found them all out.

I catch the eye of Shouty Woman number one and glance towards Veronica's office, who immediately looks down and shuffles through papers. Guilty. The three witches conspired against me to make my life difficult. I'll be moving bank now that this whole bloody process is over. And I will learn Italian. My goal now is no longer to have nice conversations and make friends here, but to argue with clerks and get through the bureaucracy.

To calm myself, I walk back home by the lake rather than through town. I can't believe I had to change my couple's meeting and Luca's Covid test so that Shouty Woman and Veronica could try to sell me house insurance. And that there are two of them. I see the man from the bank in the distance and realise who he is, by his dog. He's my golden retriever neighbour.

The fisherman is already back on shore hanging his fine lace-like nets on the fence, untangling and unhooking the fish caught, throwing them straight into a crate. I recognise the guy beside him, the restaurant owner from town. Fresh fish from the lake will be on tonight's menu. Maybe we'll go. Then I remember we can't without the Green Pass.

A cormorant stands silhouetted and still, waiting to pounce into the water. No Green Pass needed for his alfresco dining. The lake laps at the sand, still warm from summer. I'm lucky to live in such a scenic place but I need to fall in love with the essence of Italy again... if it exists at all. Perhaps it was just a facade that I should have kept in my tourist eyes rather than disillusioning myself by moving here and digging this deep into its soul.

44

TO TRUST: FIDARE

I t's All Saints' Day, which marks four years since we arrived in our camper van at Giovanni's with all our possessions and dogs. We hadn't the money nor a plan to buy a house, especially not a twenty-two roomed apparently "luxury" villa.

I thought I would be fluent in Italian within six months. I thought I would have Italian friends, nice neighbours and I thought we would spend our weekends visiting little towns and festivals around Italy. I thought I would be truly integrated into the ocean of Italian life. But I was still bobbing around the peripheral of a rock pool, sticking my toe in now and again, only to get nipped by a crab. I felt my legs hadn't even got wet yet, let alone feeling fully immersed.

Alex the Albanian is back for a second visit. He's off again, down the stairs.

"And this bathroom, who do this?" demands Alex.

"Ronan," I state.

"You want me to fix it? I fix it for you."

"Does it need fixing?"

"And this bathroom, did you do this, Mr Roman?"

"No I did this one," I say jollily, proud of my blue Spanish tiles that look much better than Ronan's bathroom effort. "It's better, hey?"

He's inspecting the grout up close.

"Do you like it?" he asks.

"Yes, I love it, do you not?"

"NO," he states and is off up the next flight of stairs.

His taste is really going down in my estimation.

He's been here thirty minutes and so far has had me up and down the stairs three times, asking me questions. First question.

"So they have taken everything of theirs?"

'They' being the last building crew that left the day before. "Yes, they have taken everything," I say as I walk behind him up the fourth and last flight of stairs. "What about this? Is this yours?" he points at some scaffolding flooring left in the corner.

"Oh no, that's theirs."

"Okay, it is mine now."

"And this? What is this?"

"It's my Christmas tree." He is moving the flat, wall-hung Christmas tree Ronan and I fondly made two years ago for our rental when we had no space for an actual tree.

"And this? This is not yours?"

He is pointing at the cement encrusted rusty wheelbarrow that was made before blow-up tyres were invented.

"Yes that's ours."

"I don't think so. That is not yours."

"Yes, it is."

"I don't think so..."

"Yes, it is... it was left in the house when we bought it."

"How did it get up here on the third floor?"

I'm wondering if I should tell them that the previous builder had it on a hoist and used it to move stuff up to the roof when they were building it. Each evening, it dangled precariously above our front door as if ready to dump hot oil on any intruders.

We've agreed to take on Alex to help us progress the house before Ronan and I lose our minds, pack up Betty and go back to Ireland with our tails between our legs. Well except Spooky. Of course, we wouldn't leave her behind, but she has no tail to put between her legs.

Alex is doing a whirlwind quiz tour of the bedroom 'they' were about to work on. He's our last resort. If he can make this room look semi okay so we can sleep without dreading opening our eyes. Then we might be able to stick at it, have hope and maybe Italy will not seem so bad again either.

"What you do here?" He points at the raw window ledge. "We put tile on it for you?"

"I don't know. I would have to see what that looks like..." My head is far from considering how to finish the window ledges.

"Or we put wood? If you want wood, I need to measure and order it. We can put narrow tile or fat tile. I think fat." He talks rapidly without pause.

"Ok," I am so glad he can speak English.

"And these, do you want to keep these?" An image of disgust is on his face as he points at the iron rods sticking out above the window lintels which held the curtain box pelmets a hundred years ago.

"We can take them down?" I say tentatively, hoping it's the right answer.

"You put something else?"

I try to be decisive. "Yes."

"Why? They are old, they are part of the history." He is looking even more disgusted at me.

"Ok leave them. I'll think of something to do with them."

"I will find you something, a nice shaped piece of metal." He draws twirls on the wall illustrating how curtains could hang.

So I'm having curtains. I hadn't really thought about this.

"And the shelves?"

I am trying to read his expression, looking at the shelves in the enclave in the corner. I like them.

"I want to-"

"We can replace them."

"keep-"

"or we can leave-"

"... them. Or replace them."

We are talking over each other. He skips past this.

"We put your bath here. Why not? We make a nice suite out of this room. When you rent your house, you get more for this room then. This house is too big for just the two of you, why not make it a B&B?"

It's interesting that he's also creating a business plan for the house where he is only supposed to be doing a bit of plumbing, after already expanding his job to the bedroom. "You need your own space. You cannot live like this," he says, looking across the hall in the direction of the room we call 'the place where our bed is at the moment'. It doesn't deserve the title of 'bedroom'.

I think he has also taken pity on me, as he has seen me perched on the left end of the diarrhoea sofa working from the tubular-legged, gold-top coffee table that has been my workspace for the last ten months. Both were rescued last Christmas Eve, from the 'definitely to be dumped' pile.

"Leave it with me. I make you something nice," says Alex, confidently. I am not holding out hope, but leave him to it as I have a book launch to organise.

The house is vibrating. There is drilling happening, banging and an angle grinder going all at the same time, which is puzzling as there are only Alex and his assistant Ivan up there.

Bits of cement fall down the chimney. The new building troop are out to make an impressive impression on their first day.

And they do. They have cleared everything out of the room. And by the end of day one they have the walls cleaned, tiles along the wall lifted and pipes laid for my freestanding bath.

The following afternoon I go upstairs in the afternoon to see if they want coffee as neither has taken a break to eat. Alex is standing on a trestle that is surrounded by fallen ceiling plaster. He chips away at the fresh plaster the other guys just finished the week before with a tiny pickaxe.

"What the hell?" I gasp.

"It's crap. We need to remove it all. They plaster over old plaster. Why they do this? They charge you for this? Why you pay for them to do this?"

"Oh my God, they charged me a fortune for that, what the hell, why did you do this? You were supposed to just paint the ceiling."

Ronan, hearing my raised voice, is now standing beside me.

"Trust me, we need to remove all the plaster, clean it and redo. They cannot plaster over metal like they have done. It will show rust soon. They cannot do this. Why they do this? And joining new plaster with old plaster does not work. It will fall eventually." He bangs the old plaster hard with his towel end. It takes a bit of effort, but chunks of plaster are soon falling away from the terracotta ceiling tiles. "They don't know what they are doing."

"And here." He is down off his scaffolding and striding towards the door.

"Why they not put a lintel here?" He wallops the cracked plaster with his gnome sized pickaxe above the doorway and a chunk falls off the only doorway that hasn't had a new lintel put in.

"They said it wasn't needed," I say weakly as the last bit of hope is eaten by more despair.

"This is dangerous. We need to put a lintel here."

Ronan agrees with them, "If all the other doors have been linteled then why hasn't this one?"

"Trust me on this room." Alex is back climbing up the scaffolding. "I do it and in a week you have a beautiful bedroom. If you don't like it, you can throw me out of the house."

I'm tired of trusting builders and throwing them out of the house.

"But how much is re-plastering the entire ceiling going to cost?

"€20 per square meter."

I'm calculating in my head and so is Ronan.

"That's €200," Ronan says to me.

"No, it's not."

Ronan has appalling maths ability. "It's €800 plus painting so we are talking about €1,000 to get the ceiling done alone."

"It is expensive but has to be done," states Alex as he continues to chip. "This room is going to cost €1,800 to €2,000 to finish, but it will be beautiful. Why you do not want a beautiful room?"

"I do... I just..."

"I also finish the bathroom you started, Roman. I make something nice there. So next week you have a beautiful bedroom and a nice bathroom to walk across to."

The temptation of promised, finished rooms is too much to bear. I don't have any hope left to pull on and as he is already chipping more of the just-finished-plaster-that-has not-yet-been-paid-for off with his little pickaxe it seems I have no choice but to go along with yet another builder.

"Okay, I am going to trust you. Make it beautiful...please. I don't want to look until it is done. It's too upsetting."

I don't have time to look. My book launch is in a week, the pre-orders are rolling in and I've a lot of prep work to do.

45

TO SHOCK: SCIOCCARE

The door of the to-be bedroom remained closed. Actually the whole first floor wasn't visited as we moved our bedroom back downstairs to what would eventually be my parents' bedroom to stay away from the dust and noise. I set up ads for the online book launch party, bought prizes for those who participate, approved the final layout, dealt with the final round of edits found by my eagle-eyed beta readers, fought with computer systems while trying to upload the final cover and manuscript in time for launch day and did all the other fifty million things that I discovered an indie author has to do besides putting words on a page.

Now and again, Alex asks about a colour or what furniture I am going to put in the room and where. Which makes me wonder if he was not painting the areas where furniture was going to be placed. But at this stage I didn't care.

Ronan takes over the role of coffee boy for the week. He is up talking with Ivan, who is Romanian but has been in Italy for thirty years. He seems to speak fluent Italian, it's the common language used between him and Alex.

Ivan is in his fifties. He has a kind face with well-defined smile lines on his cheeks. He has soft brown eyes and wears a cap similar to my dad's back in Ireland. Every morning he is first here and up the ladder working before 8am.

Somehow Ronan has full fifteen minute conversations with Ivan, even though neither can speak each other's language. I get daily reports.

"Jezuz you know your man upstairs Ivan, he fought against Ceausescu during the revolution."

"Jezuz you know your man upstairs, Ivan, he has a wife and two kids, they are grown now, back in Romania who he sends money home to every month. He used to drive back regularly. It takes twenty-two hours but with Covid he's hardly seen them at all."

"Jezuz you know your man upstairs, Ivan, his son is getting married in Romania in the summer and he's invited me to the wedding."

I'm still jealous of Ronan's ability to have full on conversations even though neither can speak each other's language.

"Rosie, Roman," calls Al the Albanian after a week of work and the day before launch day. I was fighting with the upload software for the umpteen time, trying to get it to accept the cover, which it kept spitting back at me to say it was .5mm too short and then 1mm too big.

"Come look and let me know what you think."

I was about to say "not now Al," but realised if I didn't take a break, my head might explode with the frustration.

Ronan carries up the tray of coffee he was making for himself, Al and Ivan. I expect Al will be telling us about a problem he found that means the whole house is about to collapse or something the others did before him is going to cost us a kidney to fix.

I push open the door. Al and Ivan are standing in their paint blotched work wear surrounded by finished crisp fresh cream walls. The far corner of the room has been stripped of plaster halfway up, exposing the beautiful stone the house is built from. It is the perfect backdrop to my freestanding bath with rose gold taps and my large fern they had moved in from the hallway downstairs. The terracotta floor has been cleaned and scrubbed to its original pretty colour.

Not only that, but they have moved in the antique wardrobe I had restored from Paolo's room and set up the brass bedframe Ronan had bought me for Christmas from the TV antique guy and our mattress from the room across the hall.

I throw myself on the bed and look up at the perfectly smooth white scalloped ceiling with the copper painted iron slats, which go perfectly with the intricate copper light shade I had bought over a year ago. The one that had been delivered during the early days of lockdown and I thought it was a police raid. The room was already filled with memories, our memories.

"You don't like it? Why you not say something?" Al the Albanian says anxiously.

"I don't like it... I love it." Off the bed and across the floor, I threw my arms around his neck. I didn't care about Covid I was going to hug this stranger and cry a little on his shoulder.

Across the hall they had tidied up the tiling of the bathroom, added finishing touches such as metal corner strips, hung the mirror, cleaned away the caked grout, finished the unfinished tiling around the window and installed the heated towel rail. The room is finished, and it looks fantastic. "Oh, wow... we now have two finished rooms on this floor."

"And two finished downstairs, that's four rooms, only eighteen more to go," says Ronan with the same restored hope in his voice that I am feeling about the house.

"If you like, I can work on the hallway and make it a beautiful entrance for you? It is important for your mental well-being to have something beautiful to walk into and we get rid of this." Al the Albanian waves his hand at the large blob of mould on the stairwell that is in the perfect shape of the map of Ireland.

"I have grown fond of it, but yes, if you could do the hall stairs and landings, that would be amazing."

Other rooms we can do gradually ourselves, but the hall stairs and landing were always somewhere I was going to get someone to do as Ronan nor I am good with heights.

"Okay, we start on that next week."

There is more good news, the Comune has accepted that our house is not a luxury villa and have classed it at a grade below. However, they have a year to come out and do a house inspection and should they choose to do so, they have the right to change the grading should they decide that it is indeed a luxury villa. We are at last living in one house rather than four apartments and I have a beautiful mould free bedroom.

46

TO RELEASE: RILASCIARE

Sleeping in a dust-free, mould-free, warm room for the first time in years is one thing, but waking up in a room fit for any five-star hotel brochure and realising it's yours is even better.

I give Mam and Dad a video tour of the finished rooms. "They look marvellous," says Dad. "Get him to do our rooms as well and we'll be over like a flash when the weather gets better."

Al the Albanian seems to have brought us luck as well as calmness. His wife has told us about two women in Puglia that run a business helping ex-pats get through bureaucracy in Italy. I contacted them in a last ditch of desperation about the Green Passes and, voila, they have amazingly organised them for us. Luca can now attend college and we will be able to go to a restaurant to eat.

However, I have just discovered a company that delivers recipes with all the ingredients ready to be made. I saw it on social media and ordered a trial box. This week I cooked three amazing restaurant-worthy meals and found my joy in cooking again. I might try them again in a few weeks, but I'm definitely going to get back cooking now that markets will buzz to life again, and with our Green Passes we can explore them and Italy.

But the best thing this week, besides Izzy booking her flights home for Christmas, is definitely the smell of fresh paint and cleanliness in our exquisite bedroom.

I bring my laptop up to work on in bed, like in the old days. Paddy comes up and lies on the floor beside me. It's Sunday. Winter light chinks in through the closed shutters. The ceiling is smooth and spider-free.

It's the launch day of my book with an expected 150 people attending the launch party this afternoon.

I am excited and happy... but something feels off.

I look at the launch plan schedule for the day ahead. I check through everything and all is okay.

Where is this feeling that this is not going to happen coming from? I try to shake it off. I go downstairs and by my second cup of tea; the feeling is so strong that I am wording a post in my head to say the launch has been cancelled. Something is not right. Is it nerves? No, I'm excited... or I was excited about it. There's something important happening today that I've forgotten about and I can't think what it is.

I check my calendar. I have flights booked the following week to go back to Ireland. My pre-Christmas two-week-long visit during which we would make the plans for Mam and Dad to finally come in the Spring to live in Italy, in time for my 50th birthday in March. The weather would start to warm up then and by the rate Alex works and with his help we would have a nearly finished house to welcome them into. Mam had already picked the colour she wanted their bedroom to be. Lemon.

Maybe I'll call Mam and Dad and see if there is a family birthday I have forgotten about... It's 8.25am there, perhaps too early to call, they'll still be in bed, but my anxiety has risen to the point I am pacing the floor.

I'll call them. I need to check in on Dad anyway as he has had a nasty cough for the last two days. It's Dad... that's it, that is what is causing the anxious feeling. It's about Dad.

But it's too early to call. Instead, I will move my flight forward to Monday or Tuesday and get over there. He didn't sound good yesterday, and the doctor had refused to do a house call because of Covid. I'll go over and tell the doctor what I think of him and make sure Dad is alright. I'll change my flights, that is what I'll do.

Just as I sit and open the airline's website, the phone rings. It's Jim. "Rosie.... It's Dad... he has..." there's white noise in my ear.

"What did you just say? I didn't hear the last words... did you just say..."

"Dad... has just passed away..."

47

TO BE: ESSERE

"There, I told you I didn't hit him with a hammer. That's what she said to the policeman, can you imagine?" Ingrid is laughing between breaths.

"You didn't say that, did you Mam?" I look at my 85-year-old mother who used to stand taller than me but sclerosis in her spine has bowed her like an aged olive tree to my shoulder height.

"I did," she says defiantly.

Ingrid continues the story, "And the young cop says 'I never said you did' and then he turned to the female cop with him and says 'Did you see a hammer?' and she says 'no'. And I am standing there terrified they'll turn around and see the claw hammer on the bedroom windowsill tucked behind the curtain, out of sight, but not well enough to hide a murder weapon. I didn't know where to look!"

"Ma, what the hell?" I say, distracted from my grief, standing in my parents' kitchen waiting for the kettle to boil for my first cup of tea since my arrival.

"Ah, they were annoying me with all their questions, as if I killed your Da. As if I would wait this long after sixty-six years of being together to kill him, if that is what I wanted to do."

"But why the hell did you have a hammer on the windowsill?"

"That's for me turnips." Her silver curls bob as her head jerks a little with the undulation of the last word, as if we all should know that is why it's there. "When I'm cutting a turnip for the stew, I stick the pointy knife into it and hammer it in with the hammer. It works grand. It's the only way to do it with the arthritis in my hands. Your Da would sometimes bring me in the vegetables to prepare for dinner in bed in the mornings."

She has her free hand from her stick doing mimes of hammering motion with her arthritic snarled fingers, before pausing and putting both hands back on her stick as if she was about to do a tap-dancing routine. "He always did say we should hit him over the head with a hammer if he ever got bed ridden... But he wasn't bedridden. He was only out chopping wood and feeding the birds a few days ago." Her animated voice is now low and back to soft memory mode.

We already had our moments of sadness when I initially arrived at the door with our 'My Mam', 'My Daughter' lines for real this time, with a long-lasting, sob-shaken enwrapped hug. It was too soon to go to those depths again, so I sparked in a curve ball. "Is it a common Irish thing to threaten to hit someone you are fond of over the head with a hammer, or is it just our family?"

"I don't know," says Ingrid. "I've heard it so many times from you lot. Well, your Ma and Da anyway. Your Da also always said people died of a shortness of breath no matter what they died of, even if they were murdered, hit by a car or whatever, he'd always joke everyone dies of the same thing, a shortness of breath."

And that is exactly what he did. He lay down beside my Ma after two days of a chest infection, closed his eyes and took his last breath. And died. Of a shortness of breath.

"I had a meeting with two of your brothers and Ingrid last night," Mam says, handing me my tea, "and we all agree I can't live here by myself, I wouldn't be able for it and I've never lived alone in my life, so the best thing is for me to go back to Italy and live with you there."

"Mam that is the best news, in the sad circumstances... I thought I was going to have to drag you back as I wasn't leaving here without you." I hug her again, relieved. I had never pictured my mam coming to live with me alone. I always imagined them coming together, living independently in the downstairs self-contained apartment, looking after each other and popping across the hall for a cup of tea or meeting us in the garden in the evening.

And I somehow had thought Dad would outlive her, considering he never was in hospital a day in his life with his clean living and his daily cod liver oil doses since as long as I can remember. Whereas Mam had been through cancer, a hip replacement and thought life was too short not to indulge in cream cakes, the odd cigar and whiskey regularly.

"I have my passport and me Immunity Tractor Pass and everything, so I'm all set to go."

"You mean an Immunity Tracker Pass? Your Covid Green Pass?"

"Well whatever it's called, that thing you need to go abroad with now... I think this calls for more than tea," she announces, taking my cup from me.

"What do you have?"

"Well there's me whiskey and you are not getting that... and there's a cupboard full of Guinness. He had bought it on special offer last week, ready for you all being here for Christmas."

There is no other alcohol in the house and I do fancy a drink now that I'm here and reality has struck.

"I'll have a Guinness so." I pull the tab on a can and use the technique Dad had shown me on the last visit...can in the glass's neck and then lift straight up in the air. Bonkers, but it works and creates a perfect head. Mam has walked Ingrid out to her car and the house is silent. Just me and my dad's Guinness.

I slowly walk into their bedroom where Dad had taken his last breath. He was now at the undertakers being prepared to be brought back here later on for his wake.

Beside his bed was my second mystery book I had sent to him two weeks ago, with his reading glasses stuck between the cover and dedication page. "To Dad, thanks for all the childhood stories of The Chocolate Car and the Sad Daisy." He had got to read it.

The next week is spent in a whirlwind of funeral preparation, the wake, the funeral and the party aftermath. Izzy got the day off work for the funeral and flew in and out the same day, but Ronan had to stay back in Italy for various reasons. One being that Al the Albanian was going full throttle on our house having heard my sad news. He wanted to make it nice for me to come back to. Hearing my elderly mama was coming back with me made him work even longer hours. "You don't have to pay me now, you pay me sometime, but we make it nice for the women," Ronan tells me, recounting Al the Albanians kind words in his best imitation Albanian accent.

The week after the funeral is twice as busy as the previous week. There are bills to be settled, disability aids ordered to be delivered to Italy to make my mother's life easier, a cottage to be cleaned and organised and an 85-year-old Ma to be prepped and packed for immigration to Italy and I've forms galore to complete.

"Your mum will need to fill out the widow's contributory pension form. Make sure it's the contributory one, not the non-contributory one," says the woman on the phone in the Government office.

"Ok can you post it to me?"

"No it's too big. You'll need to get one yourself."

"Ok, from where?"

"Well, a commissioner of oaths, a post office should have them or a community information centre or a health centre."

There's only one place I know the location of from her list. I'll try the post office.

I get it. It's ten pages long, so I start to fill it out on Mam's behalf. I get to the question 'did you work in Ireland pre 1979?'

'Yes.'

'If so, list all working history and dates of employment.'

I've got to answer the same for my dad.

Another form wants Mam's original birth and marriage certificates and the death certificate.

He's only dead five minutes and everyone wants the original death certificate.

Italy's bureaucracy doesn't seem so bad after all.

I decide to follow my Dad's example of dealing with death. I am going to ignore the fact that he is dead, not speak of it, not think of it and in so doing I can fool my brain into believing he is still alive.

I buy the biggest suitcase I can find and Mam fills it fast with clothes she has never worn, photo albums, tubes of oil paint, some kitchen implements she feels she can't live without, holy water, sausages, cheese, balls of wool.

I had said to my mother that we could take all the time she needs before booking our flights back, however a new Covid variant has popped up. Omicron. It sounds like a character from Flash Gordon. A baddie that is now making borders shaky again. I have my residency should Italy close its borders, but I don't know how much it would complicate Mam's entry to the country and I wasn't leaving without her. I couldn't leave without her... Ingrid has her own elderly father living with them so there was no room there for Mam, Peter lived in New York and Tony had a full house of four young children and full-time jobs. So, I was her only choice and we needed to race against the new variant. We would leave at the weekend.

48

TO CHOOSE: SCEGLIERE

Ronan keeps me going with house updates; "You should see the job he has done on the missing doors. They are absolutely fabulous. They look like new. He said in the condition they were in, they were worth about €600 but now they are worth about €1,200 each. The cousins knew what they were doing by taking them." He insists on not sending me any pictures, 'they'... as in him, and his new mates, Al the Albanian and Ivan the Romanian, want it to be a surprise.

However, two days before I am leaving for Italy, I call in to say goodbye to Laura, my neighbour and walking buddy from when I lived in Ireland. Over tea, her eyes fill with tears. "Will I ever see you again?"

"Of course." I say... But then I think... I won't be able to travel back without Mam, getting her to Italy will be a feat in itself. I am not going to be able to travel back without her. But then why would I? The only reason I came back regularly was to see Mam and Dad, top up on teabags and to have a Guinness or two. Now that Dad is gone, Mam with me and I know that canned Guinness is not too bad when poured like a lunatic, there is no reason for me to return. My brothers and their families and my friends can come visit me. I have enough space, more than them. However Laura doesn't fly. So Laura is right, I won't be returning to Ireland and we probably won't see each other again for a very long time.

And yet I am still not sure if I am ready to leave Ireland behind completely and make Italy my forever home. The bureaucracy, the language difficulties, the taxes, they have all had their fair share of wearing me down in the last year.

Covid lockdowns had kept us apart from the reasons we had chosen Italy, I had forgotten the sagre, festivals, the long leisurely strolls through the quaint little towns, visits to artisan's workshops and museums, finding a gem of a restaurant with outdoor dining and amazing views, the joy of discovering new words and getting to use them.

Now, leaving my parent's cosy cottage to return to another winter of mould and dust was no longer a choice.

As soon as Mam had gone to bed, I call Ronan in a panic. Italy was no longer an adventure. Things had become strained. It was now all or nothing. Maybe he should be the one packing up and coming here. We could live in the cottage with Mam, be close to Jim and Ingrid and familiarity. The house is smaller but we could make it work. I voice it all to him in word blubber.

"Rosie, Rosie, take it easy... Look... we were going to keep it as a surprise, but I will give you a walkthrough of the house so you can see what you are coming back to. I'll start at the front door." He switches me to video phone as he stands outside our impressive double-door entrance with the brass knobs and knockers I had so fondly cleaned with cola.

The door pushes open and the hallway that once housed three tattered sofas and a host of creatures has shining floor tiles and freshly painted terracotta-coloured walls. He leads me past the kitchen and sitting room that still look their cosy familiar selves and past the bathroom I had tiled during Izzy's passport crisis.

The guest kitchen was now free of my upholstery work and set up as a cute kitchen. Beside it, Mam's to-be-bedroom was now painted bright lemon, just like she had requested, with a grey border skirting the floor. Curtains and bedding chosen with Shelly and Karen's help draped the windows with a bird table outside, making her first experience of a single bedroom as welcoming as it could ever be. A hamper of Italian food and wine sat on her bedside table along with a condolences card from Anto and Giovanni.

"I am thinking your mam will want to sit in with us and not by herself in the front sitting room," says Ronan from behind his phone camera. "So I was thinking this room could now be the craft room for you both to work in." He pushes open one of the newly refurbished shining doors to the front sitting room where all my upholstery projects and works in progress are neatly stacked along with an easel for Mam. The walls I had stood at hopelessly knocking old plaster off only a month or two ago were now beautifully finished with a lighter terracotta shade and the old Italian rag rolled effect that chalky paint creates.

"And look, there's more." Ronan leads me by the phone back out to the hallway and up the stairs and spins me around slowly on the landing to show me the Turkish chandelier I had bought a year ago in place, illuminating newly plastered walls painted the cappuccino colour I had chosen months ago. The mouldy map of Ireland had been cappuccino-d. I didn't miss it like I thought I would. The house was beautiful, fresh, clean and ready to welcome us back. It's looking all the more twinkly through my happy tears dropping onto the phone screen.

"The top floor still has to be done, but Al said he'd have it finished before Christmas if we want him to do it."

"Oh Ronan, you guys have done so much. It's beautiful!" He turns the camera back to face him. "Rosie everyone in the world has been behind closed doors for the last year. We've just been behind grotty ones, but they are now shining! Things have changed now, things are getting better in the world, Italy is opening up again, by the summer we will be wandering around cobbled streets, eating gelato in the sun and enjoying the Italy we originally fell in love with. We will love it again... and this time, all the more, because we now have a beautiful house to call home."

He was right; it was time to fall back in love with Italy.

"Now get back here quick and get the Christmas tree up in that bloody corner." He points the phone to the stairwell where a year ago Danny's crew had pulled out all the stops to install the extra electric socket, especially for my future Christmas trees. Thinking back, maybe Danny and Anto were not too bad after all. At last the socket will have its purpose.

I slept well that night but the ease was short-lived.

49

TO GO: ANDARE

The night before our flight, I awake several times feeling panicked. How am I going to do this alone? The suitcases, check-in, getting Mam in her wheelchair to the airport, onto the plane and out the other side? Jim and Ingrid are going to drive us the two-hour trip to Dublin airport. After that, I'm on my own.

I get up at 5.30 and make tea. Tea always makes things better. I recognise the knot in my stomach, the ball in my chest. It is the same one I had four years ago when we left Ireland with three weeks' notice to go to Italy. Rising bile, indigestion without eating. Jim and Ingrid being my backbone as we made the dash.

The last time, we were running away from a natural disaster called hurricane Brian. This time we are running away from a virus called Omicron. But there's a difference. Four years ago I had Ronan by my side to take over when it all got too much. I just need to make it to him, make it to Pisa and he'll be there with his loving arms to take over. I just need to get there. At least I won't have to say goodbye to my mam and dad and wonder if I'll ever see them again. This trip has changed that.

But I needn't have worried. The disability service in airport is amazing, we skip through the lines so fast that we are at the boarding gate in no time. I have time to get us both a tea.

"Feck the tea, where's the duty free."

"I'm just telling you now," she says, sitting in her wheelchair holding a stuffed bag of last-minute items that lit up the security X-rays like Christmas had come a month early. "I drink two bottles a week, one your dad knew about, the other he didn't, and I always keep another in reserve."

"Do you ever drink the reserve one?"

"No it's just on reserve, just in case... I only need to buy a reserve bottle every two weeks."

"So what you are telling me is you drink two and a half large bottles of whiskey a week?"

"No just two the other is just a reserve bottle, I told you, will you ever listen?" Hairs bristle on the back of my neck, she's back talking to me like I'm a child getting frustrated at my math homework.

"I want to get a reserve bottle in the duty free just in case we don't get back in time."

At the duty free, a bottle of her favourite brand is €30. "That's cheap," she says taking two onto her lap. "They are €36 in the supermarket."

"Mam don't buy that here! I know from buying them for wedding guests they are only about €16 in Italy."

"€16?! Are you serious?" Her eyes light up.

"I'll be buying several reserve bottles a week at that rate. I should have moved to Italy sooner. But I'll buy one reserve bottle here anyway, so I have it to celebrate with on our arrival."

Mam is so delighted with her purchase that she happily sits people watching while I drink my tea and have time to check my book sales for the first time since it was launched two weeks ago. I'd be happy if I had made a hundred sales, but that would be a stretch, considering it was the most silent book launch in the history of books.

As soon as I heard the news of my dad, I had sent out the post I had formed in my head earlier that morning of the book launch, while I was still numb;

'Book Launch party cancelled due to unforeseen circumstances.'

My book baby was live and still for sale, but it had a very quiet delivery.

I'm looking at the numbers and rechecking. That can't be right. I check again.

"What's up with you?" Mam asks, "I can see it in your face. Has the flight been cancelled because of that new Megatron Covid invasion? Oh no... are we stuck in bloody Ireland?"

"No Mam... and it's Omicron and it's a variant of Covid not an invasion."

I'm scrolling down my sales page. There are reviews... lots of them and they are good... bloody good. People I don't know like my book.

"Then what is it? Why is the flight cancelled?" she interrupts, demanding an answer.

"The flight isn't cancelled Mam.... I'm looking at the sales of my book..."

"What book? That mystery one? I liked the second one. It was better than the first one. The first one wasn't my cup of tea at all, you should have-"

"No, Mam not that one, it's another book I've written... I think I've sold 536 copies of it?"

"Is that good?"

"That's bloody brilliant! At this rate, I'll be able to be a full-time writer within a year or two."

"Well done! You always wanted to be a writer. Born with a pencil in your hand practically. Very uncomfortable." She laughs loud. "How about we open the bottle of whiskey to celebrate?"

"Mam it's only 11am, I'd never have a drink this early and we are about to board."

"I wouldn't drink this early either. I don't have a drink until after midday, and Tuesday, Thursday and Saturday are party nights."

"How do party nights differ from other nights?"

"They don't really!" She laughs at herself. "When you make it to my age, every night is party night."

On the plane, my shoulders drop a little and I am more conscious of the deep pain that has sat on my neck and back for the last two weeks. I feel if I took my top off, people would be in awe at the tight muscles I have across my shoulders. Like I had been prepping for the Iron Man challenge for five years, but on second thoughts I decide against whipping off my sweaty top. The muscle tightness is not on the surface level it is way deeper and goes right through to my heart and lungs. As soon as we are up in the air, I take a deep breath for the first time in weeks.

"I just need to get my laptop and catch up on some work," I say reaching down feeling under the seats in front of us for my laptop bag.

"Will you ever rest yourself?" she tuts.

"Mam I need to do some work." I'm not thinking of all the wedding clients who have sat patiently waiting for my return from Ireland, I'm thinking about the next book... I am itching to get it started.

"Work, work, work, give yourself a break. You have been on the go for the last two weeks non-stop. I don't know how you did it, but you need to give yourself a rest."

I bite my lip so hard I can feel a swelling when I release. "Don't start telling me what to do," is what I want to shout at her. I am exhausted and trying to get my laptop bag out from under Mam's large bag of paraphernalia is making me sweat. It's pointless. I give up, I wouldn't be able to concentrate with her looking at my screen beside me, anyway.

I look out at the clouds and there it is, the full rainbow circle dancing along beside us. Dad with God.

I look back at Mam dozing, and think how brave she is. Three weeks ago, she was sitting with the love of her life, pretending she was on a cruise. Since then she has buried her first and only love, left behind everything she knows as normal for the last eighty-five years, packed up her belongings and is moving to an alien country, all with a positive attitude. Brave.

It's a word Karen mentioned on the phone the day before when I called to thank her for helping set up Mam's room so beautifully. I hadn't paid much heed to what she had said.

Her words were now playing in my ears. "It's the least I could do. You are brave. I love my mum, but we could never live with each other now with both of us being adults."

The drink trolley arrives. I decide not to wake her. "I'll have a tea please," I mouth at the air hostess.

As the hostess preps my tea, I wonder what Mam will make of living in Italy. She is indeed brave. She is used to being in control. How is she going to surrender that? How is she going to hand the reins of power over to me, the one she feels, for some reason, doesn't know how to do basic things to get through life? When I visit her in Ireland, usually I go around Jim's house in the evening to get away from Mam telling me what to do, what I should be doing and how fat I'm getting.

We haven't lived together as adults. Mam is independent but unsteady on her feet. She can only stand for short periods due to the arthritis in her spine. I won't be able to leave her for long periods, maybe an hour or two, but over nights will now be out of the question.

Luca has just reached the age where we were comfortable leaving him home alone and I had thought Ronan and I could start going away for the odd weekend when Italy opens up again. But not now. No more business familiarisation junkets to beautiful hotels around Italy, stays at Karen's, quick nips back to see friends in Ireland or to visit Izzy in London.

I'll need to make three meals per day. I'll need to drive her everywhere she wants to go. I'll need to be there for her 24/7 because in Italy, the land of family, I don't have extended family support. I am alone. With my mother... who still talks to me like I am juvenile.

The invisible belt is back around my chest, but this time all the tighter. Mam looks peaceful. I look out the window and try to take a deep breath, but the tightening belt is not allowing me. The air on the plane has become very much warmer.

"Is that all madam?" says the smiling eyed hostess, handing me my tea.

"Yes... I mean no... give me a gin and tonic...make it a double."

Mam's eyes flicker open, "Are you having a drink without me?" She turns to the hostess and announces loudly to all within a five-mile earshot radius, "I'll have a whiskey, and make her tonic one of those fat free ones, she's getting a bit squidgy around the middle. The menopause I'd say."

I feel my cheeks burning under my Covid mask. She takes a slurp of her whiskey.

"Oh don't you worry Rosie Girl, I'll have you fit as a fiddle in no time, pushing me around Italy in the wheelchair. It's going to be great. Lots of new experiences for us both, I'll have that fat off you in no time."

The hostess hands me my drink with sympathetic horrified eyes, glancing momentarily at my mother, then back to my hot face.

My new experiences start immediately as I do something I have never done before... I skip the tonic and knock back the double.

Oh Lord... What have I done?

———————————

If you enjoyed my story, please do post a review on Amazon, it means a lot!

Sign up for house and book updates on www. rosiemeleady.com

A Rosie Life In Italy Book 4: Potatoes, Pizza & Poteen is available for pre-order.

ACKNOWLEDGMENTS

Thanks to:

Marco Moretti for the cover illustration.

Suzy Pope for her editing skills.

My Facebook group (@arosielifeinitaly) who are a constant encouragement.

My beta readers for their feedback.

And all my author friends on Clubhouse who are a daily source of knowledge, support and laughs.

ABOUT THE AUTHOR

Dubliner Rosie Meleady has been a magazine publisher and editor since 1994. She won the International Women in Publishing Award 1996 at the ripe old age of 24. She couldn't attend the award ceremony in London as she decided it would also be a good day to give birth.

In her 'A Rosie Life In Italy' series, she writes about buying a 22-roomed derelict villa in Italy by accident, renovating it and existing in Italy.

She now lives happily ever after in Italy disguised as a wedding planner, while renovating the villa and writing long into the night.

Follow Rosie on her blog and social media: www.rosieme-leady.com

ALSO BY ROSIE MELEADY

A Rosie Life In Italy 1 : Why Are We Here?

A Rosie Life In Italy 2 : What Have We Done?

A Rosie Life In Italy 3 : Should I Stay or Should I Go?

A Rosie Life In Italy 4 : Potatoes, Pizza and Poteen

A Deadly Wedding Cozy Mystery Series:

A Nun-Holy Murder

A Brush With Death

Jingle Bones (Novella part of : Clues, Christmas Trees and Corpses: A Limited Edition Cozy Mystery Anthology)

Made in the USA
Monee, IL
03 October 2022